PENGUIN BOOKS

BEREAVEMENT

Colin Murray Parkes, MD, FRCPsyche, is Honorary Consultant to St Christopher's Hospice, Sydenham, and Consultant Psychiatrist to St Joseph's Hospice, Hackney.

After holding various clinical posts in general medicine and psychiatry, he served from 1960 to 1962 as a member of the research staff of the Medical Research Council's Social Psychiatry Unit at the Maudsley Hospital. Subsequently he worked for thirteen years with John Bowlby at the Tavistock Institute of Human Relations and, in addition, was project director of the Harvard Bereavement Study, which was conducted at Harvard Medical School. He has been Honorary Consultant Psychiatrist to the Tavistock Clinic and, from 1975 to 1993, Senior Lecturer in Psychiatry at the London Hospital Medical College.

Dr Parkes has lectured extensively in the United Kingdom and overseas and is the author of numerous articles and scientific papers. His other books include *Recovery from Bereavement* (with Robert Weis, 1983) and *Counselling in Terminal Care and Bereavement* (with Marilyn Relf and Ann Couldrick, 1996). He has contributed to and edited books on the nature of human attachments: *The Place of Attachment in Human Behaviour* (1982) and *Attachment across the Life Cycle* (1991). More recently he has edited *Cross-Cultural Aspects of Death and Bereavement* (with P. Laungani and W. Young, 1996).

With Dora Black, Parkes is Scientific Editor of *Bereavement Care*, the international journal for bereavement counsellors, and Advisory Editor on several journals concerned with hospices and bereavement. He is President of Cruse Bereavement Care, the national voluntary organization which provides counselling for bereaved people across the United Kingdom.

BEREAVEMENT

Studies of grief in adult life
Third edition

Colin Murray Parkes

PENGUIN BOOKS

PENGUIN BOOKS

Published by the Penguin Group
Penguin Books Ltd, 80 Strand, London WC2R 0RL, England
Penguin Putnam Inc., 375 Hudson Street, New York, New York 10014, USA
Penguin Books Australia Ltd, 250 Camberwell Road, Camberwell, Victoria 3124, Australia
Penguin Books Canada Ltd, 10 Alcorn Avenue, Toronto, Ontario, Canada M4V 3B2
Penguin Books India (P) Ltd, 11 Community Centre, Panchsheel Park, New Delhi – 110 017, India
Penguin Books (NZ) Ltd, Cnr Rosedale and Airborne Roads, Albany, Auckland, New Zealand
Penguin Books (South Africa) (Pty) Ltd, 24 Sturdee Avenue, Rosebank 2196, South Africa

Penguin Books Ltd, Registered Offices: 80 Strand, London WC2R 0RL, England

www.penguin.com

First published by Tavistock Publications 1972
Third edition published by Routledge 1996
Published in Penguin Books 1998
5

Printed in England by Clays Ltd, St Ives plc

CONTENTS

FIGURES

TABLES

ACKNOWLEDGEMENTS

The studies that form the basis of this book were carried out with the support of the Mental Health Research Fund (now the Mental Health Trust), the Department of Health and Social Security, the US National Institute of Mental Health (Grant 1RO1MH-12042), the Tavistock Institute of Human Relations and the London Hospital Medical College.

Thanks are due to the staff of the Bethlem Royal and Maudsley Hospitals, the Tavistock Institute and Clinic, the Laboratory of Community Psychiatry of Harvard Medical School, and St Christopher's Hospice, Sydenham, and especially to the late John Bowlby, without whose support, guidance, and constructive criticism the work would never have been possible.

Others who have made a special contribution include Richard Brown, Gerald Caplan, Marlene Hindley, Margaret Napier, and Robert Weiss. The late Olive Aisnworth criticized the drafts, Janice Uphill typed my illegible manuscripts and Rosamund Robson gave editorial assistance.

But most of all, thanks are due to the numerous bereaved people who agreed, at a time of great distress, to talk to a stranger in the hope that their experience could be of value to others.

INTRODUCTION TO THE THIRD EDITION

Since the second edition of this book was published there has been a considerable increase in scientific interest in bereavement. Psych/Lit record 440 publications on the topic in the last five and a half years and many of these papers reflect the fact that psychologists are now taking an active interest. Of course, the number of papers is not necessarily an indication that our knowledge has been increasing at a similar pace, but there have been some important developments.

Since the advancement of psychological knowledge depends, to a large extent, on the development of reliable instruments to measure psychological phenomena, it is encouraging to find several measures of 'grief' in use. Thus we have Faschingbauer's 'Texas Inventory of Grief' (Faschingbauer *et al.*, 1977, 1981 and 1987) and Sanders's 'Grief Experience Inventory' (Sanders *et al.*, 1991), both of which have been widely used to measure the psychological disturbance that accompanies bereavement. Neither of them confines itself to specifically grief-related items but Horowitz's 'Impact of Events Scale' (Horowitz *et al.*, 1979), which was developed to measure two independent components of the reaction to stress (intrusive thoughts and avoidance), contains in its 'intrusion' scale a measure which comes close to doing this. The problem is that there are important differences between the unwanted, intrusive memories that haunt people who have witnessed an horrific or terrifying event and the happier memories which preoccupy most bereaved people. Horowitz's scale does not make a clear distinction between them.

Haunting memories are one of the key features of the condition which is now known as Post-Traumatic Stress Disorder (PTSD). Ever since this condition was recognized as a diagnostic entity in the influential third edition of the *Diagnostic Statistical Manual* (*DSMIII*) of the American Psychiatric Association (1987), it has attracted a great deal of research. PTSD is a part of the reaction to traumatic bereavements as described in earlier editions of this book. The increase in our understanding of this field has justified the devotion here of an entire chapter (10) to this topic.

Several key works have appeared in the last few years. Perhaps the most notable of these has been Jacobs's treatise on 'Pathologic Grief' (1993). Jacobs makes out a strong case for the inclusion of 'Pathologic Grief' in a future edition of the *DSM*. He has also drawn attention to the frequent association between bereavement and anxiety/panic disorder and has carried out significant research into the endocrine accompaniments of bereavement. Other key works are two volumes by Margaret and Wolfgang Stroebe, *Bereavement and Health* and *Handbook of Bereavement* (Stroebe *et al.*, 1987 and 1993). This group have now moved from their former base in Tübingen to join Schut and others at the Department of Health Psychology of the University of Utrecht. They have developed a 'Dual Process' model of grief and repeated reference is made to this and to their other important work in these pages.

Other useful sources of information for those who work with the bereaved and need to be kept up to date with innovative service and research are the journals *Omega, Death Studies, Mortality* and *Bereavement Care*. There are also the biennial International Conferences on Grief and Bereavement in Contemporary Society, at which most of the major researchers and practitioners in the field meet and report their latest research.

The advent of AIDS has created a new population of people of whom many suffer multiple bereavements as well as threats to their own lives. Social pressures often cause them to conceal their situation from others and to suppress feelings of grief and fear. New methods of counselling and support have been developed to help these people and others who suffer from 'disenfranchised grief' (Doka, 1989). The epidemic has also given rise to a great deal of research into the functioning of the Immune Response System which has been shown to be affected by bereavements and other stresses.

My own research in recent years has focused on the problems which cause bereaved people to seek psychiatric help. This was the starting point of my work thirty-six years ago but it is only in the last decade that I have been able to return to this topic. Two strands have emerged as of particular importance: one, traumatic bereavement, has been referred to above; the other concerns the vulnerability which causes some people to 'break down' following bereavements that others would take in their stride. My ongoing work examines the roots of this vulnerability in the relationship between the developing child and its parents, and serves to remind us that grief is an expression of the attachments that people form with each other and that our attachments are ultimately rooted in our childhood.

Another development arising out of my own work has been the formulation of a theory of 'Psychosocial Transitions' to explain the changes in our internal world which are necessary following bereavements and other major life changes. These are spelled out in Chapter 7.

Several researchers have warned against the dangers of oversimplifying complex issues. These include the concepts of 'phases of grief' which have been widely misunderstood and treated as if they were a fixed sequence through which every bereaved person must pass in order to recover from bereavement. Equally misunderstood have been the concepts of 'anticipatory grief' and 'grief work'. Critics such as Wortman and Silver (1989) have elaborated these misunderstandings into an attack on the supposed 'Myths of Coping with Loss', ignoring the fact that few authorities at work in the field believe in the 'myths' as stated by them.

Another area of controversy concerns the dangers of medicalizing normal life crises and treating grief as an illness. My own attempts (in Chapter 1) to examine the relationship between grief and mental illness have led some to assume that I am in favour of this viewpoint. In fact I do no such thing and see it as part of the doctor's role to reassure people of the normality of grief. In a world in which doctors are expected to relieve all the sufferings of humanity it is not surprising that people today tend to go to their doctor when they are bereaved rather than to their clergyman. It is not the doctors who are empire-building but the public who are seeking medical magic. This said, doctors may justly be accused of colluding with their patients when they prescribe medication for normal grief or fail to explain the nature of the bodily effects of grief.

Three chapters now replace the former chapter, 'Determinants of Grief'. This reflects the large amount of new work that has been published on this topic. Whereas most of the initial work on bereavement was confined to studies of widows' reactions to the death of their husbands, we now have detailed knowledge of many other types of loss. These are so numerous and detailed that there was a danger that the work would become too compendious. For this reason I have continued to focus on the areas about which I have firsthand experience, and have touched only briefly on such topics as the effects of bereavement on children and the many types of loss which are not caused by death. Similarly I have not attempted to review the large literature on cross-cultural aspects of bereavement which is the subject of another book (Parkes, Laungani and Young, 1996).

The former chapter, 'Helping the Bereaved', has also been expanded into two chapters to allow for the considerable increase in research and in the number and type of organizations available to bereaved people. It would be surprising and indeed suspicious if all forms of service to the bereaved were equally effective and we should not be perturbed to find that some of the evaluations that have been carried out have had negative results. Sometimes this can be explained as resulting from inadequate methods of assessment and sometimes it implies that the services themselves were not effective. Nevertheless the number of successful evaluations of bereavement services cannot fail to impress and there is now a great need for more comparative studies that will help us to decide which services are most suitable for which people.

Perhaps the most reassuring aspect of my review of the current literature has been the recognition that, despite numerous additions to the first and second editions of *Bereavement: Studies of Grief in Adult Life*, very little of the original account of bereavement and its consequences has had to be changed.

Colin Murray Parkes
December 1995

1

THE COST OF
COMMITMENT

> But O the heavy change, now thou art gone,
> Now thou art gone, and never must return!
>
> Milton, 'Lycidas'

Psychoanalysis, or 'the talking cure', as it was first called, was discovered by Breuer in 1881 when he started treating an intelligent, imaginative girl of twenty-one, Anna O. A puritan in a puritanical family, Anna O. led a monotonous existence enlivened by the rich fantasy world she created for herself. Although she is described as moody and obstinate, Anna was a sympathetic person, fond of helping the sick and passionately devoted to her father.

Her mental illness took the form of a succession of hysterical symptoms including headaches, 'absences', and paralyses and anaesthesia in her limbs, which began during her father's terminal illness. Breuer came to see her each day and treated her by encouraging her to talk about her fantasies. These were always sad and usually involved a girl sitting beside a sick-bed. After the father's death the symptoms got worse and the stories became more tragic. Breuer discovered that each symptom was related to a particular disturbing event, and tended to improve when Anna O. had succeeded in discussing the event that was associated with it.

It was Breuer's talking cure that subsequently gave rise to the art of psychoanalysis and all the forms of psychotherapy in use today. Breuer's crucial observation was of a link between traumatic events and symptoms.

When the anniversary of her father's illness arrived, Anna O. began to relive, during her 'absences', the events of the preceding year. These episodes were precipitated by any reminder of the previous year and their accuracy was authenticated by reference to her mother's diary. It was at this time that a number of severe and obstinate symptoms disappeared dramatically after she had described the events which, Breuer concluded, had given rise to them. Breuer reinforced these recollections by causing her to relive experiences by means of hypnosis.

Sigmund Freud, who knew Breuer well, was greatly interested in this case and made use of the talking cure himself. Breuer, on the other hand, did not pursue his discovery. He had devoted so much time and interest to this one attractive girl that his own marriage was affected. According to Ernest Jones (1953), Breuer, when he realized the extent of his involvement with this patient, abruptly brought the treatment to an end. Anna O., who was by now strongly attached to Breuer, became excited and developed a fresh crop of dramatic symptoms, among them a hysterical childbirth. The subsequent course of her illness was not as uneventful as Breuer's account leads one to suppose. She appears to have continued to have 'absences' for some years and to have been admitted to a mental institution on at least one occasion – here she is said to have 'inflamed the heart of the psychiatrist in charge'. She never married, remained deeply religious, became the first social worker in Germany, founded a periodical, and started several institutes.

A description of the case of Anna O. was published jointly by Breuer and Freud in 1893, in a paper entitled 'On the Psychical Mechanisms of Hysterical Phenomena', along with a series of cases treated by similar means. Although Breuer lost interest in the talking cure, Freud took it up with enthusiasm. He made a virtue of the personal relationship between patient and physician and believed that improvement often depended upon this. Hypnosis he eventually abandoned because it interfered with this relationship and because he found the method of 'free association' equally effective in the recovery of memories of traumatic events.

Freud soon found, however, that the recovery of recent memories, as carried out in the case of Anna O., did not necessarily relieve symptoms. He therefore encouraged his patients to recall earlier periods of their lives, and he claimed that he discovered the memories of primal events in their childhoods, which he believed to have been the critical determinants of mental illness. Already by 1898, five years after the publication of the paper mentioned above, Freud had become convinced of the importance of sexual experiences in childhood and thenceforth he took less interest in the recent experiences of his patients. Nevertheless, he never gave up the view that major psychic traumata, occurring in childhood or in adult life, can be responsible for neurotic illness. He gave evidence to this effect before a commission set up by the Austrian military authorities after the First World War to investigate the harsh treatment of war neuroses by their own doctors.

It is not my intention to discuss at length the relative merits of different theories of the causation of these neuroses. I have dwelt on Freud's contribution because of its great influence, and also because I believe that it is more than a coincidence that the breakthrough to which Breuer's talking cure gave rise resulted from the investigation of a case of mental illness arising at the time of the loss of a father. There is no doubt that the symptoms that Anna O. developed resulted from a combination of causes, some relating to her father's threatened or actual death, others to her own personality and early life experiences. Her father's illness and death can be regarded as the precipitating circumstances without which the illness would probably not have arisen – at least not in the form it actually took. Thus by examining the relationship between a recent precipitating event and the particular symptoms that followed it, Breuer made his contribution to our understanding of psychopathology.

Few other attempts have been made to do just this, perhaps because the connection between a particular event and a particular symptom is often difficult to trace. Nevertheless, I believe that where major stresses are concerned (and loss of a close relative is normally a major stressor), this approach fully justifies its results.

A bereavement by death is an important and obvious happening which is unlikely to be overlooked. Less obvious forms of loss, and losses that take place some time before the onset of an illness, may be overlooked. Even if they are not, it is less easy to demonstrate that there is a causal connection between them and the illness. And even if a causal connection can be assumed, the precise nature of this connection needs to be understood.

If, by studying the clear-cut case where causation is undoubted, we can learn more about the chain of causation and its precise consequences, it may eventually be possible to understand other types of case by starting from the consequences and working backwards towards the causes.

Aetiology is the bugbear of psychiatry. There are very few mental illnesses whose causes are straightforward. A few organic diseases and illnesses caused by drugs and other chemical changes in the blood are beginning to be understood. But the majority of mental illnesses do not result from organic brain disease or changes in the blood. Psychiatrists often disagree regarding the cause of a neurotic or a psychotic illness. Even when we agree we usually have to admit that our agreement depends upon our sharing the same theories of causation. Theories of causation vary from school to school and few of them are yet amenable to testing by scientific means. They can best be regarded as useful working hypotheses. Until we can obtain a better understanding of the links between psychological causes and psychological symptoms we shall continue to work in a professional twilight.

TRAUMATIC STRESS

One exception to this rule is the field of post-traumatic stress. This has come to prominence in recent years thanks to the recognition of a complex of symptoms which are likely to arise when people experience severe threats to their lives or witness peculiarly horrifying scenes. It has been termed Post-Traumatic Stress Disorder. PTSD accounted for much of the mental illness found among veterans of the war in Vietnam and, although it had been described after many other situations in the past, it was that event, more than any other, that forced psychiatrists to acknowledge the existence of PTSD as a diagnosis. The distinctive features of PTSD are haunting memories of the traumatic event that are so vivid that the sufferer feels as if they are experiencing the trauma again and again. These occur during the day or at night in the form of recurrent nightmares. They are so painful that people will go to great lengths to avoid any reminder that will trigger them off. They feel as if they are waiting for the next disaster and are constantly jumpy and on the alert.

Clearly PTSD differs from the other psychological reaction to major traumatic events, grief. Despite Freud's insistence on the importance of mourning (1917), the reaction to bereavement had been little studied by psychiatrists until recent years. Grief, after all, is a normal response to a stress which, while rare in the life of each of us, will be experienced by most sooner or later; and it is not commonly thought of as a mental illness. But what is a mental illness?

GRIEF AND MENTAL ILLNESS

To many people mental illness is equated with madness, a kind of mental weakness which causes people to 'break down', to lose control of their behaviour, and to become incapable of acting rationally. Only psychiatrists are qualified to treat such serious conditions and people who seek their help are to be regarded with great suspicion, for mental illness is thought to be incurable.

Since grief is clearly not that kind of mental illness, surely it is not a mental illness at all, and it would be very unfair on bereaved people to label them as 'nut cases' and subject them to the social stigma that would result. What's more, if people begin to think of themselves as sick, they may begin to behave as if they are sick, to become more helpless than they need to be, and to take advantage of the excuses for withdrawal which are accorded to all those deemed to be ill.

As long as people view mental illness in this light, then these arguments are very powerful, and we would be wrong to stigmatize the bereaved as mentally ill. But the public image of mental illness bears little relation to the realities of psychiatric practice, and although some psychiatric patients are incurably mad the great majority do not conform to the gloomy picture portrayed above. Nor is it to their advantage to stigmatize them or to encourage them to think of themselves as weak or helpless. By refusing to regard grief as a mental illness, we may be perpetuating a view of mental illness which does harm to the majority of people who seek help from psychiatrists and other mental health workers.

The assertion that because grief will be experienced by most of us sooner or later it cannot be said to be an illness is not valid. There are many illnesses that most of us experience: chicken pox, measles, even the common cold. If a bruise or a broken arm, the consequence of physical injury, is within the realm of pathology, why not grief, the consequence of a psychological trauma?

But doctors don't treat grief, you may say. In fact they do. There are indications that many people go to their doctor for help after a bereavement, and a large proportion of their complaints, as I shall show, are expressions of grief. Even those who do not seek help are not necessarily 'well'; people suffer various physical complaints without requesting help, and there are numerous minor ailments such as warts, bruises, or burns for which professional care is unnecessary.

Illnesses are characterized by the discomfort and the disturbance of function that they produce. Grief may not produce physical pain, but it is very unpleasant and it usually disturbs function. Thus newly bereaved people are often treated by society in much the same way as a sick person. Employers expect them to miss work, they stay at home, and relatives visit and talk in hushed tones. For a time, others take over responsibility for making decisions and acting on their behalf. When grief is severe, bereaved people may be disabled for weeks, and relatives worry about them; later they may say, 'I don't know how I lived through it'.

On the whole, grief resembles a physical injury more closely than any other type of illness. The loss may be spoken of as a 'blow'. As in the case of a physical injury, the 'wound' gradually heals; at least, it usually does. But occasionally complications set in, healing is delayed, or a further injury reopens a healing wound. In such cases abnormal forms arise, which may even be complicated by the onset of other types of illness. Sometimes it seems that the outcome may be fatal.

Since the first edition of this book was published in 1972, the influential *Diagnostic Statistical Manual* of the American Psychiatric Association (1994) has included 'Bereavement' among a group of 'Other conditions that may be the focus of clinical attention'. In this way they allow it to be taken into consideration without committing themselves to a diagnosis.

In many respects, then, grief can be regarded as an illness. But it can also bring strength. Just as broken bones may end up stronger than unbroken ones, so the experience of grieving can strengthen and bring maturity to those who have previously been protected from misfortune. The pain of grief is just as much a part of life as the joy of love; it is, perhaps, the price we pay for love, the cost of commitment. To ignore this fact, or to pretend that it is not so, is to put on emotional blinkers which leave us unprepared for the losses that will inevitably occur in our lives and unprepared to help others to cope with the losses in theirs.

I know of only two functional psychiatric disorders whose cause is known, whose features are distinctive, and whose course is usually predictable, and those are PTSD and grief. Yet PTSD is a new discovery and grief has been so neglected by psychiatrists that, until recently, it was not even mentioned in the indexes of most of the best-known general textbooks of psychiatry. The diagnostic systems which are in use in psychiatry grew up without reference to these conditions.

When knowledge is lacking regarding the aetiology and pathology of a disease, it is standard medical practice to classify it by its symptoms. This is what has happened in psychiatry. It is the principal presenting symptom that usually determines the diagnosis, and because psychiatric patients usually complain of emotional disturbance, the diagnostic labels contain the names of the emotions involved. Thus we have anxiety states, phobias, depressive reactions, depressive psychoses, and so on. The system would work better if there were not so many patients who exhibit one feature at one time and another at another. This leads to strange combination terms such as phobic anxiety, anxiety-depression, schizo-affective, or, as a last resort, to pan-neurosis or personality disorder. When asked how to classify a bereavement reaction, most psychiatrists say 'reactive depression', and certainly depression is a common feature. Yet more prominent is a special kind of anxiety, separation anxiety, which is discussed at length in Chapter 4. In fact, I think it fair to say that the pining or yearning that constitutes separation anxiety is the characteristic feature of the pang of grief. If grief is to be forced into the Procrustean bed of traditional psychiatric diagnosis, therefore, it should probably become a subgroup of the anxiety states. But separation anxiety is not always the symptom that causes a bereaved person to seek help and it may be that PTSD and grief will open the door to a new classificatory system. We shall return to these issues in Chapter 8.

THE PROCESS OF GRIEVING

Part of the difficulty in fitting grief into existing descriptive disease categories derives from the fact that grief is a process and not a state. Grief is not a set of symptoms which start after a loss and then gradually fade away. It involves a succession of clinical pictures which blend into and replace one another. In this book we shall see how numbness, the first phase, gives place to pining, and pining to disorganization and despair, and it is only after the stage of disorganization that recovery occurs. Hence, at any particular time a person may show one of four quite different clinical pictures.

Each of these phases of grieving has its own characteristics and there are considerable differences from one person to another as regards both the duration and the form of each phase. Furthermore people can move back and forth through the phases so that, years after a bereavement, the discovery of a photograph in a drawer or a visit from an old friend can evoke another episode of pining. Nevertheless, there is a common pattern whose features can be observed without difficulty in most cases, and this justifies our regarding grief as a distinct psychological process.

I said earlier that grief is not a common stress in the lives of most of us. In saying this I should, perhaps, have written grief with a capital G. Losses are, of course, common in all our lives. And in so far as grief is the reaction to loss, grief must be common too. But the term grief is not normally used for the reaction to the loss of an old umbrella. It is more usually reserved for the loss of a person, and a loved person at that. It is this type of grief that is the subject of this book, and this type of loss is not a common event in the lives of most of us.

Even bereavement by death is not as simple a stress as it might, at first sight, appear to be. In any bereavement it is seldom clear exactly what is lost. The loss of a husband, for instance, may or may not mean the loss of a sexual partner, companion, accountant, gardener, baby-minder, audience, bed-warmer, and so on, depending upon the particular roles normally performed by this husband. Moreover, one loss often brings other secondary losses in its train. The loss of a husband is usually accompanied by a considerable drop in income, and this often means that the widow must sell her house, change her job (if she has one), and move to a strange environment. The need to learn new roles without the support of the person upon whom one has come to rely, at a time when others in the family, especially children, are themselves bereaved and needing support, can place a major burden on a woman over and above the fact of the bereavement itself.

A death occurs at a particular time and place. Of course it may have been anticipated. An illness can drag on over a great length of time and sometimes a person has been functionally dead for months before his physical death. Nevertheless, it is, in my experience, rare for there to be no reaction to the death itself. Even when patients have been unconscious for weeks and the doctors, in their alienation, have come to regard them as 'vegetables', relatives continue to visit and hope. Even when the relatives say that they know there is no hope, they betray the expectation that something can be regained or retained of the old relationship. That they may continue to do this after the death is a fact that is not generally recognized. But there are good grounds for regarding the death itself as the crucial event after which grief can normally be expected to occur. And for all that has just been said, bereaved people do have enough in common to make it worthwhile to look at bereavement as a whole and to map out the course of events that tend to follow it.

Apart from grief, two other factors that always play a part in determining the overall reaction to a bereavement are stigma and deprivation.

STIGMA

By stigma I mean the change in attitude that takes place in society when a person dies. Every widow discovers that people who were previously friendly and approachable become embarrassed and strained in her presence. Expressions of sympathy often have a hollow ring and offers of help are not followed up. It often happens that only those who share the grief or have themselves suffered a major loss remain at hand. It is as if the widow has become tainted with death in much the same way as the funeral director.

In some societies the taboo on bereaved people can be more explicit. In a paper entitled 'A Little Widow is a Dangerous Thing', Cochrane (1936) wrote:

> Among the Shuswap of British Columbia widows and widowers in mourning are secluded and forbidden to touch their own bodies; the cups and cooking vessels which they use may be used by no one else. They build a sweat house by a creek, sweat there all night and bathe regularly, after which they must rub their bodies with branches of spruce. No hunter comes near such mourners, for their presence is unlucky . . . Thorn bushes are used for bed and pillow, and thorn bushes are also laid around their beds.

The Agutainos of Polawan also find the widow a dangerous thing:

> She may only go out at an hour when she is unlikely to meet anyone, for whoever sees her is thought to die a sudden death. To prevent this she knocks with a wooden peg on the trees as she goes along, warning people of her presence. It is believed that the very trees on which she knocks will soon die.

> (Ibid.)

In the circumstances it is not surprising that many societies have found it most convenient to send the widow into the next world along with her husband. Ritual suicide has been widespread, appearing in Asia, Africa, America, and Australia. Cochrane cites traces of it in Europe also.

In our society we have less fear of the newly bereaved, but we still find it difficult to accept their need to mourn, and when forced to meet them we find ourselves at a loss. Geoffrey Gorer (1965), in his study of grief and mourning in contemporary Britain, says 'Mourning is treated as if it were a weakness, a self-indulgence, a reprehensible bad habit instead of a psychological necessity'. We do not burn our widows, we pity and avoid them. In similar vein Illich (1977) has described death as a form of 'Consumer Resistance'.

DEPRIVATION

Deprivation implies the absence of a necessary person or thing as opposed to loss of that person or thing. A bereaved person reacts to both loss and deprivation. Grief is the reaction to loss, loneliness the reaction to deprivation. Deprivation means the absence of those essential 'supplies' that were previously provided by the lost person. Our understanding of the supplies provided by love relationships is still scanty. In a sense they are the psychological equivalents of food and drink. People are necessary to people, and the loss of a loved husband, wife, or child leaves behind a gap. Our needs for interaction with a loved person are presumably rooted in instinctual needs for pair-mating and brood-rearing. They include much more than sexual intercourse and the suckling of the young. John Bowlby (1969) has discussed at length the evolution of attachment behaviour. He suggests that at the time of its inception 'protection from predators' was one of the most important functions of attachments between human beings. Although there is no longer any good reason for a widow to fear attack by hyenas, it is no surprise to find that the lack of a close attachment to another person is often associated with a subjective feeling of insecurity and danger.

When we add to these instinctual supplies the supplies of information, comfort, money, sex, and other things which may derive from love objects in our complex society, it is clear that bereavement is likely to be followed by deprivation.

The cultural evolution that has made marriage and similar partnerships integral parts of our social organization has done little to ensure that the functions that they perform will be adequately carried out after their dissolution. Increasing disregard of formal mourning has meant that bereaved individuals get little support from society at large and from their own families in particular. Automatic remarriage to the husband's eldest brother (levirate marriage), once the custom among Jews, may not have solved the problem of mourning, but it must have ensured that many of the essential needs of the widow were met. Loneliness, poverty, rolelessness, sexual frustration, and absence of the security that comes from sharing responsibilities are a few of the ongoing feelings that stem from deprivation. They can be expected to continue as long as the deprivation continues and to end when alternative sources of supply are found. Widows who no longer have small children must learn to live alone and it is no surprise to find that, in Lopata's 1979 study of widows in Chicago who had been bereaved for an average of eleven years, half said that 'loneliness' was their greatest problem.

THE ROOTS OF GRIEF

Loss and deprivation are so inseparably bound together that it is not possible to study one without the other. One can postulate that grief, the reaction to loss, will be greatest shortly after the loss, and will then decline, leaving behind the reaction to deprivation, but people even get used to being deprived.

There is one thing, however, that justifies us in treating bereavement as a unitary stress and paying less attention to secondary losses, deprivation, role change, and stigma; that is the observation that grief is so powerful a reaction that, for a time, it overshadows all other sources of difficulty. '. . . for my particular grief,' says Brabantio, 'Is of so floodgate and o'erbearing nature, That it engluts and swallows other sorrows, And it is still itself' (*Othello*, I.iii).

In the ongoing flux of life human beings undergo many changes. Arriving, departing, growing, declining, achieving, failing – every change involves a loss and a gain. The old environment must be given up, the new accepted. People come and go; one job is lost, another begun; territory and possessions are acquired or sold; new skills are learnt, old abandoned; expectations are fulfilled or hopes dashed – in all these situations individuals are faced with the need to give up one mode of life and accept another. If they identify the change as a gain, acceptance may not be hard, but when it is a loss or a 'mixed blessing' they will do their best to resist the change. Resistance to change, the reluctance to give up possessions, people, status, expectations – this, I believe, is the basis of grief.

How someone copes with the challenge of change in their life will determine not only their view of the world but their view of themselves. It is no exaggeration to assert that personality is both a resultant and a determinant of change. From the moment of birth children relate to the world around them. We are born with an innate bias to develop behaviour patterns which, if all goes well, interlock with the behaviour patterns of our mother and produce the first attachment.[1] We usually learn that our cry can be expected to fulfil its biological function of attracting our mother. Before long we have learned to charm by smiling and to cling. As our size and strength increase and we begin to crawl or toddle, our propensity to follow mother becomes apparent. From now on we can maintain a safe proximity to her at will, but we can also wander away. If we become aware that we have lost mother we will cry and search restlessly and she will respond to our cry and come in search of us.

In most human communities it is the mother to whom this first attachment takes place and most of the research which was initiated by Bowlby's important work, *Child Care and the Growth of Love* (1953) has focused on her as the indispensable parent. More recently it has

11

been shown that others can be satisfactory substitutes for the natural mother provided that they provide consistent care. Hence the term 'mother' throughout this book should be taken to refer to the person who is the primary carer.

So far there is nothing peculiarly human about the infant's behaviour. Other animals have the same or similar ties to their mothers. But already differences will be emerging and there is reason to believe that the manner in which the mother responds to the baby's attachment behaviour can determine how the baby henceforth behaves. The innate behaviour patterns that emerge in early childhood are soon modified, refined, or extinguished by early experience. For instance, it has been shown experimentally that a baby's propensity to smile at a human face will gradually disappear if the human face consistently fails to smile back. Similarly, the 'bathroom treatment' for crying babies works on the assumption that, if you ignore a baby's cry for long enough it will stop crying. No adequate study has yet been made of the long-term effects of such treatment. But there are numerous studies of the effect of separating child from mother altogether and these all point to the conclusion that such separations are potentially harmful to the developing child. Pathological effects seem most likely to occur if (a) the separation is prolonged, (b) no mother-substitute is available, (c) the child is in pain or its movement is restricted, (d) it is in an unfamiliar environment, (e) it is between six months and three years of age at the time of the separation. The recognition of the importance of this combination of circumstances has given rise to major reforms in the care of young children in hospital, which include, in many hospitals, the admission of the mother along with the young child.

The mother of a two-year-old child is a mobile base from which forays can be made into a semi-familiar world. The child is both attracted and repelled by the unfamiliar component in this world, but it is the proximity of mother that will determine whether a new object or person is approached or avoided. Periods of clinging tend to alternate with periods of exploration at a safe distance from mother, but if a stranger should appear or the child should suddenly realize that it has gone beyond the safe distance, it soon 'returns to base'.

To young toddlers, therefore, mother is a haven of safety. The behaviour that attaches them to her ensures their protection and has evolved for that reason in human beings just as it has in a wide range of other species.

It is from this personal bond between mother and child that all subsequent relationships develop, and it is probably no exaggeration to say that what the toddler learns about mother governs its expectations of future relationships. Erikson (1950) has spoken of the 'basic trust' which may or may not arise in the minds of young children, and how this will influence their future attitudes not only to people but to the world in general and to changes occurring within it. By basic trust Erikson means the development in the child of a confident expectation that when mother leaves she will return, that when she is needed she will be there, that if it cries out or searches for her she will be found.

Trust in others and trust in the world can be cemented or shattered by experiences at any stage in life, and literature abounds with tales of people who have been embittered by fate. Usually the happy ending comes when faith is restored by the love of another. But there are those who seem doomed to disappointment, and too often one finds that these people lack that basic trust which should arise in early childhood: intolerant of separation or change, they cling too hard to what they have, or, losing it, avoid all human involvement for fear of further disappointment.

The import of these remarks will become clear when we come to consider the consequences in later life of severing those personal bonds that succeed, and to some degree resemble, the primal tie to the mother. We shall not be surprised to find elements of the same behaviour patterns that were found in childhood and are found, to some extent, among a wide range of beasts, birds, and teleost fishes.

2

THE BROKEN HEART

> He only without framing word, or closing his eyes, but
> earnestly viewing the dead body of his son, stood still upright,
> till the vehemence of his sad sorrow, having suppressed and
> choaked his vitall spirits, fell'd him starke dead to the ground.
>
> > Montaigne's description of the death of
> > John, King of Hungaria

Is grief a cause of death? You will not find grief on a death certificate, not today. But the notion that one may die of grief is a popular theme among novelists, and it is not long ago that it was a recognized cause of death.

Thus, in Dr Heberden's Bill classifying the causes of death in London during the year 1657 we find:

Flox and Small Pox	835
Found dead in the streets, etc.	9
French Pox	25
Gout	8
Griefe	**10**
Griping and Plague in the Guts	446
Hang'd and made away 'emselves	24

Such figures would today be dismissed as examples of medical mythology, but is there in fact any evidence that grief is sometimes a cause of death?

GRIEF AND MORTALITY

There is, of course, no doubt that psychological factors play a part in many illnesses, but it is only in rare cases of 'vagal inhibition' and in so-called voodoo deaths that they appear to be the sole cause. Vagal inhibition is a pseudo-scientific term sometimes used by doctors for the cause of death following a sudden emotional shock. A classic example is provided in the story of some students who held a mock trial and sentenced a man to death. He was led to the place of execution, blindfolded, and hit on the back of the neck with a towel – whereupon he died. Not dissimilar are the numerous well-authenticated cases of death from witchcraft. Although the witchcraft can take many different forms, such deaths seem to follow a general pattern. The 'victim' is told that the appropriate ritual curse has been carried out; if he has faith he at once becomes deeply depressed, stops eating, and within a few days is dead. In neither the vagal inhibition type of death nor death from witchcraft is there any post-mortem finding that explains the phenomenon.

Such occurrences are fortunately very rare, but there is other evidence of the effect of psychological factors on mortality among the unhealthy and ageing. Aldrich and Mendkoff (1963), for instance, discovered a major increase in mortality among chronically sick patients when a Chicago Home for Incurables was closed for administrative reasons. Of 182 patients who were relocated in other homes, thirty were dead within three months – a mortality rate five times greater than expectation. Mortality was highest among those patients whose grasp on reality was most tenuous, particularly among the thirty-eight whom Aldrich rated as 'psychotic' before relocation, of whom twenty-four died within a year.

Apart from a few isolated cases of doubtful authenticity, I have come across no evidence that phenomena such as these are responsible for death following bereavement. The examples have been quoted simply to remind the reader that psychological factors can have profound effects even on healthy people.

For many years it has been known that widows and widowers have a higher mortality rate than married men and women of the same age. But then so have bachelors and spinsters, and it is not unreasonable to suspect that some of the fitter widows and widowers remarry, thereby ensuring that those who remain will have a relatively high mortality rate.

This explanation might certainly account for an increased mortality rate among the widowed population as a whole, but it would not explain the peak of mortality in widowers during the first year of bereavement as discovered by Michael Young and his colleagues (Young, Benjamin and Wallis, 1963). They found an increase in the death rate among

4,486 widowers over the age of fifty-four of almost 40 per cent during the first six months of bereavement. This dropped off rapidly thereafter to around the mortality rate for married men of the same age. (Further details are given in the Appendix, section 1.)

Since this study was published, a number of other studies of the mortality of bereavement have been carried out. Reviewing fifteen longitudinal studies, Stroebe *et al.* (1993) conclude:

> The bereaved are indeed at higher risk of dying than are non-bereaved persons. This seems to apply not only to the widowed but also for other bereaved relatives. Highest risk occurs in the weeks and months closest to loss, and men appear to be more vulnerable than women.

That widows may also be at risk is confirmed by a major study by Mellstrom *et al.* (1982). They found a highly significant increase in the death rate among widows during the first three months of bereavement and among widowers during the whole of the first year. The life expectancy of widowers was reduced by one and a half years and that of widows by six months.

Of other types of bereavement, Rees and Lutkins (1967) have claimed an increased mortality among parents who have lost a child, and Roskin (1984) a significant increase in mortality among grandparents.

Several diseases seem to contribute to the higher mortality, but recent work has indicated that the most frequent cause of death is heart disease. The research by Young *et al.* (1963) on the death rate among widowers was used as the basis of a further study (carried out by Parkes, Benjamin and Fitzgerald, 1969) of the causes of death among these same widowers as revealed on their death certificates. It was soon apparent that three-quarters of the increased death rate during the first six months of bereavement was attributable to heart disease, in particular to coronary thrombosis and arteriosclerotic heart disease (see Appendix, section 1). This is confirmed in Mellstrom's study and further confirmation comes from a study of sudden cardiac deaths in women aged between twenty-five and sixty-four (Cottington *et al.*, 1980). The death of a significant other person was six times more likely to have occurred during the preceding six months than it was in the control group.

The origin of the term 'broken heart' goes back to biblical times. 'Bind up the broken hearted,' says Isaiah, and the idea seems to have persisted ever since that severe grief can somehow damage the heart.

Benjamin Rush, the American physician and signatory of the Declaration of Independence, wrote in his *Medical Inquiries and Observations upon the Diseases of the Mind* (1835): 'Dissection of persons who have died of grief, show congestion in, and inflammation of the heart, with rupture of its auricles and ventricles.' Rupture of the heart is, of course, a rare condition, but when it does occur it is usually caused by a coronary thrombosis. All of which leads us to suspect that the old physicians may not have been as foolish as we suppose. (In case any bereaved reader is now clutching his chest and preparing to call an ambulance, may I hasten to point out that palpitations and a feeling of fullness in the chest are normal concomitants of anxiety and that bereaved people often experience them without developing heart disease.)

The fact that bereavement may be followed by death from heart disease does not prove that grief is itself a cause of death. We do not even know whether bereavement causes the illness or simply aggravates a condition that would have occurred anyway. Perhaps widowers tend to smoke more or to alter their diet in a way that increases their liability to coronary thrombosis. Even if emotional factors are directly implicated we still have to explain how they affect the heart. Stress is known to produce changes in the blood pressure and heart rate, in the flow of blood through the coronary arteries, and in the chemical constituents of the blood. Any of these changes could play a part in precipitating clotting within a diseased coronary artery and thereby produce a coronary thrombosis, but without further research we can only speculate.

Other causes of the increased mortality after bereavement are cirrhosis of the liver, infectious diseases, accidents, and suicides. Increased mortality from deaths by violence have also been reported by Jones and Goldblatt (1987) and Mellstrom *et al.* (1982) also report excesses for accidents. This may be explained both by lack of care – newly bereaved people often have difficulty concentrating on driving and some take deliberate risks – and by excessive consumption of alcohol which is a contributing factor to many violent deaths.

Four longitudinal studies have shown an increased risk of suicide among bereaved people (Bojanovsky, 1980; Bunch, 1972; Kaprio *et al.*, 1987; and McMahon and Pugh, 1965). This is greatest during the first week of bereavement when Kaprio *et al.* showed a ten-fold increase in suicidal deaths among women and a sixty-six-fold increase in men. Parents and sons are at risk as well as spouses (Bunch, 1972).

Osterweis *et al.* (1984) make the following point about the three principal causes of bereavement-related death – suicide, cirrhosis and cardiac arrest: 'All three conditions have clinical antecedents (depression, alcoholism, and cardiovascular disease) that could be detected before or very shortly after bereavement, thus identifying three high-risk groups for whom early intervention might be useful.' The question is, 'What kind of intervention?'

One kind of intervention is that provided by rituals of mourning. Among the Huli of Papua, New Guinea, the death rate among widowers during the first year of bereavement has been shown to be significantly greater ($p < .02$) than that among widows. Frankel and Smith (1982) suggest that this difference may be explained by persistence, among women but not men, of a tradition of intense public mourning in a 'crying house' (*duguanda*). Women are expected to engage in a day and night of keening and angry denunciation of the dead person for dying. Close female relatives continue to keen after the funeral and sometimes sleep in the crying-house for several weeks. This is seen as therapeutic.

In all known societies it is friends and families who provide most of us with psychological support after bereavement and it is fascinating to learn that, in a sample of 503 elderly British widows and widowers who were followed up for six years after bereavement, factors associated with high death rates were: having nobody to telephone; not having seen all of one's grandchildren during the first six months of bereavement; and having no living brothers or sisters (Bowling, 1988).

Another type of intervention that may reduce mortality is remarriage. Thus Helsing and his colleagues (1982) have found that widowers who remarried had a mortality rate substantially lower than widowers who did not remarry and lower even than the rates among married men in the control group! However, it may well be that this reflects the effects of good health on eligibility, rather than the effects of remarriage on health.

Is there a medical way of preventing cardiac deaths after bereavement? Well, there may be. The main way in which the emotions influence the heart is via the vagus nerve. If we could block or damp down that influence in people with known heart disease who suffer a bereavement then we might be able to protect their coronary arteries from possible damage. The use of a beta-blocking drug such as Propranolol as a preventive measure would do just that. No research has yet been undertaken to test this theory but the medication is widely used and, with proper medical supervision, quite safe.

It may be that measures aimed at reducing the stress of bereavement will also help to reduce mortality and there is some evidence that the number of suicides among the relatives of patients dying at St Christopher's Hospice, Sydenham has diminished since the introduction of a bereavement counselling service. (This is described in more detail on page 184.)

OTHER EFFECTS OF BEREAVEMENT ON HEALTH

Lindemann's interest in bereavement as a topic of study was triggered by his observation of an association between losses and the onset of ulcerative colitis (1945). What other effects does bereavement have upon health? Many physical and mental illnesses have been attributed to loss. Usually the attribution is based on the observation that the illness in question came on shortly after a loss. But since losses of one sort or another occur in the lives of all of us, a chance association between illness and loss is always possible. Furthermore, the distinction between physical and psychological symptoms soon breaks down. In the rest of this chapter I discuss, first, the types of condition that are commonly brought to the attention of a physician or general practitioner, and then I go on to look at the symptoms of bereaved psychiatric patients. But it will soon be obvious that there is a considerable overlap.

Some of the better studies of the psychosomatic effects of loss have come from the Strong Memorial Hospital in Rochester, USA, where a group of psychiatrists developed the theory that it is the feelings of helplessness and hopelessness that may accompany loss that are responsible for physical illness. In one remarkable study, women suspected of having cancer of the womb were 'diagnosed' by a psychiatrist with striking accuracy (see Appendix, section 2). These women had been admitted for investigation after a routine vaginal smear had revealed the presence of ugly-looking cells which might or might not indicate cancer. At this stage nobody knew whether a cancer was present or not, and a biopsy was necessary to prove or disprove such a diagnosis. The psychiatrist, who was as ignorant as anyone of the true situation, interviewed each woman and asked her about her feelings about any recent losses in her life. When he found evidence of both loss and feelings of helplessness or hopelessness he predicted that this woman would, in fact, be found to have cancer. In 71 per cent of cases his diagnosis proved to be correct.

The sceptic will point out that perhaps, unbeknown to the doctor, these women did have an inkling of their true diagnosis and it was this knowledge that influenced their feelings or their tendency to recall recent losses in their lives. Similar bias could conceivably explain the high rate of losses reported to Cooper and Farragher (1993) by women with breast cancers. They used a very similar method to study women attending a breast cancer screening clinic.

High rates of loss have also been reported in a number of other conditions. Thus Klerman and Izen (1977), reviewing an extensive literature, list acute closed-angle glaucoma, cancer, cardiovascular disorders, Cushing's disease, disseminated lupus erythematosus, idiopathic glossodynia, pernicious anaemia, pneumonia, rheumatoid arthritis, thyrotoxicosis, tuberculosis, and ulcerative colitis. However inconclusive they may be these results cannot be ignored and it is to be hoped that the necessary work will be done to establish the chain of causation.

In retrospective studies of this type the investigator starts with a person who is sick, or suspected of being sick, and attempts to find out whether they have suffered a loss prior to the onset of illness. Such studies always carry a risk of retrospective bias. Another way of proceeding is to start with people who are known to have suffered a loss and to follow them up in order to find out what illnesses are contracted thereafter. This approach has been adopted in several studies of bereaved people. For example, seventy-two East London widows were interviewed by Peter Marris on average two years after they had been bereaved; thirty-one (43 per cent) thought that their general health was now worse than it had been before bereavement (Marris, 1958). In another study by Hobson (1964), a similar proportion of widows (seventeen out of forty) from an English market town made the same assertion. According to both these studies the number of complaints attributed to bereavement was very large. Headaches, digestive upsets, rheumatism, and asthma were particularly frequent.

But such symptoms are common enough in any group of women and might have occurred by chance alone. Moreover, 'general health' is a woolly concept of doubtful validity. In a study of twenty-two London widows (1970) (referred to henceforth as the London Study) I attempted to obtain a number of different estimates of general health. I asked the widows to rate their own health as 'good', 'indifferent', or 'bad' at each of five interviews carried out at intervals during their first year of bereavement. I also counted the number of consultations each widow had with her GP in the course of the year, and in addition checked off on a standard list the symptoms she claimed to have suffered each time I visited her. Naturally I anticipated that the widows who said that their general health was bad would be the ones who had consulted their GP most frequently and suffered the largest number of symptoms. It came as a surprise to find that this was not the case. The only thing that was found to distinguish the widows who said that their health was bad was a quite separate series of assessments of irritability and anger. Anger and irritability, it seemed, were accompanied by a subjective feeling of ill health which was not reflected in any particular symptom or in a tendency to consult the doctor (see Appendix, section 3).

There is evidence, nevertheless, that newly bereaved people do consult their doctors more often than they did before bereavement. In one study of the case records of eight London GPs, I was able to identify forty-four widows who had been registered[1] with their GP for two years before and one and a half years after bereavement. Three-quarters of these widows consulted their GPs within six months of bereavement and this was a 63 per cent increase over the number who had consulted them in a similar period prior to bereavement. The largest increase was in consultations for anxiety, depression, insomnia, and other psychological symptoms, which were clearly attributable to grief. But it was surprising to find that the rise in consultations for such symptoms was confined to widows under sixty-five years of age. Older people did not, apparently, consult their doctor about these matters.

Consultations for physical symptoms, however, had increased in all age-groups, most notably for arthritis and rheumatic conditions. Psychological factors are known to play a part in rheumatism, but many of these widows had osteoarthritis, a condition that takes years to develop. It seems therefore that, as with coronary thrombosis, the bereavement probably did not originate the condition but aggravated one that was already present. It is possible, too, that the widows were using their arthritis as an excuse to visit their doctor and that the higher consultation rate reflected a need for help which had little to do with their physical state. (These findings are discussed in more detail in the Appendix, section 4.) They reveal the situation in Britain, where no expense is incurred by widows who consult a GP. In the USA, however, the expense of medical care seems to act as a deterrent. Two studies (Clayton et al., 1974; and Parkes and Brown, 1972) showed no increase in physician visits after bereavement, while a third (Wiener et al., 1975) showed an increase in consultations among elderly widows who were contributors to a pre-paid health plan.

A useful series of studies (1967, 1968 and 1969) which does not rely on the widow consulting her doctor was carried out by Maddison (and others) from the University of Sydney, Australia (see Appendix, section 5). He devised a postal questionnaire containing fifty-seven questions about symptoms and health care over the preceding year. This was completed by 132 American and 221 Australian widows thirteen months after bereavement, and by control groups of married women. All were under the age of sixty. Of the total sample of widows, 28 per cent obtained scores indicating 'marked' deterioration in health, compared with only 4.5 per cent of the married women.

Symptoms that were commoner in the bereaved than in the married groups included nervousness, depression, fears of nervous breakdown, feelings of panic, persistent fears, 'peculiar thoughts', nightmares, insomnia, trembling, loss of appetite (or, in a few, excessive appetite), loss of weight, reduced working capacity, and fatigue. All these symptoms are common features of grief and it is not surprising to find them complained of by a group of newly bereaved widows. But Maddison found also, in the widows, excessive incidence of symptoms that were less obviously features of grieving. These included headache, dizziness, fainting spells, blurred vision, skin rashes, excessive sweating, indigestion, difficulty in swallowing, vomiting, heavy menstrual periods, palpitations, chest pains, shortness of breath, frequent infections, and general aching.

Many of Maddison's findings have subsequently been confirmed in a study of sixty-eight young Boston widows and widowers under the age of forty-five, which I carried out with Ira Glick, Robert Weiss, Gerald Caplan, and others at Harvard Medical School. (This study is henceforth referred to as the Harvard Study. The findings are reported in more detail in Glick, *et al.*, 1974 and Parkes and Weiss, 1983.) These unselected widows and widowers were interviewed fourteen months after bereavement and compared with a control group of sixty-eight married men and women of the same age, sex, occupational class, and family size. The bereaved group showed evidence of depression and of general emotional disturbance as reflected in restlessness and insomnia, and in having difficulty in making decisions and remembering things. They also consumed more tranquillizers, alcohol, and tobacco than they had done prior to bereavement. They were distinguished from the non-bereaved group by the frequency of their complaints of physical symptoms indicative of anxiety and tension; however, they did not show, as older bereaved subjects have shown in other studies, a large increase in physical ailments.

Four times as many bereaved as non-bereaved had spent part of the preceding year in hospital, and the bereaved group sought advice for emotional problems from ministers, psychiatrists, and (occasionally) social workers more often than did the non-bereaved. (Further details of this study are given in the Appendix, section 6, and in Chapter 9.)

One study which found no increase in either self-assessments of being worried about one's health, or of illness reported during the preceding month at various times during the first four years of widow(er)hood, is that by Zisook *et al.* (1982 and 1987). They studied a sample of volunteer respondents comprising 30 per cent of the widows and widowers whom they contacted within the first month of bereavement. Their findings are so at variance with other studies that one is forced to conclude that this method of selection is biassed in favour of fitter widow(er)s.

In presenting evidence gleaned from several different studies concerning the effects of bereavement on physical health, I may be producing confusion when my aim is to dispel it. It would be so much simpler if one could state dogmatically that bereavement is a cause of headaches, osteoarthritis, and coronary thrombosis, and leave it at that; or, better still, go on to explain how it causes such conditions. But the evidence does not yet justify dogmatism. So what conclusions are possible?

I think we can justly claim that many widows and widowers seek help during the months that follow the death of their spouse, and that the professional persons they most often go to are medical practitioners and ministers of religion. I accept the evidence that bereavement can affect physical health, but it seems to me that most of the complaints which take people to their doctors are reflections of anxiety and tension rather than of organic disease. In such cases the most important role for the doctor may be to reassure people that they are not sick rather than to label them as sick.

With regard to more serious conditions, I agree with Osterweis *et al.* (1984), who conclude: 'The most extensive evidence of a link between disease in a specific organ system and bereavement exists for the cardiovascular system. Sudden cardiac arrhythmias, myocardial infarction, and congestive heart failure are the most frequently mentioned conditions in that system.' They cite Chambers and Reiser's (1953) study of congestive heart failure, Wiener *et al.*'s (1975) study of hypertension, and Engel's (1971) study of sudden cardiac arrests as evidence that threatened or actual losses of human relationships can exacerbate or precipitate these conditions. Finally, there are certain potentially fatal conditions, such as coronary thrombosis, blood cancers, and cancer of the neck of the womb, which seem in some cases to be precipitated or aggravated by major losses.

BEREAVEMENT AND MENTAL HEALTH

Is there also evidence that bereavement can produce frank mental illness? Here it is possible to speak with more confidence, since grief has been a subject of detailed study in recent years. Nevertheless, we shall soon enter the realms of speculation when we try to explain why one person recovers more easily than another from the psychological effects of bereavement. The only safe course is to review the evidence as concisely as possible so that readers can make up their own minds what conclusions are justified.

From the case summaries of 3,245 adult patients admitted to two psychiatric units during 1949–51, I was able to identify ninety-four (2.9 per cent) whose illness had come on within six months of the death of a parent, spouse, sibling, or child (Parkes, 1965). No doubt there were others among these patients who had been bereaved, but this fact was not mentioned in the case summary; and I am sure that there would be others again in whom the onset of mental illness had been delayed for more than six months after the bereavement that caused it. However, it was necessary to confine attention to those patients whose illness could reasonably be supposed to have something to do with bereavement.

Since bereavement is not an uncommon event, it was necessary to discover first whether the association between bereavement and mental illness could be due to chance alone. That is to say, would the patients have become ill at this time whether they had been bereaved or not? I compared the number of spouse bereavements which had actually occurred in the psychiatric population with the number that could have been expected to occur by chance association. The expected number of spouse bereavements was calculated from the Registrar General's mortality tables for England and Wales covering the same years as the study. It transpired that thirty of the ninety-four patients had been admitted for illness which had come on within six months of the death of a spouse, whereas only five spouse-bereaved patients would have been expected by chance alone (see Appendix, section 7).

Similar conclusions were reached by Stein and Susser (1969) in two carefully conducted studies of psychiatric care in Salford, England. These studies showed an abnormally large proportion of widows and widowers among people coming into psychiatric care for the first time in their lives and an abnormally large proportion of recently bereaved among these widowed patients. Then there are the studies of depression in London and on the island of Lewis in the Hebrides by Prudo *et al.* (1981). They found that no less than 77 per cent of chronic psychiatric disorders in Lewis had been provoked by the death of a close relative (compared with only 16 per cent in London). This may reflect special vulnerability among the islanders, many of whom are unmarried adults living with kin. By contrast, Frost and Clayton (1977) showed no significant differences between the number of recent family bereavements among 249 psychiatric patients and 249 patients from the orthopaedic and obstetric departments of the same hospital in St Louis. But, note that bereavement may be a causal factor in admissions to hospital for both orthopaedic disorder and pregnancy.

To return to my study of ninety-four bereaved psychiatric patients identified from their case notes: the diagnoses made by the psychiatrists in these cases were ascertained and compared with the diagnoses made on the 3,151 patients who had not, according to their case records, been bereaved. Two main findings were: first, that the bereaved patients had been diagnosed as suffering from many different types of psychiatric illness; and, second, that the most common single diagnosis in this group was reactive or neurotic depression. This was the diagnosis for 28 per cent of the bereaved patients and for only 15 per cent of those who had not been bereaved (see Appendix, section 7).

Further confirmation of the part which bereavement can play in producing clinical depression comes from a series of studies by Clayton and her colleagues (Bornstein *et al.*, 1973; Clayton *et al.*, 1972; and Clayton *et al.*, 1974). Using a check list of eight symptoms generally accepted as evidence of 'depressive illness' they found that 35 per cent of older widows had six or more symptoms at one month after bereavement. The proportion fell to 25 per cent at four months and 17 per cent at a year. In all, 47 per cent suffered from 'depressive symptom complex' at some time during the year compared with 8 per cent of a control group who had not been bereaved (see Appendix, section 8). Similar findings have been reported by Jacobs *et al.* (1989). Vulnerability to depression may not be confined to human beings, and Goodall (1971) has described very similar reactions among bereaved chimpanzees!

Another group of common psychiatric problems that are found after bereavement are anxiety disorders. Recent work by Jacobs (1993), who studied 102 bereaved spouses in New Haven, Connecticut, revealed that no less than 44 per cent showed evidence of generalized anxiety disorder or panic syndromes at some time during the first year of bereavement.

Post-traumatic Stress Disorder is, as we might expect, most common following unexpected and horrific types of bereavement. Schut *et al.*

(1991) followed up 281 people under the age of sixty-six who had lost a partner. He assessed them at intervals across the first twenty-five months of bereavement using a questionnaire to measure the presence of the classical symptoms of PTSD (As described in *DSMIII*). Although only 9 per cent met these criteria throughout the period of follow-up, nearly a half met them at some time during the two years.

From the case records of the bereaved psychiatric patients in my own study in 1964, it became apparent that, at the time of their admission to hospital, which was usually about a year after bereavement, many of them were still grieving. What is more, their grief had often taken an unusual form, being either more severe and prolonged than usual, or being delayed and/or complicated in ways which will be described. In these patients grief was an integral part of the illness that had brought them into psychiatric care.

In other cases, however, the mental illness did not seem to involve grieving. For instance, several patients who had always been heavy drinkers had developed alcoholic psychoses after the death of a close family member. Here the symptoms were the symptoms of alcoholism, and if there was any persisting tendency to grieve this was not an obvious part of the clinical picture. Bereavement, in these cases, had been the 'last straw', resulting in the breakdown of individuals whose previous adjustments had been precarious.

This study (henceforth referred to as the Case-note Study) revealed quite clearly the important part that bereavement can play in producing mental illness. It also indicated that the mental illnesses that follow bereavement often seem to comprise pathological forms of grieving which are specific to bereavement. In other cases, however, they comprise non-specific reactions which might have been caused by a variety of life events. The study of bereavement has led not only to a better understanding of pathological grief, but also to a greater understanding of these other events and their consequences. Bereavement is, after all, the most severe life event that most of us can expect to experience.

Most of the studies described above have concerned themselves with the first few years of bereavement – but what of the long term? Data on this is hard to come by, not only because it takes a long time to carry out long-term studies and few investigators have the stamina and resources to carry them out, but also because, as time goes by, other life events tend to occur in the lives of all of us and it becomes increasingly difficult to know for sure what contribution each one of them has made to our current problems. One long-term study, however, gives reassuring results. This was a large scale study of 14,000 American men and women who were followed over a twelve-year period. Those who became widowed during the first two years of the study were compared with the rest, and the investigators concluded: 'It may be comforting to know that human beings are highly adaptable creatures, and that, in the long run, the majority of us will be able to cope even with the most distressing and disruptive events' (McCrae and Costa, 1993).

RESEARCH INTO BEREAVEMENT

In order to understand better the ways in which bereavements can lead to psychiatric disorders and to initiate programmes of prevention or treatment, we must look more closely at the ways people react to bereavement, the circumstances in which problems can arise and the actions that can be taken to influence the situation to reduce pathology and encourage psychological growth.

Since this has been the main thrust of my own research over the years I shall first outline three of the major studies to which reference is made throughout this volume. I refer to them as 'The London Study', 'The Bethlem Study' and 'The Harvard Study'.

Case notes are not the most reliable source of research data and, while many of the case histories which I studied contained a full and convincing account of the patient's reaction to bereavement, there were others in which the reaction was not described in any detail. Obviously, a more systematic investigation of bereaved psychiatric patients was required. Research was needed, too, to determine what is a 'normal' or 'typical' reaction to bereavement. Two studies were undertaken with these aims in view, the Bethlem Study and the London Study, and they form the principal sources of information for Chapters 3–8 of this book. **The London Study** (Parkes, 1970), to which reference has already been made (see p. 20), was carried out after the Bethlem Study, but it will simplify matters if it is discussed first.

It is sometimes said that psychiatrists get a distorted view of life because they see only people who have failed to master the stresses they encounter. The London Study was an attempt to find out how an unselected group of twenty-two London widows under the age of sixty-five would cope with the stress of bereavement. It was undertaken with the intention of establishing a picture of 'normal grief' among young and middle-aged widows. Older widows were excluded because, as I explain in Chapter 9, there is reason to regard grief in old age as a rather different phenomenon from the grief of young people. Whatever the cause of this, it would have confused the overall picture too much to include older people in this survey.

Widows who agreed to help were brought to my attention by their GPs. These GPs had been asked to refer every woman in their practice who lost her husband and not to pick out those with special psychological difficulties. However, there were some widows who were not referred, either because they refused to take part or because the GP did not want to upset them. On subsequent inquiry, GPs did not think that these widows differed to any marked extent from those who were referred, and it appears that those who were interviewed were a fairly representative sample of London widows.

They were seen by me at the end of the first month of bereavement, and again at the third, sixth, ninth, and thirteenth months, a minimum of five interviews in all. Essentially I was studying the first year of bereavement. However, in order to include but not be over-influenced by the anniversary reaction, I carried out the 'end-of year' interview one month late. This enabled me to obtain an account of the anniversary reaction and also to get an idea of how the widow was adjusting now that this crisis was past.

At the outset I had some misgivings about the entire project. It was not my wish to intrude upon private grief and I was quite prepared to abandon the study if it seemed that my questions were going to cause unnecessary pain. In fact, discussion of the events leading up to the husband's death and of the widow's reaction to them did cause pain, and it was quite usual for widows to break down and cry at some time during our first interview; but, with only one exception, they did not regard this as a harmful experience. On the contrary, the majority seemed grateful for the opportunity to talk freely about the disturbing problems and feelings that preoccupied them. The first interview usually lasted from two to three hours, not because I had planned it that way but because the widow needed that amount of time if she was to 'talk through' the highly charged experiences that were on her mind. Once she found that I was not going to be embarrassed or upset by her grief she seemed to find the interview therapeutic and, although I took pains to explain that this was a research project, I had no sense of intrusion after the first few minutes of the initial contact. (Statistical findings are given in the Appendix, sections 9 and 10, and in Parkes, 1970.)

The aim of **The Bethlem Study** (Parkes, 1965) was to investigate atypical reactions to bereavement. Interviews were obtained between 1958 and 1960 with twenty-one bereaved patients at the Bethlem Royal and Maudsley Hospitals. Of the twenty-one patients, four were male and seventeen female. Most of them were seen soon after entering psychiatric treatment, at which time they had been bereaved for an average of 72 weeks (the range was from 4 to 367 weeks). (For further details see the Appendix, section 11, and Parkes, 1965.)

In both the London Study and the Bethlem Study bereaved people were asked to tell me, in their own words, about their bereavement and how they reacted to it. Questions were kept to a minimum and simply ensured that comparable information about critical events was obtained in each case. Some notes, particularly records of significant verbatim statements, were taken at the time and some assessments were made immediately after the interview. These were recorded on a survey form which was also used as an *aide-mémoire* during the interview.

Following these two studies, which revealed, respectively, typical and atypical forms that the reaction to bereavement can take, **The Harvard Study** was carried out. This investigation (referred to on pp. 22–3) had a rather different object in view. It had been established from earlier work that grief normally follows a certain pattern but that pathological variants sometimes occur, and a group of us now wanted to discover why most people come through the stress of bereavement unscathed whereas others break down with some physical or mental illness. We also wanted to see if it was possible to identify, at the time of a bereavement, those who would be likely to get into difficulties later. Since previous research (reviewed in Chapter 9) had shown that the health risk was greatest in young widows, we focused our attention on people under the age of forty-five who had lost a spouse. And because widowers had rarely featured in earlier investigations we included a group of them in this one. We contacted forty-one widows and nineteen widowers by letter and telephone, and visited them in their homes three weeks and six weeks after bereavement, and again fourteen months after they had been bereaved, when an assessment was made of their health. The results of this predictive study are discussed in Chapter 9 (see also the Appendix, sections 12 and 13). Subsequent work on both sides of the Atlantic has now confirmed many of our findings.

The Harvard Study confirmed my expectation that American widows would be found to react to bereavement in a similar manner to the British widows who had been the subjects of my earlier studies. These studies were not carried out to prove or disprove any particular theory, but inevitably I felt constrained to group certain features together and to attempt an explanation of the process of grieving which would make sense of the data.

JOHN BOWLBY

When, in 1959, I first reviewed the scientific literature on loss and grief I was struck by the absence of any reference in it to the common observation that animals, in their reaction to loss, show many of the features that are evident in human beings. One of the few people to have made this point is Charles Darwin, who, in *The Expression of the Emotions in Man and Animals* (1872), described the way in which sorrow is expressed by animals, young children, and adult human beings. His work caused me to formulate a 'biological theory of grief', which has not required major modification.

My preliminary formulation, which formed part of a dissertation for the Diploma in Psychological Medicine, had no sooner been submitted to the examiners than I was lent a duplicated copy of a paper which showed that many of the conclusions I had reached had been reached quite independently by the late John Bowlby. Bowlby's review of the effects of maternal deprivation in childhood had appeared as a World Health Organization monograph in 1951 and had been followed by a series of papers aimed at clarifying the theoretical questions to which it gave rise. By 1959 Bowlby was well-set in working out a comprehensive theory, the first part of which was already in print. I sent him a copy of my own dissertation at that time and subsequently (in 1962) joined his research staff at the Tavistock Institute of Human Relations. From that time until Bowlby's death in 1992 our collaboration was close and I made use of many of his ideas. These biographical details are mentioned because I am no longer sure which of us deserves the credit (or blame) for originating many of the ideas that make up the overall theory on these pages. All that I can say, with confidence, is that my debt to John Bowlby is great.

3

ALARM

No one ever told me that grief felt so like fear. I am not afraid,
but the sensation is like being afraid. The same fluttering in the
stomach, the same restlessness, the yawning. I keep on
swallowing.

C. S. Lewis, *A Grief Observed*

STRESS

For many years research workers have studied and written about stress.
The term has been used to characterize the effect of virtually any novel
or unpleasant experience – from doing mental arithmetic to being
involved in trench warfare, from being in an unfamiliar environment to
having a limb crushed. Human beings and animals of all shapes and
sizes have been tricked, confined, terrified, mutilated, shocked, puzzled,
embarrassed, challenged, stumped, overwhelmed, confused, or poisoned
in the widest variety of experimental conditions in attempts to track
down the consequences of this ubiquitous phenomenon. Numerous
books and articles describe the results of these experiments. The series
of volumes on stress by Selye and Horava (1950 *et seq.*), in which the
literature of that time was reviewed, illustrates the sheer quantity of
research in this field.

The outcome of all this work has not been negligible, but it has been
disappointing. Generalizations made in one setting fail to hold up in
another; results obtained with one individual are quite different with
another; and chemical changes in the blood, which seem in one
experiment to indicate the amount of stress a person is undergoing, bear
no relation to what is found in another.

Thus we are led to suppose that stress is not quite such a simple
concept as it was once thought to be. The book by Cannon, *Bodily*

Changes in Pain, Hunger, Fear and Rage (1929), was important in demonstrating that whether an animal is preparing to fight or to flee it will show a single overall physiological response. This response includes changes in body functions under the control of the sympathetic part of the autonomic nervous system and the endocrine glands in the adrenal cortex and medulla. These improve muscular performance (increase heart and respiratory rate, transfer blood to the muscles from other organs, increase muscular tension), improve vision (by dilation of the pupil and retraction of the eyelids), assist heat loss (increase sweating), cause the bristling of hair characteristic of 'threatening' (by contraction of erector pili muscles), and mobilize reserves of energy (convert glycogen in the liver to glucose). Stress also results in inhibition of activities of the parasympathetic system, which controls digestion and other non-priority functions (by stopping the flow of saliva, relaxing the bowel and bladder, reducing the flow of secretion in the bowel, and increasing the tone of the sphincter muscles). This body of knowledge is now taught as a part of elementary physiology. Clearly, sympathetic stimulation and parasympathetic inhibition have the useful function of putting the animal into a state of readiness for instant action.

Little has been added to Cannon's original description, which still serves to summarize the effects of stress. These physical effects arise at times of stress but they often persist after the alarm is past because of the chemical substances, such as nor-epinephrine, that continue to circulate in the blood for varying lengths of time.

AROUSAL

Much has been learnt of the mechanisms in the brain that govern arousal and attention. Partly this is a question of the amount of brain that is active at a given moment. During sleep, for instance, most of the central nervous system is at rest, as is evidenced by the regular synchronous electrical discharges which can be recorded from the majority of its parts. As the level of consciousness increases and the animal wakes up, a characteristic pattern of desynchronization occurs in larger and larger areas until in periods of intense activity nearly every part of the brain seems to be involved in the general process of perceiving, thinking, and directing actions.

The parts of the brain that seem to be most closely associated with the control and direction of 'arousal', as this whole process has been termed, are the reticular formation and the limbic system. They control not only the level of arousal but the particular areas of the brain that are aroused. Stimulation of the reticular formation, for instance, has been shown to produce, first, curiosity, then successively, as the intensity of stimulation increases, attention, fear, and panic.

Physiologists are tending to make increasing use in their work of measurements of the electrical activity of the brain, and a tacit assumption is often made that measures of heart rate, galvanic skin response, and sweating, which were once thought to indicate alarm, are in fact measures of arousal. Although the fit between these measures of sympathetic activity and the electro-encephalographic measures is not perfect, it is rare to have a highly aroused brain without the signs that sympathetic stimulation is present.

This is hardly surprising when one considers that in order to become fit for instant action an animal must be fully aroused. Does it follow, then, that any animal that is fully aroused is in a state of fear or rage? Common experience suggests that it does not, and reports of individuals who have been in extreme situations, even in situations which would be expected to evoke great fear, commonly indicate that it is only after the crisis is past its peak that the participant becomes aware of any 'feelings' at all. During the period of intense activity they are so preoccupied with the task in hand that emotion is redundant (at least, that is how it seems in retrospect). Having once been threatened by a man with a loaded revolver I can bear witness to this fact. I was able in that situation to note the signs in myself of autonomic disturbance – rapid beating of the heart, dryness of the mouth, and a general increase in tension; at the same time, however, I was not consciously afraid.

It should be clear, from what has been said, that there are three distinct components in the overall response to extreme situations: level of arousal, autonomic disturbance, and emotional reaction. While there is a tendency for the three to go together, the correspondence between them is not perfect and measurement of one cannot be taken as a precise index of the other two.

EMOTIONS

Emotions are commonly assumed to cause behaviour but, as we have seen, they often follow it. In alarming situations powerful emotions are soon likely to arise but the character of the emotion will be determined by our appraisal of the situation rather than preceding that appraisal. If we appraise the situation as one in which we may well be hurt or defeated then fear is likely to predominate, if we anticipate that a fight is necessary and that we have a reasonable chance of winning anger is the more likely emotion. If we are confident of our ability to master the situation the predominant emotion is likely to be one of triumph or elated excitement. If the situation is seen as our own fault or likely to lead to humiliation then a reaction of shame is to be expected. In many situations the outcome is uncertain and we may experience mixed or rapidly changing emotions.

INTERRELATIONSHIPS

To sum up the principal components on the inactive/active dimension we can set out three levels of arousal alongside their psycho-physiological and behavioural outcomes, thus:

Central nervous system	Synchronous electrical activity of most parts of CNS	Partial desynchroni-zation	Desynchronous electrical activity of most parts of CNS
Autonomic nervous system	Sympathetic inhibition; parasympa-thetic activity	Mixed picture	Sympathetic activity; parasympathetic inhibition
Subjective emotion	None	Interest; apprehension	Extreme rage, fear, or excitement
Behaviour	Asleep; unresponsive	Moderate activity; alert	Hyperactivity and hyper-sensitivity

This simplistic picture can be said to apply to all human beings at all times. But most of us spend most of our life in the middle and on the left-hand (inactive) side of the picture and can tolerate only brief periods on the right-hand side. Situations that tend to produce alarm are regarded as stressful, and if they continue for more than a short period of time we experience a sense of strain. (In physics a stressor exerts stress on an object in which it produces strain. The same terminology would seem applicable to psychology and physiology.)

Recent research into opioid peptide systems in the brain, which are known to be affected by stress, opens a new area for future studies since these are very likely to be affected by bereavement (Hamner, 1994).

THREAT AND LOSS

What are the characteristics of the situations that produce alarm in animals and human beings? While any unfamiliar or unpredictable situation is potentially alarming, there are certain types of situation that are especially so. These include situations involving the absence of an escape route or 'safe' place, or the presence of particular danger signals which the individual is 'set' to recognize at any time (cries, sudden movements or sounds, and so on). Absence of a safe escape route, lack of a haven or home in which the individual can feel secure, or, in social animals, absence of fellow-members of the species who normally provide or share defence (e.g., parents or mate) can increase the likelihood that a particular situation will be objectively dangerous and will give rise to a state of alarm with all the signs described above. To this must be added one other category of situation capable of producing a high state of alarm, namely the loss of a child or child-substitute.

All these situations threaten the security of the individual and they include situations of loss. A woman who loses her husband has good cause for alarm. Not only has she lost a source of protection but she is likely to be exposed to novel situations and problems in her new role as widow for which she may be quite unprepared. She no longer has a confidant with whom she can discuss matters, yet she will probably have to take over many additional responsibilities and roles that were formerly her husband's. It will hardly surprise us to find her showing signs of alarm.

In fact this has been found to be the case. In the London Study it was clear that for most of the widows the world had become a threatening and potentially dangerous place. During the first month of bereavement nearly all (eighteen out of twenty-two) said that they felt restless, and the degree of restlessness fell off only gradually during the year. Restlessness and increased muscle tension went together, and assessments of restlessness and tension made at the time of our interviews were highly intercorrelated (see Appendix, section 9).

There are indications from many sources that the grieving person is in a state of high arousal during much of the time and that this occasionally approaches panic. Fourteen of the twenty-two London widows described episodes of feeling panicky. One widow, for instance, found her 'nerves on edge' and trembled a great deal; she stayed with her sister throughout the first month of her bereavement, but whenever she returned home or even when left alone she felt scared and panicky. Although brief episodes of alarm occur in all our lives from time to time and do not cause more than transient distress, the persistence of lasting full arousal can have a variety of consequences which are detrimental to health.

Loss of appetite and weight, difficulty in sleeping at night, digestive disturbances, palpitations, headaches, and muscular aches and pains all seemed to reflect a general disturbance in the nervous control of bodily processes in the direction of stimulation of sympathetic activity and inhibition of parasympathetic or vegetative activities. Thus nineteen of the twenty-two London widows lost their appetite during the first month of bereavement and in fifteen this brought about recognizable loss of weight. Insomnia was mentioned by seventeen widows and was severe in thirteen; difficulty in getting to sleep at night and a tendency to wake early or during the night were also reported. Twelve widows took sedatives during the first month of bereavement and five were still taking them a year later.

The loss of interest in food and dryness of the mouth that were typical during the early weeks of bereavement were usually associated with a sense of fullness or a lump in the 'pit of the stomach' (epigastrium), often with belching and heartburn. As one widow put it: 'The whole thing has hit my stomach.' Headaches, which were mentioned by over half the widows during the first month of bereavement, were usually described as a sense of 'tension' or 'pressure' in the head. Similar symptoms of autonomic disturbance have been found by other researchers, notably by Maddison (see Chapter 2, pp. 21–2).

Around two-thirds of the London widows had a sense of time passing very quickly. They seemed to be 'on edge' and described themselves as 'jumpy' and 'irritable'. 'I get all tuned up'; 'I'm always on the go'; 'I'm at the end of my tether, I can't cope but I know I must'; 'I feel all in a turmoil inside'; 'My nerves are on edge'; 'I can't pin myself down to anything'; 'Stupid little things upset me' – these comments give a good picture of the overall restless anxiety that was found.

Anger and irritability are discussed more fully in Chapter 6, but it is worth noting at this point that assessments of these features made at the time of the interviews correlated closely with assessments of restlessness and tension and with the widow's own assessment of her state of health as bad (see Appendix, section 3).

The evidence suggests, then, that bereavement is a stressful situation and that the generalizations that stem from earlier research into stress are likely to hold good in the case of bereavement. The symptoms described above are symptoms of strain. They occur in many different types of stress situation and there is nothing about them that is specific to bereavement. They are the reason given by many widows for consulting their doctor after bereavement, and they are all symptoms with which doctors are very familiar.

Further research has confirmed many of the findings outlined above. In recent years, a number of studies by Jacobs and his colleagues have demonstrated the effects of bereavement on the autonomic and endocrine systems. Without going into further details of this complex area Jacobs's findings can best be summarized in his own words: '. . . evidence for increased adrenocortical activity, evidence for elevated adrenal medullary and sympathetic activity, the suggestion that the Prolactin system may be activated, and the findings that growth hormone dynamics were altered in some bereaved subjects' (1993). All of these resemble the physiological changes which occur in severe anxiety and depression. They are influenced by many factors in addition to bereavement and cannot be used as physiological measures of grief.

THE IMMUNE RESPONSE SYSTEM

What of the more serious disorders, the infections and cancers to which some bereaved people seem to be susceptible? Can we deduce a possible physiological explanation for these? Some of the most important research to have been conducted in recent years concerns the body's 'immune response system'. This is a complicated system of physical and chemical functions which influences our natural resistance to infections and to cancer cells arising within us. It operates in part through two types of lymphocyte in the blood, T-cells and B-cells. Schleifer and his colleagues (1983) found that the function of both types of cell was markedly suppressed in fifteen widowers during the first two months after the death of their wives. Thereafter some responses improved but others did not. Similar findings have been obtained by Bartrop *et al.* (1977), although the changes which they studied were confined to the T-cells. More recently studies have shown that bereavement can also impair the action of the 'Natural Killer Cells' which, as the name implies, play a part in destroying alien cells (Irwin and Weiner, 1987; and Pettingale *et al.*, 1994), and He (1991) has reported a number of changes in immuno-globulins and other indicators of immune dysfunction in forty-five bereaved relatives of people killed in a bus crash in China. Finally, parents who had experienced the loss of a formerly healthy child (Spratt and Denney, 1991) showed decreases in the number of T-suppressor and increases in T-helper cells.

These studies at last provide us with the beginnings of an explanation for some of the effects of bereavement on health, but they do need to be interpreted with caution. Certainly we should not assume that the changes in the immune system that have been found after bereavement are peculiar to that situation. Similar changes can occur following other types of stress and the severity of the response is more closely related to the intensity of depression than it is to the intensity of grief *per se* (Calabrese *et al.*, and Schleiffer *et al.*, 1984). Pettingale shows that the pattern of findings suggests that these changes may make the bereaved more vulnerable to auto-allergies than to infections.

One group who might be thought to be particularly vulnerable to the effects of bereavement on the Immune Response System are people with AIDS. Because of the high death rate caused by the disease, and the fact that it tends to occur in certain minority groups, many people with AIDS have lost friends from the disease. Since AIDS is a disease of the Immune Response System one might think that bereavement would be particularly dangerous to this group. Kemmeny *et al.* (1994) compared the immune response among HIV positive gay men who were bereaved and in a similar group who were not bereaved. In the non-bereaved group the immune response correlated highly with depression but this was not so among the bereaved group. Thus it appears that HIV infection interferes with the effect of grief on the Immune Response System and, in doing so, may protect the patient.

The fact that physiological reactions and psychosomatic symptoms are not stressor-specific does not justify the doctor in ignoring the special nature of the stress situations that produced them, or the highly specific psychological symptoms that accompany them. Physiology may not enable us to distinguish between 'fight' and 'flight', but it is clearly of great importance to the individual to choose correctly between these alternative actions. It is behaviour, rather than physiology, that determines the outcome of a stress situation.

CRISIS

The study of stress situations has been advanced by the development of 'crisis theory', a body of theory which is having important repercussions in the fields of preventive psychiatry and community mental health. It derives largely from the work of Gerald Caplan and his colleagues at the Laboratory of Community Psychiatry, Harvard Medical School (see Caplan, 1961 and 1964). Caplan has used the term 'crisis' to cover major life stresses, of limited duration, which endanger mental health. Such crises disrupt the customary modes of behaviour of the people concerned, alter both their circumstances and their plans, and impose a need for psychological work which takes time and effort. They present the individual with the opportunity and obligation to abandon old assumptions about the world and to discover new ones, and they thereby constitute a challenge.

Empirical observations reveal that under mild to moderate stress most people learn rapidly and are likely to accept the need to change more readily than at other times in their life. They also tend to seek help more willingly than at other times, and other people are more prepared to offer it. The support that society offers its suffering members during periods of crisis is often considerable though it may be relatively short-term.

When the strain exceeds a certain threshold of severity (which varies from one individual to another), our efficiency and learning capacity falls off rapidly and individuals find themselves unable to cope with the situation and overwhelmed by it. They may persevere in useless activities which are inappropriate to the present situation but may have been successful in the past, or they may panic and behave in a thoroughly disorganized and fragmented manner. In such circumstances old ideas and assumptions may be adhered to rigidly, and offers of help, which would involve an acceptance of the need to change, are repudiated. 'I'll never believe he's dead and you can't make me,' one widow said to me.

These two types of response, which have been observed in many different studies, are analogous to Cannon's 'fight/flight' response in so far as 'fight' involves an approach to the problems and difficulties whereas 'flight' involves withdrawal and the avoidance of problem-solving.

It seems that most animals have an inborn propensity to pay attention to unfamiliar or alarming stimuli. Subsequently, the decision to approach or to withdraw is made, depending upon the characteristics of the stimulus, the individual, and the environment. This is the first and most important decision that an animal must make in the situation, and on it survival may well depend. It is, moreover, a situation in which instinctive mechanisms are of limited value. A monkey may be born with a fear of 'snake-shaped' objects, but its decision to approach or avoid such an object will soon be determined by experience. In fact it may be that learning is never more rapid than in situations in which the decision to approach or withdraw must be made. Approach is likely if the unfamiliar or alarming stimulus is not too alarming and if it occurs in a situation in which the animal feels 'safe'. Intruders upon one's territory are more likely to be approached, and perhaps threatened, than are the same individuals when met on their own territory.

Because our survival depends upon our ability to learn about danger it should not surprise us if memories of life-threatening or other terrifying situations tend to persist even when the danger is past. Similarly people who have narrowly avoided a danger, or come close to others who have themselves been traumatized, may have a mental image of the trauma even though they did not witness it themselves. This may account for the persistence of traumatic memories and images that are a feature of PTSD. The horror may now be over but we remain haunted by its memory and we feel as if it could return at any time. We become jumpy, hyper-alert and irritable, suspecting dangers where none exist and overreacting. These reactions may seem illogical but they are part of the pattern of reaction that has enabled man to survive in a hostile world.

Human beings bring to this age-old situation, not a terrifying and dangerous set of teeth and claws, but a highly efficient memory and decision-making mechanism capable of guiding our approach to any problematic situation. It is this success in 'attacking' problems in advance that has given us a distinct advantage over other species. It also leaves us with the need to anticipate events that may never happen and to prepare ourselves in retrospect for disasters that are already past. In other words we are the only animal who worries and agonizes.

The techniques that human beings adopt to cope with emergent situations may involve approach or withdrawal, or elements of both. The theory of psychic defence rests on the assumption that there is a limit to the amount of anxiety an individual can tolerate and that when this limit is reached individuals will defend themselves by withdrawing, psychologically, from the situation that evokes the anxiety. Is it too large a jump for us to see in this behaviour an echo of the physical withdrawal of an animal in a situation of danger? In neither case does withdrawal necessarily imply failure or defeat, although it may do so. In both cases withdrawal is assumed to reduce the danger of being overwhelmed, and anxiety is the subjective accompaniment of real or imagined danger.

The intelligent human adult knows that it is fruitless to dwell on painful memories and the intrusive images of traumatic events are sometimes so painful that we will go to great lengths to avoid them. We may do this by shutting ourselves up in a safe place (usually our home), avoiding people and situations that will remind us of the trauma and deliberately filling our minds with thoughts and activities that will distract us from the horror. But it is a paradox that, *in order to avoid thinking about something we have to think about it*. That is to say, at some level we remain aware of the danger that we are trying to avoid. Hence it should not surprise us if our attempts at avoidance commonly fail. In sleep and at time of relaxed attention painful memories tend to float back into our minds and we find ourselves reliving the trauma yet again.

The case of Henry, who consulted me two months after several members of his famiy had been killed in the *Herald of Free Enterprise*, illustrates these points well. He recalled how he had left his family below and was smoking a cigarette on the top deck of the 'Herald of Free Enterprise' when the boat suddenly heeled over and then capsized outside Zeebrugge harbour. His immediate reaction was to save his own life. He managed to smash a window and escaped onto the outside of the boat that was now lying on its side and half submerged. Only now did he realize that his family were still below. In his alarm he tried to climb back into the ship but was deterred by a fellow survivor who warned him 'You'd never get out of there alive'.

Henry remained on board for five hours, helping with the rescue operation and watching anxiously as each new survivor emerged from the ship. But none of his own family came out alive and, in the course of the next two weeks he was to identify the bodies of four of them as, one by one, they were recovered from the wreck.

Throughout this period he exerted a rigid control and he was still not crying two months later when he was persuaded to seek psychiatric help. At this time he was tense and tremulous, chain smoking to control his nerves and feeling numb and depressed. He was easily upset by loud noises and was particularly sensitive to the sound of rushing water. He had shut himself up at home and seldom went out. His surviving daughters feared that he might kill himself.

Three months after the disaster a heavy thunder storm took place and, when I saw him the following day, Henry appeared haggard and exhausted. 'It was the thunder,' he said, 'It was the same noise that the boat made as it turned over. I heard the children screaming.' He then related, in great detail and with the tears pouring down his cheeks, his memories of the disaster. The experience was so vivid that I too felt caught up in the situation. After a while I said, 'You're still waiting for them to come out aren't you?'

This case illustrates well the features of PTSD. As long as Henry succeeded in avoiding the thoughts of what had happened he could not escape from the memories that were constantly threatening to emerge. The thunderstorm acted as a trigger to his memories and allowed him to begin the process of grieving.

Just how a human being reacts to a particular stressor depends on many things: on the characteristics of the stressor; on the individual's repertoire of coping techniques; on how the situation is perceived in the light of previous experience; on the capacity to tolerate powerful emotions; and on the need to maintain self-esteem.

In these circumstances it is hardly surprising that behavioural responses to stress vary widely. The number of interacting factors that determine behaviour and the difficulty in accurately assessing each of them have long been major bars to progress in understanding human behaviour. In studying bereavement we have the opportunity to hold constant one of these factors, the life event, and this makes it easier to unravel the interaction between the others.

The reaction to bereavement, as we have seen, includes components which we can term non-specific. That is to say, bereavement evokes arousal and the responses that characterize the alarm reaction; it may also evoke intrusive memories or fantasies and it may cause approach or avoidance behaviour. The form these responses take will be partly stressor-specific (i.e., they will derive from the nature of the situation) and partly subject-specific (i.e., they will derive from the personal predispositions of the subject).

In the next few chapters of this book I shall attempt to describe and explain the stressor-specific components in the reaction to bereavement. In later chapters recent studies of the subject-specific factors will be considered.

4

SEARCHING

Over a number of years K. Kollwitz worked on a monument
for her younger son who was killed in October 1914. His death
became for her a sort of personal obligation. Two years later
she noted in her diary: 'There's a drawing made, a mother
letting her dead son slide into her arms. I could do a hundred
similar drawings but still can't seem to come any closer to
him. I'm still searching for him as if it were in the very work
itself that I had to find him.'

Catalogue to an exhibition of the works of
K. Kollwitz, London 1967

THE PANGS OF GRIEF

The most characteristic feature of grief is not prolonged depression but
acute and episodic 'pangs'. A pang of grief is an episode of severe
anxiety and psychological pain. At such a time lost people are strongly
missed and the survivors sob or cry aloud for them.

Pangs of grief begin within a few hours or days of bereavement and
usually reach a peak of severity within five to fourteen days. At first
they are very frequent and seem to occur spontaneously, but as time
passes they become less frequent and take place only when something
occurs that brings the loss to mind. Finding a photograph in a drawer,
meeting a mutual friend of the lost person, waking up alone in a
double bed – happenings such as these precipitate attacks of anxious
pining.

Robertson and Bowlby (1952) called this the phase of yearning and
protest. Protest is discussed in Chapter 6, but it should be noted in

43

passing that the anger that this word implies is a likely part of the alarm reaction described in Chapter 3, which is also at its peak during this phase. Thus we find that feelings of panic, a dry mouth, and other indications of autonomic activity are particularly pronounced during pangs of grief. Add to these features deep sighing respiration, restless but aimless hyperactivity, difficulty in concentrating on anything but thoughts of loss, ruminations around the events leading up to the loss as well as loss of interest in any of the people or things that normally give pleasure or claim attention, and one begins to get a picture of this distressing and distressed phase of grief.

Pining is a persistent and obtrusive wish for the person who is gone, a preoccupation with thoughts that can only give pain – why should one experience such a useless and unpleasant emotion? I think the answer to this question gives the key to this whole phase of grief and to much that follows it. Pining is the subjective and emotional component of the urge to search for a lost object. I maintain that an adult human being has the same impulse to search that is shown by many species of social animal.

THE URGES TO CRY AND TO SEARCH

Lorenz (1963) has described the effects of separating a greylag goose from its mate:

> The first response to the disappearance of the partner consists in the anxious attempt to find him again. The goose moves about restlessly by day and night, flying great distances and visiting places where the partner might be found, uttering all the time the penetrating trisyllabic long-distance call ... The searching expeditions are extended farther and farther and quite often the searcher itself gets lost, or succumbs to an accident ... All the objective observable characteristics of the goose's behaviour on losing its mate are roughly identical with human grief. ...

Bowlby has reviewed the literature covering the reaction to bereavement in jackdaw, goose, domestic dog, orang-utan, and chimpanzee. He summarizes his conclusions as follows:

> Members of lower species protest at the loss of a loved object *and do all in their power to seek and recover it*; hostility, externally directed, is frequent; withdrawal, rejection of a potential new object, apathy and restlessness are the rule.
>
> (Bowlby, 1961; my italics)

44

The value of such behaviour for the survival of both individual and species is obvious, crying and searching both making it more likely that the lost one will be recovered. In the meantime the separated individual is in a state of danger and must be prepared to fight or to flee should the need arise; hence the importance of an alarm reaction at this time.

In his study of the vocalization of the young vervet monkey, Struhsaker (1967) describes no less than five varieties of 'lost call'. Spectrographic analysis reveals that the characteristics of these calls make them both penetrating and capable of accurate directional location over long distances. Similar studies have not, as far as I know, been carried out with the human infant, but most mothers are well able to distinguish the characteristics of the various cries of their babies. Darwin (1872) paid careful attention to the ways in which human beings and animals give visible expression to their emotions. Weeping was for him ' the primary and natural expression, as we see in children, of suffering of any kind'. Sobbing, he believed to be the partial expression of weeping – the cry is muted but the spasmodic inspiratory movement remains, as is clearly seen in the young child shortly before or after weeping. Darwin suggested that the contortion of the muscles about the eyes is necessary to protect the eyes from the rise in venous pressure that accompanies any forced expiration (it can also be discovered in laughing, shouting, etc.).

In the adult human being the facial expression of grief is seen as a compromise between the urge to cry aloud and the urge to suppress such inappropriate and ineffective behaviour. Thus the raising of the inner aspect of the eyebrows, wrinkling the forehead and the base of the nose, produces an expression similar to that of a person looking upwards towards a bright light – someone attempting to shield their eyes from the light by lowering the eyelashes but, at the same time, to look at the light by raising the brows. The resulting contraction of antagonistic muscles produces a characteristic expression that is also seen when the sorrowing person suppresses the impulse to cry aloud.

Similarly, the depression of the angles of the mouth is alleged to be necessary in crying in order to enable the maximum amount of sound to be emitted. In the sorrowing adult the mouth is not widely opened but the angles of the mouth are drawn down. Irregular sighs are thought to represent the inspiratory spasms of crying or sobbing, and the term 'choked with grief' reflects this.

Speculative though details of Darwin's theorizing may be, his general hypothesis that the expression of grief in the human adult contains elements of behaviour patterns which are more fully expressed in young children and social animals is illuminating. Just which components derive from which behaviour patterns is likely to remain a matter for conjecture but there can be little doubt that a large part of the expression of grief is derived from the urge to cry.

To say that what we see on the face of a bereaved person is no more than a suppressed cry, however, is an oversimplification. Maturing human beings learn to do more than hide their feelings. They learn to express them in ways that convey to their fellow-men shades and textures of meaning which may be very much more subtle than those conveyed by the crying child. In most circumstances in which one human being has become separated from another it is neither necessary nor appropriate for both to cry aloud. The facial expression that Darwin describes, coupled with restless searching and verbal requests for help, is sufficient to excite the serious concern and cooperation of others. The suppressed cry has thus become part of a ritualized social signal system which is still only partially under the control of the will but which enables the separated individual to evoke and direct the help of others in an orderly and constructive manner. Only when searching is useless and reunion impossible, as in the statistically infrequent event of loss by death, does the involuntary expression of grief lose its utility. In such circumstances bereaved people may attempt to 'hide their feelings' with varying degrees of success. The extent and consequences of their success are discussed in Chapter 5; the extent of their failure is the subject of this chapter.

THE GRIEVING CHILD

Before we return to the pining adult let us take one more look at the child during the same phase of grief. I quote from an article by James Robertson (1953) in which he describes the behaviour of healthy children aged between fifteen and thirty months on admission to hospital or to some residential institution.

> In this initial phase, which may last from a few hours to seven or eight days, the young child has a strong conscious need of his mother and the expectation, based on previous experience, that she will respond to his cries. He is acutely anxious that he has lost her, is confused and frightened by unfamiliar surroundings, and seeks to recapture her by the full exercise of his limited resources. He has no comprehension of his situation and is distraught with fright and urgent desire for satisfactions only his mother can give.

He will often cry loudly, shake his cot, throw himself about, and look eagerly towards any sight or sound which might prove to be his missing mother.

Each of the components described in the preceding pages is here – alarm, protest, crying, and searching. But note that what Robertson is describing is not just the effects of losing mother; it includes the effects of being lost oneself. This child is in a strange environment; its need for its mother is therefore greater than would be likely if it had been at home. Familiar territory, mother, and other attachment figures, all share 'home valency',[1] and in the absence of one the tendency to cling to the others is stronger than usual. The young child who has achieved mobility moves within an orbit whose centre is mother. In unfamiliar surroundings the orbit is small and the child will tend to cling to mother. In familiar surroundings the child moves within a wider orbit and can tolerate intermittent separations when mother disappears altogether, provided that she is not gone for too long and that no change in the situation stimulates a demand for her return. As the child grows older and more and more of the world becomes familiar, it normally learns to tolerate greater degrees of separation and at the same time develops attachments to a number of other individuals who have now taken on some of the home valency. Nevertheless it seems that the desire for attachment figures persists as does the desire for a safe and familiar environment. Separation from either or both of these gives rise to behaviour which, in the normal course of events, ensures their return or the return of the individual to them. It is this behaviour that tends to take place during the yearning phase of grief.

THE GRIEVING ADULT

Bereaved adults are well aware that there is no point in searching for a dead person, but I maintain that this does not prevent them from experiencing a strong impulse to search. Because they recognize that searching is irrational, they tend to resist the suggestion that this is what they want to do. Some bereaved adults, however, have ready insight into the irrational components of their own behaviour.

'I can't help looking for him everywhere . . . I walk around searching for him . . . I felt that if I could have come somewhere I could have found him,' said one London widow, a week after the death of her husband. She had thought of going to spiritualist meetings in the hope of getting in touch with her dead husband, but decided against it.

Another of the London widows said, 'I'm just searching for nothing'; and another, 'I go to the grave . . . but he's not there. It's as if I was drawn towards him.'

Several bereaved psychiatric patients in the Bethlem Study were aware of the urge to search. Most of them were mothers who had lost children. An Australian woman had lost her adoptive son and her true son in the war. Their deaths were announced within a few weeks of each other. When told of her son's death, she refused to believe it and eventually persuaded her husband to bring her to England in search of the boy. On arrival she thought she saw him coming towards her on the stairs. She became very depressed and cried for the first time since her bereavement.

Another mother received a message that her son had been killed in action in Belgium. She reacted severely and four years later, when the war was over, persuaded her husband to take her to visit her son's grave in order to make sure that he was dead. Returning home she said, 'I knew I was leaving him behind for ever'.

Two other women interviewed in the Bethlem Study reported conscious searching for a dead person. One, a mother, described how she repeatedly went into the bedroom in search of her dead baby. The other, a widow, had repeatedly gone to the kitchen door to look for her husband. She found this behaviour so painful that she resisted it: 'I think, there's no good going into the kitchen, he'll never come back.'

Children who have persisted in a search for lost parents extending into adult life have been described by Stengel (1939 and 1943), who believes that some wandering fugues are the result. Adoptive children often 'keep alive' the hope of finding their true parents. One whom I met in the United States[2] had spent large sums of money in hiring private investigators to locate his mother. A striking change occurred when he succeeded in finding her. She crossed the American continent to stay with him and, although she did not live up to his idealized expectations, their relationship did become quite good. Moreover, his restless anxiety which had been present for many years diminished considerably.

In the examples quoted above, searching was quite manifest, but the majority of the bereaved people I have studied were not consciously aware of the need to search. In order to show how their behaviour nevertheless revealed the urge to search, it is necessary to look more closely at what searching entails.

SEARCHING AND PERCEPTION

Searching is a restless activity in which one moves towards possible locations of a lost object. The person who is searching has to select places in which to look, move towards them, and scan them; what is to be seen must also be selected.

'Selecting what to see' is an important part of perception. At every moment of every day sense organs in all parts of a person's body are sending back 'messages' to the central nervous system. These messages arise from within and without the body itself. In states of low arousal (e.g., during sleep) only a very small proportion of them reaches consciousness; in states of high arousal a larger porportion does so. But even when a a person is alarmed, only a small number of the total pool of sensations attain conscious levels of attention.

Those messages that do reach consciousness are the residue of a barrage. One can picture them as having to pass a series of filters which cut off those that are irrelevent or capable of being acted upon at an unconcious level. By the time a message reaches consciousness it has not only passed a series of filters but undergone a process of organization which links it with memories of similar previous experiences; it has already undergone a preliminary process of recognition. A word on a page is not perceived as a succession of of black and white shapes which must be interpreted before they can be understood; it is already a concept by the time it attains consciousness. This preconscious recognition accounts for the difficulty we have in spotting misprints in a manuscript – our brain has already been 'set' to anticipate and to perceive the correct spelling; the misprints have been filtered out before reaching consciousness. (There are five deliberate misprints in the previous two paragraphs.)

The development of a perceptual set to see one thing and ignore another is necessary to any behaviour. It is essential in searching if the lost object is to be 'seen' and recognized. Searchers carry in their mind a picture of the lost object. As each possible location is approached, sensations derived from that location are matched with the picture. When a fit, however approximate, is made, the object seen is 'recognized', attention is focused upon it, and further evidence is sought to confirm the initial impression.

COMPONENTS OF SEARCHING

A woman is searching anxiously for her son; she moves restlessly about the house looking in places in which she thinks he might be found. She appears distraught and is unaware that her hair is dishevelled. She is thinking constantly of the boy and, when she hears a creak on the stair, immediately associates it with him. 'John, is that you?' she calls. The components of this behaviour are:

1 Alarm, tension, and a state of arousal.
2 Restless movement.
3 Preoccupation with thoughts of the lost person.
4 Development of a perceptual set for that person.
5 Loss of interest in personal appearance and other matters which normally occupy attention.
6 Direction of attention towards those parts of the environment in which the lost person is likely to be.
7 Calling for the lost person.

Each of these components is to be found in the behaviour of bereaved people. The first two items, which are not peculiar to searching behaviour, have already been discussed. The special quality of pining or separation anxiety, which is the subjective accompaniment of the alarm reaction, is reflected in the special quality of the restless hyperactivity. This has been well described by Lindemann:

> The activity throughout the day of the severely bereaved person shows remarkable changes. There is no retardation of action and speech; quite to the contrary, there is a rush of speech, especially when talking about the deceased. There is restlessness, inability to sit still, moving about in an aimless fashion, *continually searching* for something to do. There is, however, at the same time, a painful lack of capacity to initiate and maintain normal patterns of activity.

> (Lindemann, 1944; my italics)

I would contend that the searching behaviour of the bereaved person is not 'aimless' at all. It has the specific aim of finding the one who is gone. But bereaved people seldom admit to having so irrational an aim and their behaviour is therefore regarded by others, and usually by themselves, as 'aimless'. Their search for 'something to do' is bound to fail because the things they can do are not, in fact, what they want to do at all. What they want is to find the lost person.

There are several reasons for the restlessness. As I have pointed out, restlessness is a part of the alarm reaction. It is also associated with anger and will need to be reconsidered in that context. One young woman whom I interviewed after the death of her *de facto* husband was repeatedly glancing over her right shoulder. She did this, she said, 'because he was always on my right'. In her case the repetition of this activity seemed to represent an abortive search. A widow who wrote for advice to Cruse, the British organization for bereavement care, described how she not only felt but acted upon a restless need to search: 'Everywhere I go I am searching for him. In crowds, in church, in the supermarket. I keep on scanning the faces. People must think I'm odd.'

Preoccupation with thoughts of the lost person and with the events leading up to the loss is a common feature in bereaved people. 'I never stop missing him,' said one widow, and the tendency to return again and again to thoughts of the lost person was still present in most of the London widows a year after bereavement.

IMAGES OF THE DEAD

These memories were remarkable for their clarity. The dead person would be pictured exactly as he was when alive. Usually he would be 'seen', for instance, in his accustomed chair, and the memory would be so intense as almost to amount to a perception: 'I keep seeing his very fair hair and the colour of his eyes'; 'I still see him, quite vividly, coming in the door'; 'I can always see him'. A similar clarity was often present in memories of the husband's voice or touch: 'I can almost feel his skin or touch his hands,' said one widow.

At other times, particularly at night or when attention was relaxed, the bereaved woman would go over in her mind the events of the past in which the lost person took part. During the early months of bereavement, and again as the anniversary of the death approached, memories of the last few weeks of the patient's life were common: 'I go through that last week again and again'; 'I find myself going through it'. The experience was sometimes so clear that it was almost as if the bereaved person was reliving the events of a year ago. 'A year ago today,' said a widow of sixty, 'was Princess Alexandra's wedding day. I said to him, "Don't forget the wedding." When I got in I said, "Did you watch the wedding?" He said, "No, I forgot." We watched it together in the evening except he had his eyes shut. He wrote a card to his sister and I can see him so vividly. I could tell you every mortal thing that was done on all those days. I said, "You haven't watched anything." He said, "No, I haven't."'

When these memories are of unhappy or horrific events that the person would prefer to forget they have consequences that are very different from those that result from happy memories. In fact the bereaved may complain that the memories of traumatic events interfere with their ability to think about and to grieve for the person who has died. It seems that we must make a distinction between grief and traumatic stress reactions and that what distinguishes the two is the character of the images which come to occupy the attention of the bereaved. A mother, who had woken to find her baby dead beside her, sat in the cemetery for hours recalling her dead baby with his glazed eyes and dry mouth. Painful illnesses or accidental deaths which cause mutilation of the dead person leave behind correspondingly painful memories. On the other hand, a peaceful death and a post-mortem appearance of repose or contentment is remembered with gratitude. An exception to this general rule was found in one woman whose husband had been married twice: she had always been jealous of his first wife and after her husband's death she remarked bitterly, 'He looked so happy in death it made me think he was with her.'

If recollections in the early stage of bereavement gave pain, happier memories often came to replace them. One widow, who was initially haunted by a vivid recollection of her husband's face after death, described how, as time passed, this memory faded and was replaced by a picture of him 'when he was normal'.

If the preoccupation with happy memories is a part of searching to regain the healthy person who is lost, what is the function of the intrusive memories of traumatic loss? Nobody would *want* to search for a baby that they know is dead or relive the painful death of a spouse, although they often feel compelled to do so. I suspect that traumatic memories and images represent a kind of rehearsal. It is almost as if, by playing the memory tape again and again, one could change the way it will come out and regain control of a world that has slipped out of control. This would be a logical thing to do if the person was not already dead. If, for instance, they were in great danger it would be logical and appropriate to focus all of one's attention on the circumstances in order to work out a way of changing the course of events. The last thing we should do is to give up and mourn for a person whose life is in danger but who is not yet dead. Only after the death does it become illogical and inappropriate to behave in this way.

The tendency to recall and relive painful memories of traumatic events has been noted after many types of psychological stress and is discussed further in Chapter 5. The points that seem relevant to a consideration of searching behaviour following bereavement are the peculiar clarity of the perception and the degree to which memories of the dead person preoccupy the mind of the survivor. Although there were a few occasions when widows complained that they were unable to recall the appearance of their spouse, such episodes were more often transient blocks in recall than lasting states of mind.

MISPERCEPTIONS

It is postulated that maintaining a clear visual memory of lost people facilitates the search by making it more likely that they will be located if, in fact, they are to be found somewhere within the field of search. It constitutes a part of the perceptual set for the lost person, by which incoming information from the sense organs is scanned for evidence of the lost object.

If a woman is set to perceive certain classes of object then it is likely that she will also misperceive those objects more often than usual. Ambiguous impressions will be interpreted to fit the looked for object and attention will be focused upon them until the mistake has been corrected.

Such occurrences are common after bereavement, as studies by Rees (1971) and Kalish and Reynolds, (1973) have shown. Widows in the London Study often described illusions of having seen or heard their dead husband. These illusions usually involved the misinterpretation of some existing sight or sound. 'I think I catch sight of him in his van, but it's the van from down the road,' said one. Other widows reported identifying a man in the street – as he came closer they would realize their mistake. A creak at night was interpreted as the husband moving about the house and a sound at the door as the husband coming home. Widows who had been accustomed to listen out for their husband during his last illness would hear him cough or call out. Such illusions, though disturbing at the time, were not more frequent among psychiatrically disturbed subjects and cannot be regarded as anything but a part of the normal reaction to bereavement. Nevertheless, they are sometimes of such vividness that people need to be reassured that they are not an unusual feature.

Although the pangs of grief and the urge to search are very powerful they are not present all of the time. The pang passes, the need to cry aloud diminishes and, for a while, the bereaved can turn their thoughts to other things. Bereaved people oscillate back and forth between grieving and the other demands of life – eating, sleeping, caring for surviving children, and so on. This oscillation has recently received much attention from psychologists and has been termed the 'Dual

Process of Grieving' (Stroebe, and Van den Bout, 1994). It needs to be understood if we are to make sense of the problems that arise when it goes wrong.

Between the pangs of grief life may appear to go on as usual but in fact that is not the way it feels. The appetites and enthusiasms that normally involve us are severely depleted and much of our behaviour seems governed by habit rather than desire. The newly bereaved people I have met showed little concern for food, sleep, personal appearance, work, or family. Although no systematic information was sought regarding sexual feelings, it is my impression that sexual appetite, too, is diminished during the early stages of bereavement. This, however, is not always the case, and an increased need for someone to cling to can sometimes lead to increased sexuality (Swigar *et al.*, 1976).

LOCATING THE DEAD

Being alert, restless, preoccupied, and set to find the lost person, the griever directs attention to those parts of the environment that are most closely associated with that person. At least half of the London widows admitted that they felt drawn towards places associated with their husband and most reluctant to leave the home where he had lived; they treasured possessions and parts of the house that were especially 'his', and tended to return repeatedly to them. One widow said, 'I walk around all where we used to go', and two others expressed the feeling that they must hurry home whenever they went out, because their husband would be waiting. One of these terminated a visit to her sister prematurely because she felt that she had left her husband too long.

Another kept going through her husband's clothes, feeling in the pockets and gazing at them. She remarked that it was here that the smell of her husband lingered most strongly and she found this very evocative of his presence. A London widow regularly wore her husband's dressing-gown. This, so she said, seemed to bring him closer. A thirteen-year-old girl who had lost her father angered and disgusted her mother by taking his pyjama jacket to bed with her at night. Photographs, pipes, wallets, and other 'close' personal possessions were often prominently displayed in places where the bereaved person preferred to be. Favourite pieces of furniture, 'his chair' for instance, were objects of special reverence. One widow had found that she could not get away from the notion that her husband was still sitting in his chair. She would sit in her own chair and find herself frequently gazing at his. This was so much of an interference with her other activities that she felt she had to do something to prevent it. The solution she finally adopted was satisfying and extremely simple: she sat in his chair herself.

Most widows liked to visit their husband's grave and several spoke of the almost uncanny attraction that drew them to the cemetery. They would think of him as being located in or around the grave and feel concern for his comfort if the weather was inclement: 'It's terrible if it's raining. It's as if I want to pick him up and bring him home.' One widow who had had her husband cremated explained this on the grounds that the local cemetery was occasionally flooded during wet weather and her husband had always been 'frightened of water'. She had a fantasy of all the corpses 'floating around in their coffins' and wouldn't have liked this for her husband.

On the whole, the sense of the dead person being located in his place of burial was less strong when he had been cremated. One widow whose husband had been a municipal gardener arranged for his ashes to be scattered in the public park where he had worked. Subsequently she visited the place frequently. Even the container in which the ashes had been placed had become numinous; it was placed on a table in the widow's sitting-room, an object of fascination and awe.

At Aberfan in Wales, where 116 children died when a water-laden coal tip inundated a school in 1966, visiting the burial place of the children became an important part of the life of bereaved mothers, and the wish to stay close to the dead children was the reason given by many parents for not moving out of the village. This was despite the fact that the disaster fund made a grant to each bereaved family to enable those who wished to do so to buy a house elsewhere.[3]

People who attempt to avoid painful reminders of the dead person by moving away usually come back, and the bereaved person who avoids reminders is aware of a sense of being pulled in two directions. One widow, for instance, moved into the back bedroom of her house to get away from her memories, but found that she missed her husband so much that she moved back into the front bedroom 'to be near him'. Two widows felt drawn towards the hospital where their husbands had passed their final illnesses, and one found herself walking into the hospital ward before she realized that he was not there. Another thought of her husband as being upstairs in the bed in which he had remained for many months before his death. She found herself listening out for him and sometimes thought she heard him calling for her.

Spiritualism claims to help bereaved persons in their search for the dead, and seven of the bereaved people who were included in my various studies described visits to seances or spiritualist churches. Their reactions were mixed: some felt that they had obtained some sort of contact with the dead and a few had been frightened by this. On the whole they did not feel satisfied by the experience and none had become a regular attender at spiritualist meetings.

REUNION

A more drastic solution to the problem of grief is suicide. This is sometimes considered as a way of achieving reunion with the dead; it may also be seen as an end to present alienation and misery. As we saw in the last chapter, several investigators have found an association between suicide and bereavement. In my own studies, ideas of suicide were often expressed. Many of the London widows went through a period during which they felt they 'might as well be dead'. Typically they would say, 'If it wasn't for the children I might consider it' – but in fact only one had made any sort of suicidal attempt and that was very half-hearted.

Among the bereaved psychiatric patients there was one, a girl of twelve, who had been admitted to hospital because of serious weight loss after the death of her mother. She had refused to eat and her father had said, 'You'll become like Mummy', whereupon she replied, 'That's just what I want to do. I want to die and be with Mummy.' Death was seen as a possible means of succeeding in her search for her mother.

CALLING

There remains one other accompaniment of searching which must be considered here. Calling for the lost person, while not strictly an essential part of searching, is often associated with it.

'Dwight, where are you? I need you so much,' wrote Frances Beck (1966) in her *Diary of a Widow*. Crying is, of course, a frequent feature of grief and sixteen of the twenty-two London widows cried when discussing their bereavement with me a month after the death of their husband. The fact that they cried does not, of course, mean that they were necessarily crying for their husbands. Crying is an expression of helplessness which can arouse sympathy and offers of help in many situations. On occasion, however, the object to which the cries of these widows were directed was quite clearly the husband. Faced with the fact that she would never have her husband back again, one widow shouted out, 'Oh Fred, I do need you', and then burst into tears. A bereaved mother cried out for her dead baby during the night, and a nurse called to her dead sister at night and dreamt repeatedly that she was searching for her sister but could not find her.

In the London Study tearfulness was closely associated with preoccupation with thoughts of the lost husband (see Appendix, section 9), and this finding seems to suggest that, whatever other factors contributed to cause these widows to cry, an important one was these memories.

GOAL-DIRECTED BEHAVIOUR

In order to get the search for a lost person into perspective we have to bear in mind that a great deal of human and animal behaviour contains elements of searching. Searching fills the gap between aims and object. Traditional psychology has paid little attention to this category of behaviour and it is only with the advent of ethology that the significance of searching has been recognized.

In analysing goal-directed behaviour ethologists have found it useful to divide it into the successive acts that make it up. A particular set of circumstances gives rise to behaviour A; this behaviour alters the situation and calls forth a fresh behaviour pattern, B; this further alters the situation until, if all goes well, the goal is achieved and the behaviour sequence is terminated.[4]

Stimuli that guide behaviour towards a set-goal are termed 'orienting stimuli' and stimuli that bring the sequence to an end 'terminating' or 'consummatory stimuli'. Similarly, behaviour that leads towards a set-goal is termed 'appetitive behaviour', and the final, more or less stereotyped, activity with which a behaviour sequence terminates has been called 'consummatory behaviour'.

This classification works well enough for behaviour such as coitus, and eating and drinking, which have as their goal a specific change in the organism. There are, however, some types of goal-situation that are continuous over time, for example, occupation of territory, incubation of eggs, or maintenance of proximity to mother. In such cases there is no consummatory behaviour and achievement of the goal-situation initiates a different type of ongoing activity whose effect is to ensure that the goal-situation will be continued.

Either type of behaviour sequence can fail to reach its goal. This may occur because the goal cannot be reached by the means employed or because more pressing stimuli distract attention and initiate a different behaviour sequence having higher priority in the hierarchy of goals. In the former case the behaviour is said to be frustrated.[5] C. S. Lewis (1961) has described the frustration of the mourner:

> I think I am beginning to understand why grief feels like suspense. It comes from the frustration of so many impulses that had become habitual. Thought after thought, feeling after feeling, action after action, had H [his wife] for their object. Now their target is gone. I keep on, through habit, fitting an arrow to the string; then I remember and I have to lay the bow down. So many roads lead through to H. I set out on one of them. But now there's an impassable frontier-post across it. So many roads once; now so many culs-de-sac.

In every appetite there is an element of searching, of finding the right fit between perception and action; and in the appetitive behaviour that mediates attachment to a human being the search element is more explicit. We speak of love as a 'tie'. The strength of a tie is its resistance to severance. The behaviour patterns mediating attachment ('attachment behaviour') are patterns of interaction: clinging, smiling, following, searching, calling, and so on. They have been described at length by Bowlby (1969). Some of these patterns, such as smiling and clinging, are best regarded as 'maintenance behaviour' and require the presence of the object for their evocation. Others, such as calling and searching, are appetitive activities and occur only in the absence of the object.

The goal-situation to which these behaviour patterns normally give rise is the optimum proximity of the loved person. When this is achieved the appetitive behaviour ceases. But if the loved person is permanently lost, appetitive behaviour will tend to persist and with it the subjective discomfort that accompanies unterminated striving. This is what is experienced as frustration.

HABITS

It is not only behaviour patterns mediating attachment that are evoked following bereavement. Many other behaviour patterns require the presence of the lost person for their termination although they are not themselves examples of attachment behaviour. Some of these are habits or activities established over the years, in which both parties shared or which depended for their relevance on both parties being alive: laying the table for two, washing up together, or making decisions about expenditure, leisure activities, and so on. When these patterns are initiated after the death of one party, a sense of frustration quickly follows. But alternative means of coping are usually available and the bereaved person soon learns to wash up alone and plan his or her own activities. When, however, attachment behaviour is evoked (as when a woman misses her husband in bed or finds herself waiting for him to come back from work), no substitute is acceptable. It is this that accounts for the persistence of the impulse to search long after habits such as laying the table for two have been unlearnt. C. S. Lewis is right in regarding the persistence of habit as a cause of frustration, but it is not the only cause. The suspense he describes would seem to indicate the expectation that something is about to happen. To the griever the only happening that seems important is the return of the one who is lost. And in social animals, from their earliest years, the principal behaviour pattern evoked by loss is searching.

IS GRIEF INEVITABLE FOLLOWING LOSS?

Wortman and Silver (1989) have suggested that distress, and by implication grief itself, is not inevitable following a loss but it is clear from their paper that they are confusing 'distress' with clinical depression which is certainly *not* inevitable (and I know of nobody who has suggested that it is). Anthropological studies have failed to reveal any society in which people do not show some sign of grieving although there is great variation in the ways in which this is expressed (Rosenblatt *et al.*, 1976). The only apparent exceptions to the rule seem to be people who lack any attachment to the person who has died and they cannot be said to have suffered a loss at all. Of course people can avoid and repress their feelings, and some of the ways in which they do this will be considered in the next chapter, but there is also evidence that, in the long run, grief will 'out'.

5

MITIGATION

> . . . They think they see their dead friends continually in their
> eyes, *observantes imagines* . . . 'all the year long' as Pliny
> complains to Romanus, 'methinks I see Virginius, I hear
> Virginius, I talk with Virginius, etc.'
>
> Robert Burton, *The Anatomy of Melancholy* (1621)

When appetitive behaviour is frustrated, as we have seen, there results
an increase in the intensity and persistence of that behaviour. But even
when pining is most intense something may happen to mitigate the pain
of grief. Some sight or sound will be misperceived and, for a moment, it
seems as if the search is at an end. Or the bereaved person may feel that
the lost one is near at hand without actually perceiving them.
Sometimes this mitigation occurs spontaneously, at others it is the
bereaved themselves who find ways to reduce the pain of grief and of
traumatic memories.

Widows I have interviewed have spoken of the comfort they derive
from putting a bolster beside them in the bed at night or from
pretending to themselves that their husband can hear their prayers. 'I
talk to him and quite expect him to answer me,' said one widow. A
certain 'willing suspension of disbelief' is necessary to allow such
pretences to succeed and there is always the danger that one may 'wake
up' to the emptiness of it all. But it seems that many bereaved people
get comfort from such behaviour.

FINDING

The commonest means of mitigating the pain of grieving comprises the
maintenance of a feeling or impression that the bereaved person is
nearby although they may not be seen or heard. A comforting sense of

the persisting presence of the lost husband was reported by fifteen of the twenty-two London widows. To some extent this seemed to allay restlessness and pining. Thus one widow said, 'I still have the feeling he's near and there's something I ought to be doing for him or telling him.' Often the dead person was not in any particular place: 'He's not anywhere in particular, just around the place; it's a good feeling'; 'Spiritually he's near'; 'I still feel that he's around'.

Just as the child feels braver when mother is nearby, so the widow tends to feel more secure when the sense of her husband's presence is strong: 'When I'm washing my hair, it's the feeling he's there to protect me in case someone comes in through the door.'

One is reminded of comparable behaviour in animals whose circumstances allow the initiation but not the termination of appetitive behaviour – sooner or later, in partial or complete form, the missing behaviour sequence may take place *in vacuo*. For example, Tinbergen (1951) has described the behaviour of a male stickleback when confined in an empty tank. It comprises a sequence of zigzag movements (termed the 'zigzag dance') which, under normal conditions, takes place only when the male stickleback perceives the characteristic appearance and movements of a pregnant female. This behaviour normally induces the female to follow the male to the nest, where the eggs are laid and fertilized. In the empty tank, however, the zigzag dances may be performed alone. Similarly, captive starlings have been observed to carry out the movements of fly-catching even when no flies are present (Lorenz, 1937). It is, of course, impossible to state dogmatically that these 'vacuum activities' are homologous with similar behaviour in human beings. All we can do is note with interest that, in many species, when 'seeking' behaviour is evoked at high intensity, 'finding' behaviour will often occur even in the absence of the object sought.

We have no means of knowing if the vacuum activities of social animals are accompanied by a sense of the presence of the sought-for object, but it seems likely that they are. Tinbergen points out that in many species deprivation lowers the threshold for the perception of 'releasing stimuli' whereas satiation raises that threshold.

Could some such process explain the misperception of the newly bereaved woman who 'sees' her husband approaching in the street, only to find when she goes to greet him that it is somebody else, or the behaviour of a woman whose infant has died who goes into the child's room in order to rock an empty cradle?

In the newly bereaved widow the perceptual element is very strong: 'He's with me all the time. I hear him and see him although I know it's only imagination.' 'If I didn't take a strong hold on myself I'd get talking to him.' Occasionally hypnagogic (half-waking) hallucinations occur. One widow was resting in her chair on a Sunday afternoon when she saw her husband, quite clearly, digging in the garden with only his trousers on; another saw her husband coming in through the garden gate; a third saw her dead father standing by her bed at night.

That 'searching' and 'finding' go together is not surprising. A 'sense of the continued presence of the deceased', 'a clear visual memory of him', and 'preoccupation with thoughts of him' were statistically associated (see Appendix, section 9); that is to say, widows with a strong sense of their husband's presence also tended to recall him with great clarity and to be preoccupied with his memory. All these phenomena, which have been referred to as components of searching, are also components of finding.

THE SENSE OF PRESENCE

Confirmation of this evidence comes from Rees's well-conducted study of 227 widows and 66 widowers of all ages (1971). He found that 39 per cent had a sense of the presence of the dead spouse and 14 per cent experienced hallucinations or illusions of his or her presence from time to time.

Those who experienced such illusions or a sense of their spouse's presence reported significantly more loneliness than those who reported no such illusions; and they also missed the dead person more, and thought and dreamt of him or her more often. But 69 per cent of those with a sense of the presence of the dead spouse felt helped by their illusions and they had significantly less sleep disturbance than the rest. Furthermore, illusions and a sense of the dead spouse's presence were more common in those who were over forty, of 'hysteroid' personality type and higher social class, who had been happily married, and had been bereaved for less than ten years at the time of the study. There was no relationship between the prevalence of illusions and religious faith, mode of death, social isolation, depression, appetite, or weight disturbance.

It seems that while searching and finding cannot, logically, occur simultaneously, they are often so closely juxtaposed as to be inseparable. Thus a widow may be preoccupied with a clear visual memory of her husband: at one moment she is anxiously pining for him, and a moment later she experiences a comforting sense of his presence nearby; then something reminds her that this sense is only an illusion and she is pining again.

As time passes, if all goes well, the intensity of pining diminishes and the pain and pleasure of recollection are experienced as a bitter-sweet mixture of emotions, 'nostalgia'. By this time the two components seem to be experienced simultaneously.

Mrs P was the devoted, thirty-year-old daughter of an assertive and somewhat dominant woman. When her mother died Mrs P consciously directed her search towards making contact with the departed spirit. In company with her sister she improvised a planchette with which she 'received' messages which she believed came from her mother.

At a seance she noticed a toby jug which seemed to resemble her mother. She felt that her mother's spirit had entered into this jug and she persuaded her sister to give it to her. For some weeks she kept the jug near at hand and had a strong sense of the presence of her mother. However, the jug proved a mixed blessing since she found that she was both attracted and frightened by it. Her husband was exasperated by this behaviour and eventually, against her will, he smashed the jug. His wife noticed that the pieces, which she buried in the garden, 'felt hot' – presumably a sign of life.

Mrs P did not give up her search. Shortly after the jug was broken she acquired a dog. Her mother had always said that if she was ever reincarnated it would be in the form of a dog. When I interviewed Mrs P three years later she said of the dog: 'She's not like any other animal. She does anything. She'll only go for walks with me or my husband. She seems to eat all the things that mother used to eat. She doesn't like men.'

It is easy to dismiss the behaviour of Mrs P as 'abnormal', but is it so remote from the behaviour of other bereaved people who build memorials to 'keep alive' the memory of the dead? They derive the same comfort, the same sense of having found the lost person, from such memorials as that which Mrs P derived from her toby jug and her dog. Moreover, as Gorer (1965) has pointed out, a majority of people in the world believe in reincarnation, and even in Britain today this belief is more common than the teachings of the established churches would lead us to expect. Thus Gorer found that 9 per cent of 359 bereaved people from all parts of Britain believe in reincarnation.

THE BEREAVEMENT DREAM

The recovery of the lost person may also be achieved in dreams. Half the London widows reported dreaming of their husband after his death, and half of these dreams had a peculiarly vivid and realistic quality.

It was just like everyday life – my husband coming in and getting his dinner. Very vivid so that when I woke up I was very annoyed.

Most commonly these dreams were happy dreams of interaction with the dead husband. Less frequently he was dying or going away, but even in the happy dreams there was usually something to indicate that all was not well.

The third week after he died I dreamt I was lying in bed and he came up and sat on the bed. I frowned up at him and he said, 'Take care of the children, because I'm going back home.' He wanted to take J and I said, 'No, you can't have him because there's no one to look after him at home [in the West Indies].' He banged the door and went off. I had a feeling that he's no more, he shouldn't be around here.'

He was trying to comfort me and putting his arms round me. I kept turning away and crying and crying. Even in the dream I know he's dead . . . But I felt so happy and I cried and he couldn't do anything about it . . . When I touched his face it was as if he was really there – quite real and vivid.

He was in bed. I was saying, 'Come on P, you're going to be all right.' Then I woke up and it wasn't. It was quite a shock.

Such dreams are not just wish-fulfilling fantasies; they all contain intimations of the husband's death. Even in a dream, reality insists upon asserting itself.

He was in the coffin with the lid off and all of a sudden he came to life and got out. And I was so overjoyed to think that he was here that when I woke up I wondered where I was. It was so clear I was crying and laughing. I looked at him and he opened his mouth. I said, 'He's alive. He's alive.' I thought 'Thank God, I'll have him to talk to.'

These examples typify the bereavement dreams originally described by Waller (1951). As in waking life the imagery is vivid, dead people are thought of as if they are alive, but the shadow of their death falls over all. Hadfield (1954) has spoken of dreaming as a form of problem-solving behaviour, and it is no surprise to find that bereaved dreamers continue to go over in their minds the vivid mental images that preoccupy their waking hours and, out of them, create the action, setting and cast of their dreams. Unfortunately the 'problem' of bereavement, the recovery of the lost object, is one that cannot be solved (even in dreams). No matter how happy the dream, there must always be a 'sad awakening'.

DISBELIEF

But there are other ways of mitigating the pain of grieving. These enable the bereaved person to avoid, consciously or unconsciously, the thoughts that are so painful, or to dissociate the pain from the thoughts.

One of these ways, perhaps the most frequently encountered, is to disbelieve that the loss has occurred. 'I can't believe it's true' was a sentiment expressed, in some form, by most widows in the London Study, and even a year after bereavement half of them still said that there were times when they could not believe what had happened: 'It's like a dream. I feel I'm going to wake up and it'll be all right. He'll be back again.' Others felt that they were waiting for their husband to come back after a temporary absence.

Disbelief in the fact of loss was seldom complete. As one man whose wife had died said: 'I just didn't want them to talk about it, because the more they talked the more they'd make me believe she was dead.'

This tendency to disbelieve the true situation was evident prior to the death, during the terminal illness. Nineteen of the twenty-two London widows had been warned of the seriousness of their husband's illness before his death; twelve later admitted that they had not believed what they had been told. Either they did not believe that the doctor had diagnosed their husband's illness correctly or they accepted the diagnosis but thought that their husband was not as seriously ill as they were told. Even among the seven who said that they had believed what they were told there were three who subsequently distorted the information or 'pushed it to the back of their minds'.

Whereas, in the normal course of events, a person who has reason to doubt the correctness of a doctor's diagnosis will ask for a second opinion, this was not the case when the disbelief was an attempt to avoid realization of incipient loss. At one level of awareness these women knew very well that their husbands were dying and they dealt with that knowledge by splitting it off and continuing to think, and to some extent act, as if they were not. But, while they continued to pretend to their husband and to themselves that he would recover, they did not fail to inform other relatives of the seriousness of the situation or to make essential plans for the contingency of his death. This capacity to hold in the mind two contradictory beliefs has been termed 'double knowledge' (Weisman, 1972). It is commonly seen in patients with terminal illness whose insight into their prognosis seems to vary in a bewildering way.

The fact that the wives of seriously ill men regularly minimized the gravity of their husband's illness does not mean, therefore, that they were completely unprepared for the death when it occurred. After they had been informed of the seriousness of their husband's condition, each woman came to terms with the illness in her own time and in her own way. Some, whose husbands had been ill for a long time, had observed a gradual deterioration and the doctor's words simply confirmed their own fears. But nearly all of them were unrealistically optimistic and continued to hope for recovery long after the medical authorities had given up.

NUMBNESS

If there are advantages to be obtained from denying the true situation during the terminal illness one would think that the death itself would put an end to all self-deception. But, as I have said, this is not the case. In half the London widows the actual bereavement was followed by a feeling of 'numbness' or 'blunting'. This experience is so common that it can be regarded as the first phase of bereavement as described on page 7. It did not necessarily come on at once, but usually within a few minutes; it then lasted from a few hours to a few days. During the period of numbness outbursts of extreme distress may 'break through' or the bereaved person may feel 'ill' or 'solid'.

One widow whose husband died alone during an attack of a rare form of asthma had found his body hanging over the banisters. Her first thought was to get the children out of the house. As the door closed behind them, ' I suddenly burst. I was aware of a horrible wailing and I knew it was me. I was saying I loved him and all that. I knew he'd gone but I kept on talking to him.' She went into the bathroom and retched. Then the feeling of numbness came over her. 'I felt numb and solid for a week. It's a blessing . . . everything goes hard inside you . . . like a heavy weight.' She felt that the numbness enabled her to cope with the children and arrange the funeral and family gathering without crying.

Even in cases when the death came as a relief, numbness and difficulty in accepting the fact of its occurrence were likely. One woman, who had felt as if she were living on the edge of a precipice during the long series of coronary thromboses suffered by her husband, had an immediate sense of relief when he died. At the same time, however, 'It didn't register at all. It didn't seem real.' She shut her mind to the idea that he would not be coming back from the hospital and carried on behaving automatically.

Outright disbelief was rare, but some widows tried to convince themselves that there had been a mistake and it was not until they saw their husband's lifeless body that they were forced to believe him dead. 'I wouldn't believe it till I saw him on the Monday [four days after his death].'

For several widows it was the funeral service that 'brought home' the reality of what had happened. This was particularly so when the remains were cremated, since this seemed somehow 'more final' than burial. Two widows described fantasies of their husband being alive inside his coffin and one had to be restrained as the coffin was moved away.

PHYSICAL SYMPTOMS

The incompleteness of the defensive numbness is indicated in the sense of impending disaster and tension that hangs over the bereaved person at this time. 'It's like walking on the edge of a black pit,' said one. Others felt pent up, 'As if my head was going to burst . . . I was in a dream . . . just couldn't take it all in . . . I couldn't believe it.'

Despite the lack of overt emotion, several developed physical symptoms at this stage. Thus one widow felt 'ill and shivery' and took to her bed for two days. Another felt 'as if my inside had been torn out'. But they were usually able to carry on and behave in a controlled and automatic manner: 'There was so much to do, but I didn't feel like I was doing it for anyone – not for him, if you see.' Or, 'It didn't seem real.'

DEPERSONALIZATION AND DEREALIZATION

Depersonalization occurs when bereaved people feel as if they are themselves unreal, whereas derealization implies that it is the world that seems unreal. Either or both of these phenomena can occur following bereavement. These feelings of unreality were transient and seldom severe except in two of the London widows. In both cases derealization persisted throughout much of the first year of bereavement.

A woman of fifty lost her husband after nursing him at home for over six months. During this time she kept her knowledge of his condition from him. She was, she said, fully prepared for his death, which came after he had been unconscious for two days. Nevertheless, she cried profusely and was in 'utter despair' for the next two days. She then experienced a sense of unreality and emptiness, all her reactions seemed blunted, and she was unable to feel anything for her children although she described their behaviour as 'marvellous'. When I first saw her, a month after bereavement, she spoke in a hushed voice and often seemed distant, mishearing my questions and seeming dazed. 'I feel I'm waiting for something to happen, for the unreal feeling to pass,' she said. 'I feel this as a different life . . . as if there's another life going on somewhere else and I'll waken up.' In this 'other life' her husband was alive and well.

She kept her mind occupied as much as possible to avoid thoughts of her loss. When forced to think of her husband, she was aware of a sense of dread, almost panic. Because of this she tried to avoid people who would remind her of his death and she found our interviews an ordeal. But she continued to take part in the study. By the sixth month the real world was beginning to re-establish itself, and at the end of a year she no longer felt the need to avoid people who reminded her of the past. The feeling of unreality had almost gone and returned only occasionally when she was on her own.

AVOIDING THOUGHTS OF LOSS

As seen in this case, another way of mitigating the pain of grief is to avoid all thoughts of the lost person and to avoid people and situations that will act as reminders. Two-thirds of the London widows said that they attempted to avoid reminders from time to time during the first month of bereavement, and six were still avoiding them a year later, though to a marked degree in only one case.

Thoughts of loss can be avoided by filling one's life with activities, and several widows deliberately kept themselves busy and worked until late at night for this purpose. Others put away photographs or personal effects which they found particularly evocative of their husband and many went through a period during which they were unable to pluck up courage to sort out or dispose of their husband's clothing. They usually remained at home because they feared that if they went out they would meet sympathetic people and they were afraid of showing their distress in public. On the other hand, a few moved away from the home which held so many reminders of the past and stayed, for a while, with relatives.

These conscious attempts to escape the pain of grief contrasted strangely with the way in which the bereaved were preoccupied, at the same time, with thoughts of their loss. They felt drawn back again and again to thoughts and situations associated with the lost person. For example, one widow who left home to escape painful memories returned there after only two days in order to be closer to her husband. Activities that were taken up in order to keep the mind occupied were often abandoned because of the difficulty of concentrating upon them.

That is not to say that attempts to avoid the pain of grief were uniformly unsuccessful. One woman of fifty-eight lost her husband suddenly and unexpectedly from a cerebral haemorrhage. She found it very difficult to believe him dead and kept breaking down and crying during the first week. She then discovered that she could stop crying by deliberately keeping her thoughts occupied with other things. She avoided going into her husband's room and persuaded her son to dispose of most of his possessions. When I first saw her a month after bereavement she broke off several times, unable to talk for fear that she would cry. A year later her overall state was much calmer but she still avoided possessions that would remind her of her husband and disliked visiting his grave. 'If he comes in my mind I try to get – to think of something else,' she said.

As time passed, and the intensity of grief diminished, those who had been avoiding things found it less necessary to do so and those who had been preoccupied with thoughts of the death found it easier to think of other things. Going through the husband's clothes or sorting out his belongings was viewed as a turning-point by some widows; others felt that their turning-point was reached when they redecorated the parlour and rearranged the furniture for the first time. Thus while searching and avoidance of searching occupied much of the widow's time during the early months of her bereavement, both became less intense with the passage of time, and other interests returned.

SELECTIVE FORGETTING

One other means of mitigating the pain of grieving was 'selective forgetting'. Lindemann (1960) has described how 'the image of the deceased disappears from consciousness'. In my own studies this was a very rare occurrence and the opposite was the rule. That is to say, the image of the deceased was retained with great clarity. The one exception was a widow of twenty-six who was unable to recall the face of her husband during the first month after his death. She complained bitterly of this and by the time of the second interview, three months after bereavement, she had recovered her memory and now had a clear visual picture of him. Unlike most of the other psychological features of grieving, the memory of the dead person tends, if anything, to increase in clarity in the course of the first year of bereavement (see Appendix, section 10).

CHANGES OVER TIME

In talking to widows about their memories of their husband I had the impression that it took time to order these and to see him as a whole person; the harder they *tried* to recall him the more difficult it was. C. S. Lewis, shortly after his wife's death, wrote in his diary of his fear of forgetting her and angrily denounced as 'pitiable cant' the idea that 'she will live forever in my memory'. Later, he described an experience that was not uncommon among the widows I have met:

> Something quite unexpected has happened. It came this morning early. For various reasons, not in themselves at all mysterious, my heart was lighter than it had been for many weeks. For one thing, I suppose I am recovering physically from a good deal of mere exhaustion . . . and after ten days of low-hung grey skies and motionless warm dampness, the sun was shining and there was a light breeze. And suddenly *at the very moment when, so far, I mourned H least, I remembered her best*. Indeed it was something (almost) better than memory; an instantaneous, unanswerable impression. To say it was like a meeting would go too far. Yet there was that in it which tempts one to use those words. It was as if the lifting of the sorrow removed a barrier.
>
> Why has no one told me these things? How easily I might have misjudged another man in the same situation? I might have said, 'He's got over it. He's forgotten his wife,' when the truth was, 'He remembers her better because he has partly got over it.'
>
> (1961)

Does this contradict my notion that the clarity of visual memories of lost people is related to the need to search for and to find them? I think not. Two factors seem to me to contribute to the gradual increase in the clarity of memories as reported by widows and widowers.

First, there is the reduction, over time, of conscious monitoring of the search. Just as it is often hard to remember names if we are trying too hard to recall them, so it seems that too intense a conscious wish to recall the features of a lost person inhibits the recollection. It is impossible to search when we are preoccupied with thinking how impossible it is to search. 'Is it,' says Lewis, 'the very intensity of the longing that draws the iron curtain, that makes us feel we are staring into a vacuum when we think about our dead?' Often, when we stop striving to remember, the memory come back to us unbidden.

Second, it seems to take time for us to begin to recall 'as a whole' people whose lives have been so close to our own that we have experienced them in a thousand fragmented parts. I have a clear memory of Mr Harold Wilson, whom I never met, looking at me out of my television set and talking in a serious, weighty voice. But my wife has become so complex and so familiar a person that I cannot view her as a whole at all. I suspect that it would take a long period of absence for me to fit together my numerous fragmentary recollections of her to make anything like a consistent picture. I am too close to see the wood for the trees.

BUILDING A NEW IMAGE OF THE DEAD PERSON

Viewed in this light the work of grieving becomes a creative activity. A gradual piecing together of the pieces of a jigsaw that, eventually, will enable us to find an image and a place in our lives for the people we have loved and lost. One aspect of this task is the re-evaluation of the dead person, an activity sometimes termed 'idealization', since it is the happy memories and valued aspects of the relationship that we treasure and wish to perpetuate.

Memories of the negative aspects of the dead are lost and idealization is carried out by most bereaved people and encouraged by society. Attempts to establish the reliability of the widow's view of her marriage by interviewing other members of her family had to be abandoned early in the London Study because it was clear that questions on so charged a matter were likely to be resented and that the information obtainable from other relatives would be just as distorted as that obtainable from the widow. It is not possible, therefore, to make any reliable estimate of the degree of idealization that was usual.

A woman of fifty-nine had quarrelled frequently with her husband and left him on several occasions during their married life. She blamed his alcoholism and gambling for their poor relationship and was rather surprised to find that she missed him at all when I first saw her: 'I shouldn't really say so, but it's more peaceful now that he's gone.' In the course of her first year as a widow her two youngest daughters got married and left home. She was left alone in her flat and became increasingly lonely and depressed. She spoke nostalgically of the old days and at the last interview, a year after bereavement, was hoping to marry again – 'to someone kind like my husband'.

As long as her husband had been alive this lady had been caught up in a long series of quarrels which had coloured her view of him. If 'idealization' implies a rose-tinted view of reality, the opposite is also possible. This lady seemed to have 'monsterized' her husband and, at the time of his death, she could see little good in him. Later she came to regret this alienation and the new image of her husband may have been no more distorted in a positive direction than her previous memories had been distorted in a negative way. Since nobody can be all good or all bad, the opportunity for monsterization and idealization is always present and it may be that one of the things we need to do when somebody dies is to redress the balance in a positive direction. Most of the time this does no harm but occasionally, as we shall see on page 128, it can create problems.

FINDING A BALANCE – APPROACH AND AVOIDANCE

To the psychiatrist it is all too easy to see the mental processes by which the bereaved reduce some of the pain of grief as 'defences'. Freud's concept of defence arose from his studies of neuroses and he first used the term in an article entitled 'The Neuro-Psychoses of Defence', published in 1894. Because repression and other defensive processes play a large part in neurotic illness, and because psychoanalysis was developed as a means of helping patients to abandon their defences, a somewhat negative view of defence prevails today. A subtle ethic has crept into much of our thinking which seems to imply that ego defences are a 'bad thing' and that we would all be much better off without them.

Studies of bereavement throw doubt on this assumption. In short, it seems to me that most of the phenomena we lump together as defences have an important function in helping to regulate the quantity of novel, unorganized, or in other respects disabling information an individual is handling at a given time. We see this most clearly in the nursery when young children are scanning, manipulating, and exploring an environment whose complexity varies greatly. In the face of new or large or threatening stimuli they withdraw or hide, or call upon their mother for support; then, gradually and warily, they begin to make familiar those very stimuli they at first found alarming.

In a similar way the widow, whose world has suddenly changed very radically, withdraws from a situation of overwhelming complexity and potential danger. Lacking her accustomed source of reassurance and support, she shuts herself up at home and admits only those members of her family with whom she feels most secure. She avoids stimuli that will remind her of her loss and attempts, in the ways I have described, to regain some part of her lost spouse. At the same time, and to an increasing extent as time passes, she begins, little by little, to examine the implications of what has happened and in this way to make familiar and controllable the numerous areas of uncertainty that now exist in her world.

Thus we have two opposing tendencies: an inhibitory tendency, which by repression, avoidance, postponement, and so on, holds back or limits the perception of disturbing stimuli, and a facilitative or reality-testing tendency, which enhances perception and thought about disturbing stimuli. At any given time an individual may respond more to one of these tendencies than to the other, and over time, he will often oscillate between them, so that a period of intense pining will alternate with a period of conscious or unconscious avoidance of pining.

Viewed thus, 'defence' can be seen as part of the process of 'attacking' a problem, of coming to grips with it in a relatively safe and effective way. That it may not always enable the individual to succeed in mastering the problem, and may at times become distorted or pathological, does not detract from its proper function, which is, presumably, the restoration of control by distancing an individual from a situation that threatens to become overwhelming.

The term 'coping' is nowadays preferred to that of 'defence' but there are also problems in the use of this term. 'Coping' implies an element of choice, we choose to cope in a particular way. Yet bereaved people who experience a sense of numbness or unreality in the face of overwhelming grief are not consciously choosing to cope with their grief by shutting it out. Their reaction is automatic and outside conscious control.

Psychotherapists sometimes speak of a person as being 'highly defended' or 'poorly defended'. The underlying assumption is that there is a general 'defensiveness', akin, perhaps, to the 'g' factor of intelligence. This would lead us to suppose that people who defend themselves against the pain of grieving by intense numbness during the early stage of grief would also have greater difficulty than most in accepting the fact that loss had occurred and a greater tendency to avoid reminders of loss; hence measures of 'numbness', 'difficulty in accepting the fact of loss', and 'avoidance of reminders' would intercorrelate. In the London Study, however, there was no significant correlation between quantitative assessments of these three defences (see Appendix, section 9).

Another hypothesis would be that these defences are alternatives – for instance, that a person who disbelieves in the reality of the loss does not need also to avoid reminders. If this was the case, however, one would expect to find a negative correlation between the defences: widows who scored high on 'disbelief' would score low on 'avoidance', and vice versa. But again there was no significant negative correlation between the three defences.

It may be that both these hypotheses are partially correct and that the effect is to cancel out any correlation, positive or negative, that might have occurred were only one of them applicable. The only justifiable conclusion would seem to be that defences are not simply an additive matter and that assessments based on one do not permit us to make assumptions about other defences or about 'defendedness' in general.

The searching behaviour described in Chapter 4 can occur only if the bereaved person disregards the fact that the dead person is permanently lost. Is it, therefore, a consequence of a defence? At the same time searching is a very painful process which is associated with intense anxiety – so much so that conscious efforts are often made to avoid situations likely to evoke the urge to search. Are the bereaved people, at this point, defending themselves against the consequence of a defence?

OSCILLATION

The problem here is that the lost are gone and the bereaved want them back. Reality-testing tells them that this is impossible. But immediate acceptance of this would involve an instant and major change in their identity or rather a host of major changes in their identity which cannot take place in a moment – it takes time. In order to buy time the mind has its own ways of limiting the input of disorganizing information. If this limitation was complete individuals could not begin to adjust to the problem (achieve a fresh identity). Most of the time, therefore, defences are partial blocks which alternate or coexist with painful realization. The 'Dual Process' of oscillation which was described on page 53f is, therefore, a part of a gradual process of realization. In this context the searching that follows bereavement is a form of facilitative behaviour whose function is the recovery of the lost object. It is not itself a defence although it depends upon a defence (partial denial of the permanence of the loss) for its occurrence.

It is clear that in this instance the behaviour does not eliminate pain or anxiety. It may reduce it but it also prolongs it. Provided that the balance of facilitation and defence is right, however, the grief work will continue, patterns of thought and behaviour which have been recognized as redundant will be habituated, and new appropriate patterns will be developed.

In like manner, repeated reviewing of the events leading up to the loss, which is described below, is an attempt to attack the problem of loss which would be inappropriate if the individuals had fully accepted the fact of loss. In denying the reality of the loss they provide themselves with the opportunity to prepare for it.

REVIEWING AND WORRYING

For bereaved people, time is out of joint. They may know, from the calendar, that a year has passed since their bereavement, but their memories of the lost person are so clear that it seems like 'only yesterday'. Of the twenty-two London widows, eighteen said that time had passed quickly, and the first year of bereavement was looked back upon as a limbo of meaningless activity.

Much more real was the memory of the period leading up to the bereavement, and bereaved people found themselves repeatedly reviewing, going over in their minds, the events leading up to the death, as if by so doing they could undo or alter the events that had occurred. 'I go through that last week in the hospital again and again,' said one widow, 'it seems photographed on my mind.'

These reminiscences obtrude upon the mind much as anticipatory worrying preoccupies people who fear a possible misfortune. And since, as we have seen, the newly bereaved are rarely able to accept, in full, the reality of what has happened, it may be that they have the same need to prepare themselves for disaster as those who have not yet experienced one. This type of anticipation has been called 'worry work' (Janis, 1958), and when it occurs before a misfortune it has the effect of focusing the attention on possible dangers and providing an opportunity for appropriate planning. It also enables individuals to begin to alter their views of the world and to give up some of the assumptions and expectations that have been established; this, of course, is a painful process.

Human beings are seldom surprised. Their ability to anticipate important changes in their lives enables them to make the necessary changes in their expectations in advance and to experience a part of the emotion appropriate to the disaster before it occurs. When it occurs they are to some extent prepared for it both intellectually and emotionally; their behaviour is correct and emotion adequately controlled. It is the capacity for worry work that makes this possible.

REALIZATION

The change having taken place, one might think that the need to worry about it had come to an end, and in respect of minor changes this is probably the case. But we have seen that a major change such as bereavement cannot be fully realized at one time. Bereaved people continue to act, in many ways, as if the lost person were still recoverable and to worry about the loss by going over it in their mind. This activity has been termed 'grief work' by Freud (1917), and it can be assumed to have the same function as worry work in preparing bereaved individuals for a full acceptance of their loss. An important difference between worry work and grief work is that worry work is based on anticipation whereas grief work is based on memory. People who anticipate an event may get it wrong; they may pretend to themselves that a particular outcome cannot occur; or they may worry unnecessarily about dangers that never arrive. Grief work, on the other hand, arises largely from memory, although bereaved people may use their imagination to fill in the gaps – to provide pictures of events that they have forgotten or have never witnessed.

At such a time there is a conscious need to 'get it right', and getting it right is not just a matter of recalling the traumatic event correctly; it includes the need to 'make sense' of what has happened, to explain it, to classify it along with other comparable events, to make it fit into one's expectations of the world. 'I think, if only I'd woken up early, perhaps I could have saved him.' Trying out new solutions, searching for clues to explain 'why did it happen to me?', and repeatedly, monotonously, remembering the sequence of events leading up to the death – these are what make up the process of grief work. Painful reminiscence has been described following major psychological traumata such as terrifying battle experiences, and it is, as we have seen, one of the prominent features of Post-Traumatic Stress Disorder. The same restless need to recall and describe the trauma is found and, under abreactive drugs or in a state of hypnosis, the battle may be relived in dramatic form as if the patient were fighting it over again.

Freud has described how, in grief work, each memory that bound the survivor to the lost object must be brought up and 'hypercathected'. By

76

this he means that 'energy' must be used to sever the link with the lost object and thereby set free the energy that is bound up with it (cathexis). It is important to bear in mind that Freud is not here speaking of real physical energy but of a hypothetical psychic energy (libido) which obeys similar laws. His libido theory, of which this is a part, is a cybernetic model which is useful in so far as it fits the observed data, but it should not be taken too far.

In recent years energy models of this type have come under scrutiny (see, for instance, Bowlby's critique (1969) of libido theory) and it seems to me that they add little to our understanding of bereavement. No one would deny that real physical energy is involved in all mental processes, but the concept of mental energy begs too many questions. It seems very reasonable that when an event occurs which threatens our life or produces a major change in our assumptions about the world we need to devote time and physical energy to appraisal of the event and its consequences. If the event takes place suddenly or unexpectedly, then the appraisal can take place only after the event.

I suspect that the repeated recollection of traumatic experiences has some such function and the extent to which it persists may well reflect the extent to which the individual has failed to complete the painful process of replanning which such experiences necessitate. Presumably appraisal of a trauma normally enables people to establish in their minds, as realistically as possible, the true external situation so that they can make appropriate plans to cope with it. If they find themselves with no suitable plans for dealing with the fresh situation it may be that they will be unable to complete the process of appraisal. They may then find themselves repeating the chain of memories again and again rather than giving way to the depression that would arise if they admitted to themselves their own helplessness. Looked at in this way, post-traumatic reminiscences are similar to obsessions, ruminations, and compulsions; these recurrent patterns of thought or activity seem to enable people to ward off anxiety while at the same time attempting to grapple with the problem.

COMPONENTS OF GRIEF WORK

It seems, then, that several components go to make up the process of grief work:

1 There is preoccupation with thoughts of the lost person, which, I suggest, derives from the urge to search for that person.

2 There is painful repetitious recollection of the loss experience, which is the equivalent of worry work and which must occur if the loss is not fully accepted as irrevocable.

3 And there is the attempt to make sense of the loss, to fit it into one's set of assumptions about the world (one's 'assumptive world') or to modify those assumptions if need be.

These are not three different explanations of the same phenomenon but three interdependent components of a larger picture. Attempts to make sense of what has happened would seem to be one way of restoring what is lost by fitting its absence into some superordinate pattern. These attempts may succeed or they may not. If they do not, then the preoccupation will increase and may indeed become obsessive.

DOES ANTICIPATORY GRIEF TAKE PLACE?

It is this which has caused some writers to question the validity of the concepts of anticipatory grief and of grief work. Thus, Levy (1992) has shown that people with high scores on a measure of 'Anticipatory Grief' were more depressed after bereavement than were those with lower scores. He concludes that 'Anticipatory Grief may be a risk factor for early bereavement adjustment'. But this study was confined to the relatives of patients with cancer who normally have every opportunity to anticipate the death of the patient and, even if this were not the case, we should not be surprised to find that those who were most distressed before bereavement were also the most distressed afterwards.

In similar vein, Wortman and Silver (1989) quote figures from my work as well as their own which indicate that intense yearning for a lost person and preoccupation with thoughts of the loss during the early period after a bereavement predicts later problems in adjustment to loss. This they see as casting doubt on the value of grief work. In fact my own studies suggest that high degrees of pining and preoccupation often reflect a type of dependent attachment which overrides and interferes with the working through of grief and leads to a form of chronic grieving which will be described in more detail in Chapter 8. Conversely, people who showed little or no evidence of having expressed grief also do badly. It is the moderate grievers who seem to cope best and who can be said to be carrying out the grief work successfully. (Further details of these findings are given on page 141 and in the Appendix, section 17.)

LOSS AND CREATIVITY

Rochlin (1965) has written at length on the hypothesis that much creative activity and philosophico-religious thought has the purpose of restoring, in some form, the love objects we fear to lose or have lost. 'We shall meet again in the afterlife'; 'He will survive in the works he created'; 'They died so that the world might become a better place for those who come after them'. Each of these sentiments reflects a wish to preserve or restore some part of the person who is lost. To what extent this is in fact possible is a matter for debate and I would certainly not suggest that such activity is meaningless. On the contrary, there may be very real ways in which a person can survive physical dissolution, and the manner in which the survivors carry out their grief work may influence this outcome. In a study of 121 people bereaved by accident, suicide, homicide or natural death, Smith *et al.* (1992) found that belief in an afterlife was associated with more recovery, greater well-being and less avoidance of grief than was lack of belief.

Lifton *et al.* (1979) say:

> A *sense* of immortality is not simply a denial of death. Rather it reflects a compelling and universal inner quest for a continuous symbolic relationship between our finite individual lives and what has gone before and what will come after. It is a search for symbolizing continuities, despite the discontinuities of death.

Lifton goes on to describe five general modes in which this striving can be expressed: biological, theological, creative, natural and experiential transcendence. Any or all of these modes is likely to become part of the attempt to find meaning in bereavement.

But for most people in the early stages of bereavement the world is in chaos. Because they are striving to find what cannot be found they ignore what can be found. They feel as if the most central, important aspect of themselves is gone and all that is left is meaningless and irrelevant – hence the world itself has become meaningless and irrelevant. In their heart of hearts they often believe that the dead do not return yet they are committed to the task of recovering one who is dead. It is no wonder that they feel that the world has lost its purpose, and no longer makes sense.

6

ANGER AND GUILT

Blow, winds, and crack your cheeks; rage, blow.
You cataracts and hurricanoes, spout
Till you have drench'd our steeples, drown'd the cocks.
You sulph'rous and thought-executing fires,
Vaunt-couriers of oak-cleaving thunderbolts,
Singe my white head. And thou, all-shaking thunder,
Strike flat the thick rotundity o' the world;
Crack nature's moulds, all germens spill at once,
That makes ingrateful man.

King Lear

The expression of irritability and anger in bereavement varies from one person to another, from one family to another and from one time to another. Sometimes it is directed against others and sometimes against the bereaved themselves, as self-reproaches or guilt.

PROTEST

On the basis of his observations of young children separated from their mother through admission to hospital or residential nursery, Robertson (1953) coined the term 'protest' for the first phase of their response. And in a study comparing children aged sixteen to twenty-six months in a residential and a day nursery, those in the residential nursery showed violent hostility of a type hardly seen in the day nursery (Heinicke and Westheimer, 1966). Examples of aggressive behaviour in animals as a reaction to separation are included in a paper by Bowlby (1961) exploring the psychological processes engaged in mourning and their biological roots. He quotes from the literature the case of Stasi, a mongrel bitch described by Lorenz (1954), who after being separated from her master for the second time became disobedient, unruly, and increasingly ferocious. He also cites the raging and screaming of Yerkes's apes when taken forcibly from their companions (Yerkes, 1943).

Bowlby sees protest as the means whereby the child punishes its mother for desertion and he claims that the experience may be so unpleasant for the mother that the likelihood of her deserting the child again is greatly reduced. Hence the phase of protest has survival value and effectively strengthens the bond between mother and child. As an integral part of the normal reaction to separation it is also to be expected following bereavement in adult life.

From the London Study it would appear that, in human adults, irritability and anger are a feature of the early (yearning) phase of grief and that loss of aggressiveness occurs in a later (despair) phase. Excessive anger was reported by all save four of the London widows at some time during the first year of bereavement. Nevertheless, there were only seven who showed their anger at the time of the first interview, and only two to four showed anger at subsequent interviews. Anger should not, therefore, be regarded as a continuous state.

BITTERNESS

The most frequent form, described by over half the widows, was a general irritability and bitterness. This was commonly associated with a feeling that the world had become an insecure or dangerous place, an attitude that often persisted throughout the first year of bereavement.

Anger was closely associated with restlessness and tension and, as noted in Chapter 2, those widows who felt most irritable and bitter commonly regarded themselves as physically unwell even though they reported no more overt physical symptoms than the rest.

The general impression was one of an intense impulse to action, generally aggressive, which was being rigidly controlled. Restless widows were likely to 'flare up' at any time and to fill their lives with activities. 'I feel all in a turmoil inside'; 'I'm at the end of my tether'; 'Stupid little things upset me'; 'My nerves are on edge'. These remarks illustrate the generally irritable mood. When tension was severe, an irregular fine tremor was often present and sometimes a stammer.

These features are a part of the general, non-specific reaction to stress described in Chapter 3. All that we can conclude from them is that the bereaved individuals are behaving as if they are in a situation of danger. But what is the danger? It will be clear from the preceding chapters that until the reality of the loss has been fully accepted one danger is the danger of the loss itself. The bereaved person still feels that the dead person is recoverable and anything that brings home the loss is reacted to as a major threat.

RESISTANCE

Relatives and friends who try to induce a widow to stop grieving before she is ready to do so, or even those who indicate that grief will pass, are surprised at her indignant response. It is as if they are obstructing the search for the one who is lost. Marris (1958) mentions one widow who beat the doctor who brought news of her husband's death. While such incidents are rare, the impulse to resist the bearers of evil tidings is strong, and anyone the bereaved person meets is likely to make real the fact of the loss. Those who come to console the widow recognize her antipathy and are deterred by it: 'What can one say?' In such circumstances there is a tacit agreement not to utter the word 'dead' but to speak of the dead person in hushed tones as if he were sleeping near at hand. Funeral directors learn to treat the dead as if they were asleep and the Anglican funeral service refers to the dead as resting or asleep in the Lord pending eventual resurrection (rest is mentioned three times and resurrection thirteen).

To speak of the goodness of the dead person and to ignore negative attributes diminishes the risk that the comforter will be seen as an enemy. It also reassures the bereaved that the dead person is worth mourning for, that loved ones were not deserted as an act of hostility. 'Why did he do this to me?' said one widow; and another, reminded nine months after bereavement that her husband really was dead, burst out, 'Oh Fred, why did you leave me?' and, later, 'If he'd known what it was like you'd [sic] never have left me.'

BLAMING

One can detect in these remarks some of the reproach and protest to which Bowlby refers, and it is true that widows often seem to regard the pain of grieving as an unjust punishment and to feel angry with the presumed author. The death is personalized as something that has been done to them and they seek for someone to blame. The blame is directed against anyone who might have contributed to the suffering or death of the husband and the husband may himself be reproached. Thus one widow blamed her husband for not telling his GP about his headaches. Another felt angry with the hospital authorities for sending her husband home by bus when he was not fit to travel; she also expressed great anger towards a nurse who had hurt her husband by ripping off an adhesive dressing, and towards God for taking her husband away. God and the doctors came in for a lot of angry criticism since both were seen as having power over life and death. 'I still go over in my mind the way those doctors behaved,' said one widow who accused them of ignoring significant symptoms.

Failure or delay in diagnosis was a common cause of complaint. While some of this anger may have been justified much of it seemed as irrational as its opposite, an uncritical adulation of the medical profession.[1] One widow who was very angry with the hospital staff at the time of her bereavement later retracted her accusations and added ruefully, 'I wish there was something I could blame.'

Seeking someone to blame was often associated with going over memories of events leading up to the loss, as described in Chapter 5. Presumably there was still a feeling that, if the person responsible could be found, the loss could somehow be prevented or undone. This feeling was vaguely expressed in terms of finding out what went wrong, as if life had suddenly been diverted from its orderly course and needed to be put back on the right track.

Anger is an emotion that is not always directed towards the object that gives rise to it. It was expressed over a wide variety of matters, many of them quite trivial. Quarrels arose with old friends who 'did not understand' or who failed to give support; one widow was constantly bickering with her teenage daughter, who had had a particularly close relationship with her father; another quarrelled with her mother over the disposal of a jointly owned car and provoked a series of quarrels with her employer which she later regretted.

THE SPREAD OF ANGER

What distinguished such behaviour from the quarrelling and angry feelings that any of us might experience at times was the frequency of the quarrels and the atmosphere of bitterness and irritability in which they took place; one could only regard them as part of the reaction to bereavement. It was sad that the other members of the family, who might have been able to help the widow to get things in perspective, were so often unable to be any more objective than the widow herself. They too were bereaved and found it hard to contain feelings of irritability and anger. Thus a mother-in-law, who had had a long-standing antipathy to her son's wife, accused her of being responsible for his death. The widow was badly hurt and reacted by telling the mother-in-law what she thought of her. The two then refused to see each other and split the family. The husband's relatives sided with the mother-in-law and the wife's with the wife. A series of angry altercations broke out over the rights and wrongs of the situation and the widow was left without the support and friendship of people she had previously liked. This example illustrates the way in which splits can occur, reputations can be damaged, and sources of support withdrawn.

There is clear evidence from the London Study that the widows who expressed the most anger became more socially isolated than those whose anger was less severe (see Appendix, section 9). Whether they drove their friends and relatives away or whether they dealt with their angry feelings by shutting themselves up at home, the result was loneliness and insecurity.

SELF-BLAME

Anger, in the early phase of bereavement, was often associated with self-reproach. The irrational component in their anger was recognized by many widows, who felt guilty at the way they behaved. 'I get furious with myself,' said one. Another reproached herself, 'You tend to magnify, look for trouble.'

Thirteen of the twenty-two London widows expressed self-reproachful ideas at some time in the course of the year. In its mildest form this was no more than a tendency to go over the events of the death in order, apparently, to seek reassurance that all was done that could have been done. 'I think "What could I have done?"' 'I think to myself, "Did I do right?"' 'My friend said, "You couldn't have done more."' 'I wonder whether we could have done any more.' 'Is there anything I could have seen early on?' Again, one finds the widow retrospectively trying to get things right, to find a reason for the catastrophe that will somehow bring order out of chaos and restore her faith in the meaning of life.

Seven widows expressed self-reproachful ideas centred on some act or omission which might have harmed the dying spouse or in some way have disturbed his peace of mind. In agonizing over events which were often quite trivial they seemed to be looking for a chance to castigate themselves, as if by accepting blame they could somehow reverse the course of events and get back the missing spouse. One widow attributed her husband's illness to over-tiredness and blamed herself for not learning to drive: 'If I'd have drove [sic],' she said, 'he'd probably be here today.' Another had had a hysterectomy shortly before her husband developed a cancer of the colon – she thought that his illness might have been caused by worry over her and blamed herself for this. Several reproached themselves for failing to stand the strain of the terminal illness. One had nursed her husband at home for a year before his death. Eventually she had lost her temper with him after he had awakened her during the night. Although she apologized and her husband forgave her he died a few days later. 'I felt as if God had given him to me to look after and when I couldn't cope he took him away.'

Regret at failure to satisfy expectations was a source of self-reproach in another widow who felt guilty because she had never made her husband a bread pudding. Another blamed herself for failing to encourage her husband's artistic talents during his lifetime. She endeavoured to make restitution after his death by finding a market for his paintings. Regarding their relationship she said: 'We were both always on the defensive. Now I can see how often he was right.'

INSECURITY

The death of a loved person is so important an event that it is difficult to shrug it off as the result of an accident or ill luck. To accept the fact that death can strike anywhere and that illness is no respecter of persons or deserts undermines one's faith in the world as an ordered and secure place.

All the widows in the London Study were under the age of sixty-five and their husbands were not much older. This meant that most of the deaths that occurred were untimely; they occurred before the usual life-span was complete. Untimely deaths cast doubt upon the 'reasonable expectations' upon which all of us base our lives. We know that disasters happen, but we cannot afford to worry about possibilities which are statistically unlikely. We continue to cross the road despite the danger that we might be run over; we travel in cars, trains, and aeroplanes knowing full well that they may crash. To worry about the possibilities would make life intolerable and most people rely upon the knowledge that accidents are statistically rare and feel that they are protected from disaster.

A major bereavement shakes confidence in this sense of security. The tendency to go over the events leading up to the loss and to find someone to blame even if it means accepting blame oneself is a less disturbing alternative than accepting that life is uncertain. If we can find someone to blame or some explanation that will enable death to be evaded, then we have a chance of controlling things. It is easier to believe that fate is indifferent, or rather positively malevolent, than to acknowledge our helplessness in the face of events. God is not subject to the laws of statistical probability, he is a 'cosmic sadist' who punishes unjustly (C. S. Lewis, 1961). Railing against God or Fate is, of course, another way of trying to control the order of things. It is not so much an expression of helplessness as an attempt to influence events by browbeating their author. The thought that the loved person's death was accidental is unacceptable because it makes us feel so impotent.

PSYCHOANALYTIC THEORIES

In 'Mourning and Melancholia' (1917), Freud points to the sadistic impulses present in all ambivalent relationships. In melancholia, which he regarded as a pathological form of grief, these sadistic impulses are commonly turned against the self. As evidence of this, Freud claims that the terms of abuse the patient uses about himself 'always' fit the love object rather than the patient. Ambivalence, says Freud, gives rise to a wish for the other's death, but it is not unusual for the ego to tolerate a wish as harmless so long as this exists in fantasy alone and seems remote from fulfilment, while it will defend itself hotly against such a wish as soon as it approaches fulfilment and threatens to become an actuality.

In order to defend themselves against what Melanie Klein (1940) has called the 'triumph' over the dead, bereaved people turn their anger against themselves or direct it outwards towards others who are to hand. Hence guilt and anger are thought particularly likely to follow the dissolution of an ambivalent relationship and, because of their destructive nature, to lead to pathological forms of grief.

Whether or not the self-reproaches of the London widows also reflected a dim awareness of death wishes towards an ambivalently loved husband is uncertain. My interviews seldom permitted the analysis, in depth, of unconscious motivation. It did appear, however, that at least one woman in the London Study, and a large proportion of those in the Bethlem Study, expressed intense feelings of guilt which could be explained in this way. In fact it was the frequency and intensity of feelings of guilt that most clearly distinguished the bereaved psychiatric patients of the Bethlem Study from the unselected widows of the London Study. We return to this issue again in Chapters 8 and 11.

PASSIVITY AND DEPRESSION, AN ETHOLOGICAL THEORY

In contrast to these feelings of anger and guilt we turn now to a consideration of the opposite phenomenon, loss of aggressiveness, which seems to occur along with feelings of apathy and despair once the intense pangs of grief are past their peak.

Lorenz continues his description of the behaviour of a greylag goose who has lost its mate: 'From the moment [the partner is missed] . . . it loses all courage and flees from even the weakest geese.' Sinking rapidly in the ranking order of the flock, the bereaved goose becomes shy, fearful, and panicky.

John Price (1967) provides an explanation, in ethological terms, for this behaviour, which he assumes also takes place in man. He points out that man is a social animal whose place in the dominance hierarchy is maintained by means of alliances with his mate and other loved persons. Loss of such a person can be expected to lead to a fall in status, and decline in status produces loss of courage and depression. To be effective a dominance hierarchy must be stable. Leadership must be clear and members of the social group must be aware of their own place in the hierarchy. This makes unnecessary the determination of a new precedence every time the interests of two members conflict. A strong dominance hierarchy is found, according to Price, in practically all species which do not limit their aggression by the strict division of territory. Attitudes of, on the one hand, submissiveness to and anxious withdrawal from individuals higher than oneself in status and, on the other, of irritability and threat towards those lower than oneself, ensure that the hierarchy is maintained and that, when conflicts do break out, the lower-status individual will usually be defeated without bloodshed.

Changes in social structure, however, are bound to occur when age or sickness reduces the powers of the higher-status members or when alliances are dissolved. In such circumstances, says Price, those whose status is declining are overcome by a depressive mood which counteracts their normal tendency to fight to defend their position and allows them to decline in status without the danger of combat with each individual in the group who attempts to supersede them. The advantages of this peaceful solution to the problem of status change are obvious and in the long run would tend to operate to maximize the chances of survival of individuals and of the social group of which they are members.

Unfortunately, no attempt has yet been made to assess systematically the extent to which bereaved people 'lose heart' and adopt a submissive, defeated attitude. But experience suggests that they usually do this during the periods of apathetic withdrawal which follow the pangs of grief. It has seemed to me – but further confirmation is necessary – that anger is most likely to be expressed during episodes of pining for the lost person. Between these episodes, and after the phase of intense pining is past, depression and an attitude of defeat intervene. 'I don't want to fight it any more,' said one widow nine months after bereavement. She was clinging to a friend of her former husband: 'I just let Bob lead me.' But from time to time she would feel aggressive and attack him, 'because he's not Jim'. Other widows who are depressed have described feelings of panic when they would like to run away if only they had somewhere to go.

IS THERE A DEPRESSIVE PHASE?

The suggestion that a phase of yearning and protest is normally followed by a phase of depression and submission has proved difficult to establish. There is no sharp end-point to yearning, and pangs of grief can be re-evoked even years after a bereavement. It does seem true, however, that as time passes anger and pining grow less, while episodes of apathy and depression remain. The situation is complicated by the wide range of variation in the readiness with which individuals express aggression. There is good reason to believe that dominance/submission is closely related to personality and that there are some individuals who habitually express aggressive attitudes while others are more submissive. Individuals are also extremely sensitive to the attitudes and expectations of others, so that there are many interacting factors that influence the expression of aggression after bereavement.

Finally, there is the problem of measurement. In the London Study every effort was made to assess the intensity of expressed anger and it was usually possible to find out when this exceeded the normal for the individual. But no attempt was made to measure anger or assertiveness that was less than normal. The fact that anger and guilt are common components of grief does not, of course, mean that they may not also have a special significance in pathological developments.

7

GAINING A NEW IDENTITY

You that are she and you, that's double shee,
In her dead face, half of yourself shall see;
Shee was the other part, for so they doe
Which build them friendships, become one of two.

* * *

For, such a friendship who would not adore
In you, who are all what both were before,
Not all, as if some perished by this,
But so, as all in you contracted is.
As of this all, though many parts decay,
The pure which elemented them shall stay . . .

John Donne, 'To the Lady Bedford'

It comes as rather a shock to hear an unsophisticated London widow (Mrs J) describing her feeling of identification with her dead husband in the following words: 'My husband's in me, right through and through. I can feel him in me doing everything. He used to say, "You'll do this when I'm gone, won't you?" . . . I enjoy the things my husband used to do . . . It's like a thought in my head – what he would say or do.' She cited watching the Cup Final and Goodwood racing on television as examples of activities deriving from him. 'I quite enjoy it because he liked it. It's a most queer feeling . . . My young sister said, "You're getting like Fred in all your ways . . ." She said something about food. I said, "I couldn't touch that," and she said, "Don't be stupid, you're getting just like Fred" . . . There's lots of things I do that I wouldn't think of doing [before Fred's death] . . . I suppose he's guiding me the whole of the time.'

Much has been written, in the psychoanalytic literature and elsewhere, about the way in which people who have suffered a loss sometimes seem to take into themselves certain aspects of the lost person. Freud at one time regarded identification as 'the sole condition under which the id will give up its objects' (1923). But ten years later he says: 'If one has lost a love object or has had to give it up, one *often* compensates oneself by identifying oneself with it . . .' (1933; my italics).

These statements describe but they do not explain the phenomenon of identification with a lost person, which remains as mystifying to us today as it was to John Donne. How can my husband be part of me? What does a widow mean when she says, 'My husband's in me, right through and through'? How can her husband be guiding her the whole of the time?

Equally mystifying is the experience of loss of self which is reported by many widows. 'I feel as if half of myself was missing,' said one widow, and another spoke of 'a great emptiness'. What do these statements mean? How can a person be 'full' or 'empty'? Why should the loss of someone 'out there' give rise to an experience of the loss of something 'in here'?

It would seem that the experience of bereavement may throw light on some fundamental questions concerning the nature of identity. It is my purpose in this chapter to present some of the data and to formulate some hypotheses which seem to begin to make sense of such phenomena.

PSYCHOSOCIAL TRANSITIONS

Before discussing the change of identity that follows bereavement, let us look at what it is that changes. When somebody dies a whole set of assumptions about the world that relied upon the other person for their validity are suddenly invalidated. Habits of thought which have been built up over many years must be reviewed and modified, a person's view of the world must change. This transition has been termed a Psychosocial Transition (PST) and it inevitably takes time and effort.

PSTs are not confined to bereavement, they take place whenever we are faced with the need to make major changes to our assumptions about the world; the amputee has to learn to stop trying to use a leg that is no longer there before he can learn to use the artificial limb that is now provided for him; the blind person must learn new ways of perceiving the world and the cancer patient can no longer take for granted a whole series of assumptions. Each of these situations confronts the sufferer with the need to give up one set of habits and to develop another.

The loss of a loved person inevitably creates a host of discrepancies between our internal world and the world that now exists for us. This is true not only at the superficial level (Who will be there when I get in from work in the evening?), but also at the deeper level of basic assumptions (If I am no longer a married man or woman, what am I?). Bereaved people are repeatedly surprised at the number of habits of thought which involve the other person and the extent to which things take their meaning from the presence of another person. (Often the person who has died is the one we would have turned to at times of trouble, and here we are, in the biggest trouble we have ever experienced, repeatedly turning to someone who is not there.). Small wonder that bereaved people often feel as if life itself has lost its meaning.

Changing the assumptive world

All of us, from the moment of our birth, have been building inside ourselves a model of the world, a set of assumptions on the basis of which we recognize the world that we meet and plan our behaviour accordingly. Because this model is based on reality it is, most of the time, a valid and useful basis for thought and behaviour. We rely on the accuracy of these assumptions to maintain our orientation in the world and to control our lives. Anything which challenges the model incapacitates us. Yet discrepancies between the world that is and the world that should be (on the basis of our internal model) do arise and cannot be ignored. Our internal model must be constantly monitored and updated.

Minor changes in the model do not challenge basic assumptions and are relatively easy to make. They may even be pleasurable and give us the feeling of increasing our knowledge and extending our repertoire of ways of coping with the world. Hence the popularity of overseas holidays and participation in sports and pastimes that extend us.

Only if the change is very great or challenges deeply held assumptions is it likely to be difficult and to be resisted. Not only does a major PST require us to revise a great number of assumptions about the world, but most of those assumptions have become habits of thought and behaviour that are now virtually automatic. A widow will come down for breakfast in the morning and find that she has laid the table for two when there is now only one person to eat it. Faced with a problem she will catch herself thinking 'I must ask my husband about that'. In either case she has continued to operate a set of assumptions that are now obsolete. For a long time she will have to watch what she thinks and what she says; nothing can be taken for granted any more. The familiar world suddenly seems to have become unfamiliar, habits of thought can let her down, she has lost confidence in her most essential possession, her internal model of the world, and because of this she may lose confidence in herself.

Since we rely on the possession of an accurate internal model of the world to keep us safe, people who have lost confidence in that model feel very unsafe. And because anxiety and fear cloud our judgement and impair our concentration and memory, our attempts to make sense of what has happened are likely to be slow and inefficient.

Not that bereavement affects all aspects of our world. Those who have invested themselves in jobs and other activities that did *not* involve their partner will find that they can continue to manage these worlds relatively easily. In fact they may feel that, when they are working, they are able to escape, for a time, from the problems of bereavement. Similarly a mother who has lost her husband may find that the care of the children who survive him provides her with a sense of purpose and meaning in her life that contrasts with the desolation that emerges after they have gone to bed at night.

In the circumstances it is not surprising if, as we saw in Chapter 5, people attempt to avoid reminders as a means of mitigating some of the pains of grief. By the same token too much avoidance means that we are not tackling the problem of relearning that is necessary if we are to adapt our model of the world to fit the world that now exists. Freud called this process of reviewing the internal world 'the work of mourning' (1917) and, in many ways each PST is a job of work that needs to be done. But *the mind that is doing the reviewing is also the object that is being reviewed*. A person is literally lost in their own PST, and the more disorganized one's thinking the more difficult it is to step aside from the disorganization and to see clearly what it is that is lost and what remains.

Resistance to change

Because we can only bring to new situations assumptions that arose out of the old, we cannot easily abandon the past. For this reason major changes are usually resisted and this is not necessarily a bad thing. Our old model of the world may be imperfect but it is the best we have and, if we abandon it, we have nothing left. Our first effort, therefore, in the face of change, must be to interpret the change in the light of our old assumptions. 'I can't believe it's true' is an understandable reaction to massive change and we should not be surprised if newly bereaved people find it hard to accept the facts of the situation. At such times the bereaved are disorganized and disabled by loss. They may need the protection and support of others whose world has not been similarly shattered to provide the security that will enable them, little by little, to take in the reality of what has happened and make it real. It then becomes possible to modify our assumptions and with them our sense of identity.

A more detailed exposition of the field of Psychosocial Transitions is given in Parkes (1993b).

THE EMPIRICAL SELF

What is this identity, this self which can be invaded, changed, or lost? William James (1892) distinguished the 'empirical self', the self that can be the object of one's own scrutiny, from the 'conscious self', the self that does the scrutinizing. The latter, that-which-experiences, can never, paradoxically, itself be experienced. We can experience the world that strikes or impinges upon us and we can experience the memories and thoughts deriving from that world (thoughts too can 'strike' us), but we can only infer the 'I' that experiences these phenomena. When we speak of changes in the self, therefore, we must be speaking of changes in James's 'empirical self'. How do people come to recognize this self, see themselves as an individual separate and different from their fellow human beings?

Human beings are multicellular organisms. That is to say, they are groups of individual living organisms which are more or less closely linked together to form a single structure. Within that structure, and part of it, is a subgroup of nerve cells, the brain, organized in such a way that it receives signals from the rest of the organism and from the outside world which enables it to make predictions about that world and to direct the organism to act appropriately. Among the signals it receives from the world are some that indicate the presence of other multicellular organisms similar to ourselves. The similarity is so great that the nerve cells in one person find themselves able to see the world through the eyes of others. They also become able to see themselves through the same eyes. The being that each of us infers from observing our own organism and behaviour and comparing it with that of others is what we call the 'self'.

Components of the self

I see myself as a psychiatrist, husband, commuter, and writer – each of these aspects of my identity stems from my roles. I am also identified by my bodily characteristics – tall, white, male, etc. – and by my behaviour – unpunctual, even-tempered, cat-loving, etc. Finally, I have the attributes of my social group – I am middle class and English. Each of these characteristics defines both similarities to and differences from other people. They enable me to be identified and they indicate to the world and to me that I have a certain status, certain powers and responsibilities, and certain possessions which are essentially my own.

Nearly all of these roles, bodily characteristics, powers, and possessions may be affected by a major loss such as a bereavement. Let us consider first how the thirty-year-old wife of an estate agent coped with the changes that followed her husband's sudden death. In Mrs B's case it was the changes in role that were seen as the major problem. She had been left with two children, a boy aged eight and a girl of five. After her husband's death she grieved deeply and lost two stones in weight. She had a strong sense of his presence near at hand and could not get the thought of his dead body out of her mind. Her grief reached its peak about two weeks after the death and a marked improvement set in during the fourth week when she went to stay with friends on the coast.

At this stage and during the next six months she felt 'totally inadequate', tense, physically tired, and irritable. She remained at home most of this time and became very reliant upon a man much older than herself who had been a friend for many years. At the same time she resented her dependence, she quarrelled with her mother-in-law and with several other members of her husband's family, and seemed to regard the world as dangerous and potentially hostile.

About the middle of the year she began to realize that she was tougher than she had thought. She took a part-time job as a shop assistant and enjoyed the work. She redecorated the house and started judo classes 'for a bit of a giggle' (and also because she wanted to be able to defend herself if any man should 'get fresh'). Episodes of grieving became less frequent and her pleasure in her new-found independence increased. This reduced her reliance on the old friend who had done so much for her during the early months, and although he had always insisted that there was nothing 'romantic' about their relationship he became very upset when he found her drinking with another man and he terminated the relationship.

A year after her husband's death, Mrs B said: 'I think most of the time I've got over it. But if I go over it in detail . . . I get panicky again.' Her weight was steady and her health good although she still had 'blinding headaches' from time to time and had thought of asking her doctor for a tonic. She rated her overall happiness as 'up and down' but was optimistic about the future. Although she had many problems to work out she felt she could master them and enjoyed doing so. She took every opportunity to go out and said that if the right man came along she would consider remarrying.

One can see from this account the sequence of stages by which a new set of roles began to be established for Mrs B. At first her preoccupation with pining for her husband drove all but the most urgent problems from her mind. After a brief retreat to the care of her friends she returned to an insecure and dangerous world feeling 'totally inadequate'. For a while she remained reliant on her man friend while taking stock and planning her life afresh. Her decision to take up judo seemed to reflect both her fear of the dangers of the world and her determination to master it. As her confidence increased her need to rely upon her man friend diminished and she experienced a sense of achievement and a relaxation which were visibly different from the restlessness and tension witnessed at earlier interviews.

ROLES AND SOLUTIONS

The roles that a person performs in life are made up of a complex series of focal action patterns which constitute a repertoire of problem solutions. This repertoire, because it is based on experience, assumes that reasonable expectations of the world will be fulfilled. As time goes by, the individual's stock of 'solutions for all eventualities' grows greater, and novel situations requiring novel solutions become rarer.

However, a major change in life, such as that produced by the death of a spouse, not only alters expectations at the level of the focal action patterns (How many teaspoons to lay on the breakfast table?), but also alters the overall plans and roles of which these form a part. A widow is no longer a wife; she is a widow. Suddenly, and always in some degree unexpectedly, 'we' has become 'I', 'ours' has become 'mine'; the partnership is dissolved and decisions must be made alone and not by a committee of two. Even when words remain appropriate, their meaning changes – 'the family' is no longer the same object it was, neither is 'home' or 'marriage'; even 'old age' now has a new meaning.

In large measure the newly bereaved widow confronts the same problems as the adolescent school-leaver. A new set of expectations and roles faces her and she must learn a new model of the world and a new repertoire of problem solutions before she can again feel safe and at ease. Like the adolescent she may feel that too much is being expected of her and she may react with anxiety, insecurity, and irritability. She may attempt to hold on to the idea that she is still the cherished wife, protected from the world by a loving husband. Even when this assumption is given up, there will be other aspects of the new situation that she cannot accept. 'I hate it when people use the word widow,' said one widow. The very word implied an identity she was not willing to assume.

DISORGANIZATION

Besides assuming a new identity, it is necessary to give up the old, and, as I have said, this can be a long and painful business and one that is never complete. But as pining diminishes and each role or focal action pattern is recognized as inappropriate, there seems to follow a period of uncertainty, aimlessness, and apathy which Bowlby (1961) called the phase of disorganization and despair. The characteristic emotion is depression, and the widow is likely to remain withdrawn from contact with those who will make demands upon her and to rely upon relatives and close friends who can be expected to protect her. Only when circumstances force her to do so or when depression is minimal will she venture out to find a job, meet people, or attempt to re-establish her place in the hierarchical society to which all social animals belong.

This period of disorganization is not a clear-cut phase of grief but occurs again and again in one context or another. Once habituation has taken place and the old assumptions and ways of thinking have been given up, the individual is free to take stock and to make a new start. Making a new start means learning new solutions and finding new ways to predict and control happenings within the life-space. It also means seeking a fresh place in the hierarchy, reassessing one's powers and possessions, and finding out how one is viewed by the rest of the world.

THE SOCIAL SELF

Cooley (1909) defined the self as those things that individuals conceive as belonging peculiarly to them. William James's 'social self' (my view of the world's view of me) he termed 'the looking-glass self'. Clearly these two views are closely allied since many of the possessions, attributions, and characteristics we term ours are ours only by consent. The work of Lifton and others who have studied 'thought reform' or 'brain-washing' has revealed the extent to which individuals' views of themselves are dependent upon the confirmation of others. Writing of circumstances before the Cultural Revolution in China, he noted:

> In thought reform, as in Chinese Communist practice generally, the world is divided into the 'people' . . . and the 'reactionaries' . . . The thought reform process is one means by which non-people are permitted, through a change in attitude and personal character, to make themselves over into people. The most literal example of such dispersing of existence and non-existence is to be found in the sentence given to certain political criminals: execution in two years' time, unless during that two-year period they have demonstrated genuine progress in their reform . . .
>
> For the individual, the polar conflict is the ultimate existential one of 'being versus nothingness'. He is likely to be drawn to a conversion experience, which he sees as the only means of attaining a path of existence for the future.
>
> (Lifton, 1961)

While the extent, pervasiveness, and duration of the subjective changes in the individuals' views of themselves vary greatly according to their life circumstances and previous experience, the powerful influence of extreme social pressures such as these cannot be denied. It comes, therefore, as no surprise to find that changes in the world's view of me are likely to be associated with changes in my view of myself. This is particularly likely when changes take place in those things I view as most intimately mine.

While there are grounds for preserving the distinction between my view of the world and my view of myself, the tools by which I act upon that world, 'my hands', 'my language', 'my motorcar', span the boundary between me and the world and blur the distinction between my 'self' and 'others'. Since I can share many of these 'possessions', what is the boundary of me?[1] Is my little finger a part of me? Is my wife a part of me? Am I a part of her?

At once it is apparent that although I think I know myself there is a hinterland between 'self' and 'other' which is not clear cut and which may change. If my little finger is cut off it ceases to be a part of me; if I lose my job I cease to be a psychiatrist; if I lose my temper I cease to be even-tempered; if my wife dies I cease to be her husband and she ceases to be my wife.

Such changes may be forced upon me or I may choose to bring them about. I may dissociate myself from my government, I may divorce my wife, or I may give away my money. Conversely, I may refuse to acknowledge in myself changes which should alter me. I may live above my income, pretend to be a better golfer than I am, or refuse to regard myself as a widower after my wife has died. Who is the real me? Am I the person I believe myself to be or the person the world believes me to be? Is there an essential, unalterable me?[2]

My body is constantly changing. Old cells die and new ones are born to replace them. Only a minority of the living beings that make up my multicellular organism were alive five years ago. Within my brain the changes are more slow. As I grow older nerve cells die but none replaces them. The part of me that perceives, directs, and remembers is gradually dwindling. Age is carrying out a series of minute lobotomy operations on me, and my personality is slowly being altered. Fortunately the change is gradual and it is possible for me to maintain the illusion that I am the person I thought I was five years ago. Unless, that is, something occurs which suddenly proves to me that I am not.

If the possessions and the roles by which we control, order, and predict the world can be shared, changed, or dissolved, then it may be that the self that depends so much upon these tools and tasks to provide an image is also capable of experiencing change. If I lose my ability to predict and to act appropriately, my world begins to crumble, and since my view of myself is inextricably bound up with my view of the world, that too will begin to crumble. If I have relied on another person to predict and act in many ways as an extension to myself then the loss of that person can be expected to have the same effect upon my view of the world and my view of myself as if I had lost a part of myself.

MUTILATION OF THE SELF AND THE PAIN OF GRIEF

From this standpoint, we can begin to understand why widows speak as if they had lost a part of themselves. When the loss has been sudden, large, and forced upon the attention, words implying mutilation and outrage tend to be used. One widow described her feelings on viewing the body of her husband: 'It's as if my inside had been torn out and left a horrible wound there.' A comparison is sometimes made to amputation: widows say that their husband has been 'cut off', 'as if half of myself was missing'.

In less violent terms the loss of self is often referred to as a 'gap' – 'it's a great emptiness', 'an unhappy void'. These words illustrate how the people we love seem to become part of our self, a view that is often held by poets but one that others may find hard to accept – perhaps because it makes us so much more vulnerable. It is more comfortable to think of the self as a separate, independent, and therefore safe, entity than to accept, with John Donne, that 'any man's death diminishes me'.[3]

Apart from this conjecture we do not yet have any satisfactory explanation of why widows sometimes refer to the experience of bereavement in physical terms. 'It's a horrible feeling here [pointing to her chest],' said a sixty-five-year-old widow. Another described a pain in her throat: 'Like something was pulling . . . I think it was because I wouldn't let myself cry . . . if I could cry it did relieve it.' One can only guess why some should locate the 'pain' in one place and some in another. In most cases the pain of grief is viewed as psychological and seems to have no clear physical location. On the face of it there appears to be empirical justification for Grinberg's belief (1964) that the pain of grief, like physical pain, is the experience of damage to the self.

REORGANIZATION

As will be clear from the foregoing chapters, it takes time for individuals to realize and accept the change in themselves which follows a major loss. External objects may change rapidly but it will be many weeks before corresponding changes have taken place in the plans and assumptions which are their internal equivalents and the changes that do occur may never be complete. Widows continue to think of their husbands as if they were still alive although they know, at the same time, that they are really dead. The corresponding feeling in the self was expressed by one: 'I don't feel that I am a widow.'

But the illusion that nothing has changed can be retained only as long as the widow avoids placing herself in situations in which the 'gap' will show. She looks backwards to the past and makes no plans for the future; in a sense she may try to stop living, to arrest time. Emergence from this state was described by the widow who had earlier spoken of her inside as being torn out: 'I think I'm beginning to wake up now,' she said, a year after bereavement. 'I'm starting living instead of just existing. It's the first time I've had a positive thought. I feel I ought to plan to do something. I feel as if I was recovering from a major illness or a major operation – you suddenly wake up. It's physical – I felt I was hollow inside, as if my heart had been torn out and left a ragged hole. Now I feel more like a person.'

Kuhn (1958) points out that mourners have the feeling that it is not the dead person but they themselves who have been ejected from the world hitherto familiar to them. The 'real' world seems 'unreal', desolate, or empty, and they behave in a careful, muffled way, just as people do at night: 'The mourner has turned away from the real world of everyday life towards the past.' In point of fact the mourner really has been ejected from the assumptive world that existed before bereavement, and the careful movements and the hushed voice sometimes adopted by newly bereaved people could be the same phenomenon as the timorous behaviour of a person who is physically ill. In both cases patients, and their relatives and friends, are afraid of damaging the sufferer by impinging too directly or strongly upon them, by making too real the painful thing that has happened and the consequences of it for their identity.[4] As one widow put it: 'I feel terribly fragile. If somebody gave me a good tap I'd shatter into a thousand pieces.'

CHANGES IN FAMILY ROLES

Let us return from these difficult psychological problems to look more closely at the changes in role that commonly follow bereavement. If one regards the bereaved family as a social system which has lost one of its members, then there are four possible outcomes:

1 The roles and functions previously performed by the missing member may remain unperformed.
2 A substitute for the missing member may be obtained from outside the family.
3 The roles of the missing member may be taken over by other members of the family.
4 The social system may break up.

Any of these events may take place, or a combination of them.

Consider the effects of loss of a family leader. Although it would be possible, though time consuming, to look at this from the point of view of the whole family I shall confine attention to the ways in which the loss of the husband's roles affects the widow herself.

1 Roles unperformed

Among the roles that are likely to remain unperformed are sexual and companion-protector roles. It is likely that the widow's sexual needs will remain unmet because her persisting attachment to her dead husband will make sexual liaisons with other men almost as strictly forbidden after his death as they were before it. More consciously missed is the companionship of the husband and the emotional security and opportunities for interaction which this previously provided. Loneliness was complained of by most of the twenty-two London widows and it was most pronounced at night. A year after bereavement nine were still sleeping badly and five of these were taking sedatives.

2   Substitutes from outside the family

Substitutes for a missing husband are not readily acceptable. Only one widow in the London Study became engaged within the first year of bereavement; three others said that they had hopes of remarrying. Reasons such as age and the difficulty of finding an eligible suitor were given for this lack of interest in remarriage, but many of the widows still seemed to regard themselves as married to their dead husband and remarriage would have been a form of infidelity. Children often resented any male who seemed to them to be usurping the place of their dead father. By contrast, widowers often remarry, and Helsing and his colleagues (1981) found that at least half of the widowers whom they studied had remarried within twelve years of bereavement.

Only three of the twenty-two widows moved out of the home they had shared with their husband, and the number living alone increased from five to seven in the course of the first year of bereavement (owing to the marriage of children). Despite their loneliness only four widows now spent more time in social contact with friends and relatives than they had done before bereavement, and seven of them said that they now spent less time in social contact. Thus it seems that they did not seek social relations as a substitute for the companionship of their husband. It may be, however, that a follow-up of these widows over their second and third years of bereavement would have revealed a change in this pattern.

3   Substitutes from within the family

The role of principal wage-earner was normally taken over by the widow. Over half (thirteen) of the bereaved London families suffered a drop in income after the death of the wage-earner and in four cases this was severe and caused great anxiety. Most widows, in consequence, took a job, and fourteen were going out to work by the end of the year (five more than before bereavement); in addition, two of those who remained at home took in paying guests. Half of the widows had children under fifteen living at home and these constituted an additional burden. Responsibility for family affairs, finances, house, and children weighed heavily on a similar proportion a year after bereavement.

Roles that were, of necessity, taken over by the widow herself thus included: principal wage-earner, family administrator and planner, and disciplinarian of the children. The overall responsibility for the future of the family rested squarely on her shoulders and opportunities for discussion and joint decision-making with her husband no longer existed.

The increase in self-esteem which might have resulted from taking over a leadership role often seemed to be cancelled out by the widow's own feelings of personal inadequacy in this role and by the decline in status of the family as a whole which resulted from the loss of the principal male.

4 Family disintegration

The fourth outcome that can follow loss of the family leader, disintegration of the family as a close-knit social unit, occurred immediately in five cases, where the children had already left home before the father's death, and shortly afterwards in three cases, where the children got married and left home soon after the death. In a further five cases it seemed probable, a year after the death, that the children would leave within the next two to three years. Thus over half the families were broken up or about to be broken up after the death of the father even though, in all cases, the surviving widow was under sixty-five years of age. In the case of older widows and widowers the social isolation caused by bereavement is a common problem and loneliness is often described as the besetting problem of old age.

Whether the family broke up or stayed together, a gap was left by the death of the father. If the family stayed together it was usually the widow who eventually came to fill the gap. If the family disintegrated the sense of a gap remained, but many of the roles formerly carried out by husband and wife were no longer required. In such a situation the widow was likely to feel unneeded and unwanted. Although it has not been possible to follow up such functionless widows for more than a year, experience with Cruse – Bereavement Care suggests that for some this aspect remains a problem which may continue unsolved for many years.

IDENTIFICATION

In those cases in which it was necessary for the widow herself to fill the gap left by her husband's death the responsibilities involved often constituted a great strain. Several widows deliberately modelled themselves on their husband and went out of their way to take over his interests and carry out activities in the way in which he would have carried them out. Their efforts were accompanied by a feeling of satisfaction and closeness to the husband.

The practical necessity for the widow to take over roles and activities previously carried out by the husband may coincide with her own wishes and provide her with an opportunity to maintain her sense of proximity to her lost husband, but is there more to it than this? Ever since Freud put forward the notion in 'The Ego and the Id' (1923) that withdrawal of the libido that attaches one person to another can take place only when the lost person is 'reinstated' within the ego, some psychoanalysts have regarded identification with the lost object as a necessary component of mourning. Abraham, writing a year later, saw the object as 'hiding in the ego' – 'The loved object is not gone, for now I carry it within myself and can never lose it.'

Krupp (1963) regards identification as deriving from the repeated frustrations and losses of early infancy: 'The infant tries to become the loved one to prevent further loss . . . Out of bits of the personalities of others [the growing child creates] the unique mosaic of the self.' In this view, identification with the lost person is not just another way of postponing the realization of loss; it is the necessary condition without which grief cannot end and a new identity be developed. The object is never truly given up; it is made into a part of the self. In this way 'figures who appear to be given up or lost are permanently held with bonds that are impervious to being severed' (Rochlin, 1965).

What, then, are the forms of identification that have been found among the widows studied? In the London Study one of the questions regularly asked was: 'Do you feel that you have got more like your husband in any way?' The usual response was for the widow to admit that she had come to resemble her husband during their marriage but that there had been no increase in resemblance since his death.

This reply is borne out by the work of Kreitman (1964 and 1968), who has shown that married people tend to develop the same neuroses; what is more, the longer they have been married, the more similar their symptoms will be. The most likely explanation seems to be that married people learn from each other; they gradually come to see the other's point of view and to make it their own. Attitudes, preferences for certain television programmes, taste in food, fears and hopes of the world, all these tend to be shared by husband and wife so that it becomes possible for either one to use the word 'we' and speak for both. Thus the identification of husband and wife goes on throughout married life and grows stronger as time passes. It is not something that occurs only after the dissolution of the relationship. Nevertheless, there were in the London Study two widows who showed quite clearly an increased tendency to behave and think like the dead person, and a further eight in whom there was inconclusive evidence of such a tendency at some time during the year. One, Mrs J, was referred to at the beginning of the chapter; and evidence concerning two others is given below. At no time did more than four of the twenty-two widows admit to this type of identification.

Mrs H's husband was a gardener and a very practical man whose main interest was the care of his house and garden. After his death his wife remained at home with her daughter and son-in-law. Within three months, however, her mother-in-law, of whom she was very fond, died and the daughter and son-in-law moved away leaving her alone in the house. During the next nine months Mrs H spent most of her time repairing and decorating her house: 'Dad done [sic] it well,' she said. 'I've got to do it the same as him.' Her lawyer remonstrated with her because she could not afford to spend so much on the house, but she remarked, 'If I do what my husband wanted I don't mind if I spend every penny I've got.' 'I've become more like him; I have to now he's not here to do things.' She learnt to drive, 'because I don't want to sell the van, he prided it so much'.

Another widow, Mrs T, also enjoyed decorating the house. 'I can see him doing it,' she remarked. 'I find myself doing jobs around the house the way he would have done them' – she found this comforting.

Another phenomenon, which was very striking when it did occur, was a sense of the husband's presence inside the surviving widow. Mrs D, whose attempts to make restitution to her dead husband were described on page 85, had been at odds with him throughout their married life and had felt her security threatened by behaviour which she regarded as irresponsible. Her husband had sometimes sacrificed his family's interests in order to satisfy his artistic inclinations and his wife had repeatedly pressed him to settle down. 'At dawn,' she said, 'four days after my husband's death, something suddenly moved in on me – invaded me – a presence, almost pushed me out of bed – terribly overwhelming.' Thereafter she had a strong sense of her husband's presence near her and sometimes inside her. She adopted his sense of values, accepted his criticisms of her bourgeois attitudes and planned to try to market his paintings. At the end of the year she now saw many things 'through his eyes'.

The sense of the presence of the dead husband is a common phenomenon which was discussed in Chapter 5. Sometimes it consisted of a general feeling that the husband was somewhere near at hand; at other times he would be located in a specific place, a particular chair, a bedroom, or the grave in which his body was buried. Occasionally, however, the husband was sensed to be within the widow herself.

This was a pleasant feeling which seemed to minimize grief. 'It's not a sense of his presence,' said one widow when asked if she felt that her husband was nearly at hand. 'He is here inside me. That's why I'm happy all the time. It's as if two people were one . . . although I'm alone, we're sort of together if you see what I mean . . . I don't think I've got the willpower to carry on on my own, so he must be.'

This widow solved the problem of locating her dead husband in space by finding him in herself. Five others found him in somebody else. For instance, one widow had been married to a black West Indian man. She had two children: the first, a boy, was dark skinned, but the second, a girl, was fair. The girl was born shortly before her father's death and 'was meant to replace him'. After the death, Mrs H was disturbed to find herself identifying the girl with her husband: 'She has his hands – it gives me the creeps.'

The respondent who married eight months after the death of her *de facto* husband, Bill, soon became pregnant. She was 'dead keen' on having a baby and identified her unborn child with Bill. 'Giving birth,' she said, 'will be like getting Bill out of me.' She seemed in this statement to express her wish both to have and to get rid of Bill.

Another type of identification phenomenon, the development of symptoms resembling those of the husband's last illness, is obviously pathological. It is considered in the next chapter.

THE NEW PERSON

In sum, it appears that the ways of identifying with the husband which have been described achieve two ends: they enable the widow to get back, in some sense, the man she has lost, and they help her to take over the roles he has vacated. But however attractive these ends may appear to be, it was only a minority of widows who, at any time during the first year of bereavement, were conscious of coming to resemble or contain the dead spouse. These widows got through their grief no faster than the widows who reported no evidence of identification, and there was nothing to suggest that identification is a necessary part of the process of recovery. It seems, rather, that identification with the lost person is one of the methods that bereaved people adopt to avoid the painful reality of loss; as such it may delay acceptance of the true situation, but, like most other coping mechanisms, it is only intermittently effective. The sense of the husband 'inside' is a transient phenomenon, and those who experience it are likely to locate him in some other person or place on other occasions. Similarly, the adoption of roles or attitudes of the dead person is seldom permanent and never complete; episodes of comfortable 'closeness' are followed by periods of grieving and loneliness, and it is only intermittently that identification occurs.

Golan (1975) speaks of the process as a progression from 'being a wife to being a widow to being a woman' – growth is completed as she gives up her view of herself as being a 'partnerless half' and becomes an autonomous individual. This progression is aided by the gradual return of bodily appetites. The appetite for food is often the first to reassert itself, perhaps because starvation begets hunger. Sexual and other interests come later and lead eventually to a resurgence of interest in the world and a willingness to plan for a new future.

The London widows seemed at last to find their new identity emerging from the altered life situations which they had to face. New friends and new workmates provided role models and several widows remarked that they had been much helped by talking to other widows with whom it was easy for them to identify.

This does not mean that the identification with the husband which had grown up during the years of marriage was altogether lost. Clearly, the points of view, values, and modes of problem-solving which had been established over the years did not all cease to be appropriate, and the first thought of many a widow when faced with a new problem was often, 'What would my husband have done about this?' But the answer to this question is not always apparent and the use of the remembered husband as an ever-present referee tends to diminish with time. As the old assumptions about the world prove ineffective and a fresh set of assumptions is built up so the old identity dissolves and is replaced by a new and different one.

8

ATYPICAL GRIEF

> The grief hath craz'd my wits.
>
> *King Lear*

We know that a proportion, albeit a small one, of bereaved people 'break down' after bereavement and are referred for psychiatric help. In this chapter the forms that such 'breakdowns' may take are described, and in the next chapter we consider why it is that some people react in these ways while the majority come through the stress of bereavement without seeking psychiatric help.

As indicated in Chapter 2, the problems which bring people into psychiatric care after bereavement fall into two categories, non-specific and specific. The non-specific problems are not special to bereavement and comprise a wide range of psychiatric conditions which can be caused by a variety of stressors. The specific conditions are types of pathological grief and it is this group which we shall be examining more closely in this chapter.

The situation is further complicated by the fact that many of the people whose presenting symptoms were of a non-specific type also showed evidence of pathological grief and many of those presenting with pathological grief also had evidence of non-specific reactions. Mixed pictures, as we have seen, are not uncommon in psychiatry.

Be that as it may, it is clearly necessary to study more closely the types of symptom that follow bereavement if we are to find out which ones are indicative of pathology. Let us, therefore, look at the constellation of psychological symptoms experienced by a group of patients who came into psychiatric care after bereavement and compare them with the symptoms shown by unselected widows.

HOW DO WIDOWS WITH PSYCHIATRIC PROBLEMS DIFFER FROM OTHER WIDOWS?

No very systematic comparative data are available, and comparisons are of doubtful validity when they are based on different studies of different populations using different symptom criteria and carried out at different time-intervals after bereavement. Nevertheless, quantitative assessments made in studies of 'normal' and psychiatrically disturbed widows do confirm the observations of clinical practice and some of these findings are reported in the Appendix, section 11.

They indicate first of all that the widowed psychiatric patients had experienced more or less the same grief symptoms as the widows in the normal samples studied. Only one symptom, ideas of guilt or self-reproach, was markedly more frequent in the psychiatric group.

However, when account was taken of the intensity and duration of the symptoms, the psychiatric and non-psychiatric groups were clearly distinguished. Two types of reaction became apparent in the disturbed group: one was a tendency for grief to be prolonged; the other was a tendency for the reaction to bereavement to be delayed. Some of the delayed reactions were also prolonged.

CHRONIC GRIEF

Thus out of twenty-one bereaved psychiatric patients (four male, seventeen female) interviewed in the Bethlem Study (see p. 28), there were fifteen whose grief seemed more prolonged than I would have expected. These patients suffered from what Anderson (1949) had termed 'chronic grief'. Years after bereavement many of them were still preoccupied with memories of the dead person, pining intensely and severely distressed by any reminder that brought him or her to mind. Eight patients cried uncontrollably and several others said that they felt 'too hurt to cry'. Agitated and aggressive outbursts occurred in four cases and four admitted to having suicidal preoccupations. The intensity of grief impaired working capacity in eight cases and caused most to shut themselves up at home or withdraw in some way from contact with their friends and relatives. Osterweis *et al.* (1984) point to a feature of these patients which seems to distinguish them from other bereaved people: 'Not only is there no movement but there is a sense that the person will not permit any movement. It is the felt intensity of anger, self-blame or depression that makes the reaction pathologic.'

'I miss him every moment of the day'; 'I want my husband every minute of the day but neither you nor anybody else can give him to me' – these statements would be normal enough if made a few weeks after bereavement but in fact they were made one and a half and nine and a half years later (the latter case being the most prolonged chronic grief reaction that I have ever seen). Even allowing for exaggeration they reflect a sad state of affairs and one that may not be very uncommon. Gorer, in his study (1965) of a random sample of people from all parts of Britain, interviewed eighty who had been to the funeral of a close family member within the previous five years. He found that nine (11 per cent) were still severely depressed a year or more after bereavement. He was struck by the solitariness of these people, who sat at home alone and did not seek psychiatric help.

Gorer distinguishes between those who suffer such chronic depressive reactions and those who say 'You never get over it', while at the same time leading effective and reasonably satisfying lives. The latter, he believes, regard unlimited mourning as a duty to the dead and are not truly grieving though they continue to mourn.[1] The distinction is, of course, hard to make and I believe that the two categories overlap to a considerable degree. In the case of Queen Victoria, who can be regarded as the exemplar of chronic grief, the intense pining that was apparent during the first few years after the death of Prince Albert grew gradually less even though she continued to mourn his loss for the rest of her life (Longford, 1964). Nevertheless, it would be untrue to regard her perpetual mourning as nothing more than a duty to the dead.

Mrs S lived for eleven years with a man twenty years older than herself. She described their relationship as 'ideal – everything – it was so right – he was so fine . . . I'd absolutely found myself'. Even during his life she was intolerant of any separation from him and when he died after a long illness she 'never stopped crying for months'. 'For years I couldn't believe it, I can hardly believe it now. Every minute of the day and night I couldn't accept it or believe it.' She stayed in her room with the curtains drawn: 'For weeks and weeks I couldn't bear the light.' (One is reminded of the widow who spoke in a whisper for fear of making reality too real.)

She tried to avoid things and places that would remind her of her loss: 'Everywhere, walking along the street I couldn't look out at places where we were happy together . . . I never entered the bedroom again . . . can't look at animals because we both loved them so much. Couldn't listen to the wireless.' But she retained a very clear picture of her *de facto* husband in her mind which she was unable to shut out: 'It goes into everything in life – everything reminds me of him.' For a long time she went over and over in her mind the events leading up to his death.

At first she used to agonize over minor omissions and ways in which she had failed him, but gradually these preoccupations lessened and she tried to make a new life for herself. However, she found it difficult to concentrate on her work and hard to get on with other people: 'They've got homes, husbands and children. I'm alone and they're not. I'm so unhappy, they're not.' She tried to escape by listening to recorded music and reading a great deal, but this only increased her isolation.

A friendly chaplain advised her to seek psychiatric help but 'I had the idea that psychiatrists can't help with real-life problems'. Her GP treated her for bowel symptoms (spastic colon), but 'You only get three minutes and you can't talk about psychological problems in that time'. Eventually she sought help from a voluntary organization, and it was the people she met there who finally persuaded her to seek psychiatric help.

DELAYED GRIEF

The second feature that distinguished the psychiatric patients from other bereaved people was a tendency for their reaction to bereavement to be delayed. There were eight patients in the Bethlem Study who had suffered from delayed grief. In all these cases a period of two weeks or more had elapsed between the death and the onset of pangs of grief. In three cases this seemed to be a prolongation of the phase of numbness described in Chapter 5, but the remaining five behaved as if nothing had happened – not even numbness was acknowledged.

When told of the death of her husband, Mrs K remarked, 'Oh, would you give me a cigarette?' She went about her household tasks automatically and her sister thought, 'It hasn't penetrated; how awful when it does and she realizes.' Mrs K said, 'I just couldn't believe it. I didn't realize he was not coming back.' About two weeks later she became more subdued and depressed, but she was still unable to cry: 'Tears came to my eyes but I was unable to let them go.' Her depression gradually got worse and she became socially withdrawn and preoccupied with self-reproachful ideas centring on another widow to whom she had been unkind during her husband's illness. It was in this state that she was admitted to a psychiatric unit six months after bereavement.

In this case it was depression and suicidal thoughts that brought the patient into the care of the psychiatrist and in fact all the patients I had seen with delayed reactions eventually developed depression. It is not surprising that some psychiatrists prefer to regard this as a depressive illness caused by bereavement rather than a delayed grief (Osterweis *et al.*, 1984, p. 56).

In his classic paper 'The Symptomatology and Management of Acute Grief', Lindemann (1944) described various *formes frustes* of grief which may occur during the period of delay, and in my own series I have come across complaints of insomnia, panic attacks, irrational angry outbursts, and social withdrawal. However, these can equally well occur after the period of delay and they did not in themselves bring about psychiatric referral.

The forms of atypical grieving shown by the bereaved patients in the Bethlem Study were often associated with panic attacks, persisting and intense guilt, or a peculiar kind of hypochondriacal condition in which the patient developed symptoms closely resembling the symptoms suffered by the dead person during the last illness.

ANXIETY AND PANIC ATTACKS

Panic attacks were described by six of the twenty-one patients studied. They were brought on by reminders of death and by loneliness at loss of support, and included 'choking sensations', breathless attacks, and other somatic expressions of fear.

Mrs C was fifty-six when her husband died from lung cancer. Her mother had died the previous year and her only daughter had left home to get married at about the same time. Consequently, when her husband died she was left alone in the house. 'I tried to go on as before. I said "Goodnight mate" just as if he was there.' After a few weeks she got a job as a kitchen-maid to get herself out of the house during the daytime. She began to sleep badly and to dread returning to the empty house. She experienced attacks of trembling, with sweating, palpitations, and pains in the stomach. These were brought on by thinking about the empty house and by reminders of her loss. She became increasingly depressed, tense, and agitated, feeling that she had let people down by getting depressed and blaming herself for her illness.

It was in this state that she was admitted to hospital five months after bereavement. 'It's definitely connected with his death,' she told me. 'I love too hard, I love so much, that's why I get hurt. I think, "There's no good going in the kitchen – he'll never come back."' She still found her memories so painful that she tried to avoid them, but she felt that there was something wrong about this. 'I can't think about him now as I

111

should . . . I don't talk about him. I avoid thinking about him. It's easier to die than to keep on like this.'

Loneliness and social isolation seemed to make it more difficult for this widow to tolerate the pain of grief. She tried to go on as if nothing had happened and to avoid thinking or talking of her husband, but it became difficult for her to control her thoughts in this way and the attacks of severe anxiety from which she suffered seemed to reveal the intensity of her fear of being overwhelmed by grief.

These two features, intense separation anxiety and strong but only partially successful attempts to avoid grieving, were evident in all the forms of atypical grief I have come across. The degree of disbelief and avoidance varied considerably, but whatever its degree there was always an impression that the underlying separation anxiety was severe.

SELF-BLAME

Ideas of guilt or self-blame in relation to the deceased were expressed by two-thirds (fourteen) of the bereaved psychiatric patients. Sometimes this consisted of mild self-reproach as when a widow felt that she could have done more for her dying husband. Other patients were convinced that they were directly responsible for the death.

Over half (eight out of fourteen) of the patients who expressed ideas of self-reproach also expressed marked hostility towards other individuals, usually doctors, nurses, or clergy, who had attended the dying person during his last illness. This had sometimes caused problems, since it had led to immoderate outbursts. Fortunately, social controls in Western society seem strong enough to prevent the more extreme outbursts of anger which can be a danger in other cultures. Thus Westermeyer (1973) has described eighteen Laotian men who ran amok and exploded grenades in public places. Sixteen of these cases had followed recent losses (five by death of a wife). There was no great difference between the forms of guilt and anger expressed by these bereaved psychiatric patients whom I studied and those shown by the unselected widows, as previously described. But both guilt and, to a lesser extent, anger were reported more commonly in the psychiatric group and were more often seen as a major problem.

Mr M was sixty-eight when his wife died. They had been married for forty-one years and according to a member of the family he had 'coaxed and coddled her' throughout their married life. She died, unexpectedly, after a brief illness. For several days he was 'stunned'. He made all the funeral arrangements, then shut himself up at home and refused to see anyone. He slept badly, ate little, and lost interest in all his customary pursuits. He was preoccupied with self-reproachful thoughts and had fits of crying during which he blamed himself for failing her. He blamed himself for sending his wife into hospital (fearing that she had picked up a cross-infection on the ward), and was filled with remorse for not having been a better husband and for having caused his wife anxiety by himself becoming ill.

At the same time he was generally irritable, blaming his children for hurting their mother in the past and blaming the hospital for his wife's death. When he went to meetings of a local committee he lost his temper and upset his fellow-members. His son took him on a trip abroad in the hope of getting him out of his depression but he became more disturbed than ever and broke off the holiday to return to the home which he had cared for fastidiously since his wife's death.

Ten months after bereavement he was admitted to a psychiatric hospital where, after spending some time in psychotherapy talking about his loss, he improved considerably. It was at this time that I saw him and I was struck by the way in which he talked of the deficiencies of his wife while denying any feeling of resentment. 'I looked forward so much to when I retired – that was one of the things that cracked it. I wanted to go on holiday abroad but I couldn't get her to see eye to eye with that. She had been brought up to believe that to go without was essential. I never cured her of that.' He bought her a home but 'she regarded it as a millstone' – nevertheless she became very attached to her home, 'happier there than anywhere'. Her timorous attitude was reflected in numerous fears. 'She was afraid of the sea – I never pressed her to go abroad. The children would ask her to do things and automatically she'd say "No". No man could have wished for a better wife.'

One might expect that this man would now feel free of the restraints placed upon him by forty-one years of marriage to a difficult woman, but his conscious attitude can be summed up in his own words. 'Supporting my wife gave me a purpose in life. I've always been able to exert my will through her. Now I don't need to any more.' We can speculate that the anger which formed so marked a part of his reaction to bereavement may have been displaced from the wife herself on to others, including himself. The trip abroad with his son may have been a bid for freedom, but it was defeated because this man was still influenced in some degree by the assumptions and expectations which had become 'built in' throughout his married life. To take advantage of his wife's death to do the things that he had failed to persuade her to do in life would have been an insult to the part of her that still survived in his mind.

SOMATIC SYMPTOMS AND IDENTIFICATION

If the anger and guilt expressed by Mr M have their counterpart in the recriminations expressed by the unselected widows (see Chapter 6), the hypochondriacal symptoms which are considered next seem likely to be related to the identification phenomena discussed in Chapter 7. Such symptoms were found among five of the twenty-one patients in the Bethlem Study and I have since encountered six other cases in which there seemed to be a relationship between hypochondriacal symptoms and the symptoms experienced by a dying relative during his last illness. They were usually aches and pains in the site of a pain that had been prominent during the illness of the relative whose death preceded their onset.

Six of these eleven patients with hypochondriacal symptoms complained of chest pain, and in four of these cases the pain resembled the pain of coronary thrombosis, one patient had pain simulating lung cancer, and another the supposed pain suffered by a son who had died in a car accident. A further three showed the apparent effects of a stroke, and there was one case of recurrent vomiting.

In a few cases it seemed that the identification symptom was an exaggeration of symptoms that are common enough after bereavement. Thus palpitations frequently accompany anxiety and a woman whose husband had just died from heart disease may easily imagine that she is suffering from the same condition. Mrs I, for instance, became very panicky after the death of her husband from a coronary thrombosis. She thought that the palpitations and gasping she experienced at the time, and the sense that her heart was bursting, indicated that she too had a coronary thrombosis.

Many of the symptoms shown, however, bore no resemblance to those that commonly result from the physiological disturbance accompanying bereavement. (In psychiatric terminology the individuals concerned would be regarded as suffering from hysteria rather than hypochondriasis.) Mrs H, for example, when told of her husband's death, immediately lost the use of her voice for ten days. Her husband had died from the second of two strokes, the first of which had left him unable to speak.

The link between the terminal illness and the identification symptom appeared most clearly in a woman who was in psychotherapy at the time when her father died from a stroke which had paralysed the left side of his body. She had nursed him at home for several weeks before his death. The day after this event she related to her psychotherapist a dream which had occurred the previous night. In it she saw her father lying in his coffin; he had reached up at her from the coffin and 'stroked' the left side of her body whereupon she woke up to find that the left side of her body was paralysed. The paralysis wore off over the course of the next hour and she had no further symptoms of this nature.

This example shows clearly how the struggle to realize, to make real, the father's sickness and death was expressed in a bereavement dream. The father, neither alive nor dead, reaches out and, in a gesture that contains and expresses the ambivalence of their relationship, strokes his daughter and passes on to her the stroke that killed him. It is perhaps no coincidence that a recurring problem for this woman, which came up repeatedly in psychotherapy before and after her bereavement, was her feeling of having been harmed by her father.

In two bereaved psychiatric patients the hypochondriacal illness itself resembled a hypochondriacal illness suffered by a close relative. Thus Miss O, an American spinster of middle age, had lived with her sister for many years. After her sister's death her grief was delayed for three months and then broke through with great severity. She had not recovered from this phase when, seven months later, she became paralysed and anaesthetic from the waist down. These dramatic symptoms bore no resemblance to the symptoms of her sister's last illness but they did closely resemble an illness her mother had suffered, apparently as a reaction to bereavement. This illness had greatly affected the patient's life. Her mother had developed a paralysis of both legs after the death of the patient's two brothers. She had become a cripple, in the care of the family, and had thereby succeeded in dominating them. Whether or not the mother's illness was in fact a reaction to bereavement, it was believed by the family to have been so, and the patient shared this belief. After the mother's death her place had been taken by the patient's sister, who resembled her mother in many respects. Miss O's illness perpetuated the pattern and caused great concern in the family.

The second case of a hypochondriacal illness occurred in a woman whose father was said to have vomited every morning for thirty years. When seen seven months after his death she claimed that she had taken over the habit. She was preoccupied with his memory and said, 'I do exactly the same things as my father.'

These examples illustrate some of the forms that identification symptoms may take. As with the other symptoms commonly experienced by bereaved psychiatric patients, they bear a close resemblance to similar phenomena reported by unselected widows in the London Study. In fact, one of the London widows had a hypochondriacal illness described by her GP as 'mimicking her husband's illness', and four others, at one time or another, complained of symptoms suspiciously similar to those of their husbands. Four of these five also showed other identification phenomena[2] of the types described in the last chapter.

CONCLUSION

Of the presenting symptoms of bereaved psychiatric patients listed at the beginning of the chapter, it is clear that some – such as depression, hypochondriacal symptoms, phobic symptoms, insomnia – may be a part of the special forms of grief which have been described. Others – such as alcoholism, asthma, and loss of hair are not specifically related to bereavement; like the various psychosomatic conditions described in Chapter 2 they could have occurred in a variety of stress situations, and there is nothing about them *per se* that would lead us to suspect pathological grief. It is only when we look at the history of the events and reactions that led up to the presenting symptom that the nature of the problem becomes clear.

The overall conclusion from this chapter must be that among the various mental disorders that can be precipitated by bereavement the most frequent are likely to comprise atypical forms of grief. Although these atypical forms differ in intensity and duration from the more usual reactions to bereavement, certain aspects of which may be exaggerated or distorted, they do not differ in kind. There are no symptoms that are peculiar to pathological grief although it seems reasonable to view extreme expressions of guilt, identification symptoms (as opposed to other phenomena of identification), and delay in the onset of grief of more than two weeks' duration, as indicators that the reaction to bereavement may take a pathological course.

What causes these reactions, and why some people come through the experience of bereavement without breaking down while others need psychiatric or other medical help, are considered in the next chapter.

9

DETERMINANTS OF GRIEF I
Relationship, gender and age

No different, I said, from rat's or chicken's,
That ten-week protoplasmic blob. But you
Cried as if you knew all that was nonsense
And knew that I did, too.

Well, I had to say something. And there
Seemed so little anyone could say.
That life had been in women's womb before
And gone away?

This was our life. And yet, when the dead
Are mourned a little, then become unreal,
How should the never born be long remembered?
So this in time will heal

Though now I cannot comfort. As I go
The doctor reassures: 'Straightforward case.
You'll find, of course, it leaves her rather low.'
Something is gone from your face.

David Sutton (b. 1944), 'Not to be Born'

Those who are concerned with the effects of bereavement have to take into consideration many possible factors when trying to explain the differences between individuals in their response to this event. It is not enough to say that the loss of a love object causes grief, and leave it at that. Grief may be strong or weak, brief or prolonged, immediate or delayed; particular aspects of it may be distorted and symptoms that usually cause little trouble may become major sources of distress. These points have been illustrated in previous chapters and the cases cited will already have indicated a few of the antecedent influences that seem to play a part in determining people's reactions to bereavement.

117

In some cases it may seem that a particular response is the consequence of a number of circumstances each of which contributes to the outcome; in others, one factor may appear to be the chief determinant.

For example, in the case of a young woman with a previous history of psychiatric illness whose husband dies suddenly and unexpectedly, there are several factors – her youth, her predisposition to mental illness, and her lack of opportunity to prepare herself for bereavement – that would be likely to have a determining influence on her reaction to his death.

On the other hand a unitary cause is exemplified by Queen Victoria. Her strong, dependent attachment to Prince Albert was such that she became upset by the briefest of separations throughout their married life. This fact alone is sufficient to explain the severity of her reaction to his death although cultural and other considerations have to be taken into account if we are to explain the form this took. We also have to explain why she established this type of attachment to the prince in the first place.

A complete explanation for any psychosocial event would be possible only if we knew everything that had preceded it – which clearly can never be the case. We shall never be able fully to understand any piece of human behaviour, nor can we expect to identify major factors that are important to outcome in every case of bereavement. But we can, I believe, learn something of the factors that play a part in most cases and a major part in some.

Relevant data can be obtained from detailed studies of a few people or from statistical studies of larger samples. Ideally, the two types of study should complement each other, for it is only by studying large numbers of people that we can generalize, and only by intensively studying a few that we can evaluate the significance of the mathematics of many.

Thus in the Case-note Study (see Chapter 2, pp. 24–7, and Appendix, section 7) statistical information was obtained from the case records of ninety-four bereaved psychiatric patients. More detailed information was obtained from the twenty-one psychiatric patients interviewed in the Bethlem Study, the twenty-two unselected widows in the London Study, and the nineteen widowers and forty-nine widows in the Harvard Study (see Chapter 2, and the Appendix, sections 6, 9, 11, and 12). Reference will be made in this chapter to a number of other studies which have been carried out in recent years. Taken altogether these studies point to certain of the major determinants of outcome after bereavement.

It was indicated in the last chapter that many of the patients who come for psychiatric help after bereavement are suffering from intense and prolonged forms of ordinary grief. It seems reasonable, therefore, to consider first what factors affect the overall magnitude of grief before going on to try to explain more specific variables.

ATTACHMENT

It would seem, on the face of it, a truism to say that the intensity of grief is determined by the intensity of love. But this is easier to state than to prove. In our society 'love' is so much a virtue that you will seldom find a widower or widow willing to admit that he or she did not love his or her spouse. Besides, what do we mean by 'love'? The meaning is imprecise.

Since love is a tie and the strength of a tie is its resistance to severance, one might suppose that intolerance of separation could be taken as a measure of love. But this would be to equate love with the particular type of clinging we see in young children who will not allow their mothers out of their sight. As Bowlby (1953) has pointed out, a well-established love relationship is one in which separation can be tolerated because the loved one can be trusted to return when needed. Ainsworth refers to this as 'security of attachment' (Ainsworth and Wittig, 1969).

The situation is further confused by the ambiguity of the term 'dependent', which is used sometimes to mean 'intolerance of separation' and sometimes to indicate 'reliance on someone for the performance of particular roles or functions'. Thus I may be 'dependent' on my wife because I cannot bear to be parted from her or because I need her to get me up in the morning.

Finally, there is the question of 'involvement'. By this I mean the extent to which one person's roles, plans, and repertoire of problem solutions depend upon the presence of the other person for their relevance and practicality. Thus the greater the area occupied by A in the life-space of B, the greater the disruption that will result from A's departure.

Determinants of the outcome of bereavement

ANTECEDENT
Relationship with the deceased
    Kinship (spouse, child, parent, etc.)
    Strength of attachment
    Security of attachment

Degree of reliance
Involvement
Intensity of ambivalence (love/hate)
Childhood experiences (especially insecure parenting and losses of significant persons)
Later experiences (especially losses of significant persons)
Previous mental illness (especially depressive illness)
Life crises prior to the bereavement
Mode of death
Timeliness
Multiple deaths
Previous warnings
Preparation for bereavement
Violent or horrific deaths
Disenfranchised deaths
Culpable deaths

CONCURRENT
Gender
Age
Personality
Grief proneness
Inhibition of feelings
Socio-economic status (social class)
Nationality
Religion (faith and rituals)
Cultural and familial factors influencing expression of grief

SUBSEQUENT
Social support or isolation
Secondary stresses
Emergent life opportunities (options open)

Relationship with the deceased

It would be hard to tease out the contribution of the four components of human relationships – strength of attachment, security of attachment, reliance, and involvement – to a particular relationship, and all we can hope to do is to examine instances where it seems that one or other component predominates.

In our society, partners, be they married or unmarried, tend to form small close-knit family units with their children, and to have a lesser degree of involvement with their parents and siblings than they did in the past. The woman's roles, plans, and problems tend to be family and husband-centred and she is usually more reliant on her partner for money, status, and company than he is on her. It comes as no surprise, therefore, to find that **loss of a husband** is the commonest type of relationship loss to give rise to psychological difficulties. Among 171 people who have been referred to me in recent years for the treatment of psychiatric problems following bereavement, 45 per cent had lost a spouse (35 per cent a husband, 10 per cent a wife), 22 per cent had lost a parent, 14 per cent a child, and 11 per cent other people. The remaining 9 per cent had multiple bereavements.

In my earlier Case-note Study, the number of women psychiatric patients whose illness had come on following the death of their husband (twenty-five) was seven times greater than would have been expected had the bereavement not been a causal factor in determining illness. On the other hand, the number of men whose illness had followed the death of their wife (six) was only four times greater than expected; and the illnesses that followed the death of a parent showed hardly any excess over expectation.

Losses of children in the Case-note Study were not sufficiently numerous to enable statistical probability of mental disorder to be calculated, but I have no doubt that they can cause psychological problems and Neidig and Dalgas (1991) showed that bereaved parents showed higher scores on the Texas Inventory of Grief than are found after other types of bereavement. Wretmark (1959) remarks that 'extremely severe and incapacitating reactions were found among mothers who have lost small infants', and Gorer (1965) describes the loss of a child at any age as 'the most distressing and long-lasting of all griefs'.

Clayton (1980), found that the death of a child had occurred within six months in a surprisingly high proportion of depressed psychiatric patients and Mann (1987) reported that 8 per cent of women who had lost a child attempted or committed suicide.

The reaction of parents to the death of an adult child in a road traffic accident has been studied by Shanfield and his colleagues (1984a and 1985). Although parents regularly agreed that the death of the child had been more painful than the death of a sibling or parent, those who had lost an adult child *and* a spouse did not regard one as being more painful than the other. Lundin (1984b), however, in an eight-year follow-up, found more evidence of persisting tearfulness and mourning among parents who had lost a child than among widows and widowers, but the latter were more likely than parents to continue to think about the dead person and to express feelings of guilt.

In my own study of thirty-five women and five men who sought psychiatric help after the death of a child (Parkes 1996a), the ratio of seven women to one man suggests that women are more vulnerable to the death of a child than men. Even so these psychiatric reactions did not follow ordinary bereavements and none of these parents were secure people who had lost a child by a predicted death. All showed evidence of prior vulnerability (as in Chapter 11) and/or had suffered particularly traumatic bereavements further details of which will be given in Chapter 10.

It is only in the present century that loss of a child has become a rare event, and what evidence there is suggests that during earlier days, when most parents would expect to lose up to half of their children in infancy or early childhood, they accepted their losses more readily than we do today. Hence Montaigne can write: 'I have lost two or three children in their infancy, not without regret, but without great sorrow.'

Granted that there has been a change in the reaction to the death of children, how can it be explained? Since we have fewer children to a family today than in the past, it may be that the tie between each child and his mother is correspondingly greater. Could it be that each mother has a total amount of potential for attachment and that it is therefore easier to lose one child out of a family of ten (10 per cent of one's children) than it is to lose one child in a family of two (50 per cent of one's children)? Another important factor is likely to concern the expectation of loss. In a society in which deaths of children are statistically rare we are more likely to be unprepared for those that do occur.

By comparison, the **loss of a parent in adult life** seems, as a rule, to cause much less distress but it is, of course, much commoner than loss of a child. Thus Moss and Moss (1995), reviewing the literature on this subject, state that the loss of a parent in adult life is 'rarely pathological'. Even so, psychiatric problems can be triggered in adults by the death of a parent, and they constitute the second commonest reason for people to seek my psychiatric help after a bereavement and the second commonest reason for people to seek help from Cruse – Bereavement Care. (In both instances death of a spouse is the most common.)

I studied twenty-two women and five men who were referred for psychiatric treatment after the death of a parent (Parkes, 1995b). A third of them had never married and, of those who had, only one had a marriage that was satisfactory. Nearly a half described themselves as having been unduly dependent on the parent who died and it was often this that had caused their marital problems. Seventy per cent were lacking in self-confidence and, without a supportive marital relationship, had found the death of their parent particularly hard to tolerate. On the other hand, the parent's death did present them with a chance to discover that they were not in fact as weak and helpless as they had feared and most of them eventually did well, a finding that is in keeping with Moss's conclusion that the death of a parent in adult life is often an opportunity for personal growth.

Birtchnell (1975b) found that among patients referred to psychiatric services in North-East Scotland with depressive illness, the proportion of women who had lost a father and men who had lost a mother in the preceding five years was over half as much again as in the general population. The death of a father was also common in alcoholic patients of both sexes.

In general, marriage seems to protect people from the traumatic effects of the death of parents. Thus in Jacobsen's and Ryder's (1969) study of the marriages of ninety people who had lost parents, it was found that the death of a parent in teen or adult life was associated with increased 'closeness' to their partner, whereas people who had lost a parent early in life often had less 'closeness'. However, a minority (about 19 per cent) of late-bereaved women were unable to enjoy sexuality and a few men were said to have 'retreated into childish and effeminate activities' following the death of a father.

Further evidence for the potentially traumatic effects of the death of a parent comes from Bunch *et al.*'s (1971) study of suicide. Among single men who committed suicide, 60 per cent had suffered a maternal bereavement during the preceding three years. This compares with only 6 per cent of single men who had not committed suicide. Loss of parents among married male suicides and among female suicides was relatively uncommon. It would seem from these studies that adult men who remain unmarried and continue to live with mother are particularly vulnerable to suicide when she dies.

Most studies do not indicate that the **loss of a sibling** in old age (which is when most of us lose siblings) is a major loss for most people. One exception seems to be the death of a twin and, more particularly, the death of an identical twin. Segal and Bouchard (1993) studied the intensity of grieving in forty-nine monozygotic (identical) and nineteen dizygotic (non-identical) twins after the death of the twin and other relatives. The intensity of grief expressed by twins significantly exceeded that for mothers, fathers, grandfathers, grandmothers, and other relatives. Monozygotic twins grieved more intensely for the death of their twin than dizygotic. The authors argue that this shows that grief intensity increases with genetic relatedness and confirms their theory that grief has evolved as a Darwinian adaptive mechanism. This may not be as far-fetched as it sounds if we accept the theory proposed in Chapter 3 of this volume, that the essence of grief is the cry for a lost person which has its roots in the attachments which enable us and our families to survive.

Loss of a sibling in middle life has been described as having a 'considerable impact' (Perkins and Harris, 1990), and Moss and Moss (1995) emphasize the part which siblings play in preserving the meaning of family and the identity of older people.

Loss of a grandchild is rare but can be traumatic when it occurs. Ponzetti and Johnson (1991) indicate that grandparents grieve not only for the child who has died but also for their own child, the grandchild's parent, and Roskin (1984) has reported that Israeli grandparents suffer an increased risk of mortality in the special circumstances of the loss of a grandchild in war.

Gender

One way or another women usually come out of bereavement with more psychological problems than men. By contrast it is men who are more likely than women to die of a heart attack after the loss of their spouse. There was only one man among the twenty-five bereaved patients who attended the Old-Age Counselling Service at McGill University in 1945–51 (see Stern, Williams and Prados, 1951), and 83 per cent of 171 bereaved patients who were referred to my psychiatric outpatient clinic were women. In that setting women outnumbered men in all categories of bereavement by a ratio of four or five to one. A study of forty relatives of patients who died in a St Louis hospital showed significantly more crying and a greater consumption of sedatives and tranquillizers among women than men (Clayton, Desmarais and Winokur, 1968).

In the Harvard Study, which comprised forty-nine widows and nineteen widowers under the age of forty-five living in Boston, Massachusetts, it was clear that the women showed more overt distress after bereavement than the men and that their psychological and social adjustment a year later was less good than that of the widowers. However, our measures of psychological and social adjustment also revealed large differences between married men and women in a matched control group of married people, and when this is taken into account it seems that the widowed women showed no greater decrement in adjustment after bereavement than the widowed men; moreover, at follow-up two to four years after bereavement, it was the men who were found to have taken longer to recover than the women. This suggests that a large part of the difference reported above is attributable to the tendency of men to hide their feelings and to their reluctance to seek help, a finding that is confirmed by Brabant *et al.* (1992) and by Tudiver *et al.* (1991), both of whom have carried out studies focused on widowers.

Why widowers should be more likely than widows to die of heart attacks following the death of their partner is not known. It is at least possible that men repress their grief more rigorously than women and that the increased mortality reflects some psychosomatic effect on the heart of this repression. Support for this hypothesis comes from Bonnano's (1994) study of conjugal bereavement which showed that bereaved people with *low* scores on grief-related symptoms had more rapid heart rates than people with high scores.

Men are less likely than women to seek psychiatric help following all types of bereavement and they often see themselves as having responsibility to contain their own grief in order to look after their wives. This is particularly likely following the death of a child. Thomas and Striegel (1995) who studied twenty-six couples who had lost a baby by stillbirth conclude that 'Mothers and fathers grieve differently, mothers grieve for their babies, fathers grieve for their wives'.

Age

Other factors that might be expected to affect the magnitude of the reaction to bereavement are the timeliness or untimeliness of the loss and the opportunities for anticipatory preparation that precede it. This is most obvious in **old age**. There is a great difference between the quiet slipping-away of an old person and the tragic cutting-off of a young one 'in his (or her) prime'. This is reflected in the reactions to bereavement of those who survive.

Stern, Williams and Prados (1951), describing the reactions to bereavement of twenty-four bereaved women and one bereaved man between fifty-three and seventy years of age who attended the Old-Age Counselling Service at McGill University, Montreal, found 'a dearth of overt mental manifestations of grief'. Similarly, in my study of the consultations that forty-four London widows had with their GPs (see p. 21), I found that, whereas widows under the age of sixty-five frequently consulted their GPs, for help with emotional problems during the first six months after bereavement, this was not the case with older widows. Furthermore, the consumption of sedative drugs was no higher among the older widows after bereavement than it had been beforehand, whereas there was a seven-fold increase in sedative consumption in the under-sixty-five age-group during the first six months of bereavement, which declined only slightly over the following year. (Cases were not followed up for more than eighteen months.) (See the Appendix, section 4, for statistical details.)

These findings are confirmed by Maddison's and Walker's study (1967) of 132 American widows between the ages of forty-five and sixty. The widows completed a questionnaire about their physical and mental health thirteen months after bereavement. Although the questionnaire asked for information about no fewer than fifty-six social factors, each of which might have been expected to contribute to their state of 'health', the only two that were found to bear a statistical relationship to outcome were the age of the widow and the age of her husband (these two were, of course, closely related). Thus younger widows had a higher illness score than older widows.

But not all studies come up with similar results and the association between young age and bereavement outcome was not confirmed when Maddison *et al.* replicated the study in Sydney, Australia (1969), nor was it confirmed in a study by Sable (1991) in which older widows were found to have higher levels of distress one to three years after bereavement than younger widows. None of these studies used non-bereaved controls and it may be that the increased incidence of illness and infirmity which is normal in the older age group explains some of these findings.

On the other hand, Kay, Roth and Hopkins (1955), who examined 184 psychiatric patients over the age of sixty with 'affective' (depressive or manic) disorders, found that the incidence of bereavement as a precipitant was higher in those whose first attack of the illness occurred when they were over the age of sixty than in those who had attacks at a younger age. Of course this could be because bereavements become more frequent as people get older, but it is reported that even in this age-group the emotional disturbance of the illness 'went far beyond any reaction that could be regarded as normal to the relevant misfortune'. It seems that bereavements in old age, however timely, were still capable of precipitating emotional disturbance designated as 'illness'. Van Rooijen (1978) observed that although older widows showed no less depression than younger widows, the intensity of their grief and the somatic distress that goes with it was less severe in older than in younger widows.

It seems then that, while young age may be associated with greater intensity of grief, pathological reactions are not confined to the young. Bereavement is certainly a cause of depression in old age and at least three studies have demonstrated that between 10 per cent and 17 per cent of elderly widows can expect to experience levels of depression equivalent to those found in psychiatric clinics at some time during the first year of bereavement (Clayton *et al.*, 1972; Duran *et al.*, 1989; and Lund *et al.*, 1989). Clegg (1988) has reported that of seventy-one patients admitted to a psycho-geriatric ward, twenty-two (31 per cent) had suffered one or more bereavements and an additional ten (45 per cent in all) had suffered other losses such as loss of health or roles. Furthermore the influence of bereavement on mortality rate, which was described in Chapter 2, is greatest in this age-group, presumably because of the bodily frailty that is most prevalent at this age.

One possible explanation for psychological problems following bereavement in old age is the multiplicity of losses which often concur at this time. Gass (1989) has shown that widows who face other threats in addition to the loss of their spouse are at greater risk of psychological difficulties than those for whom the spouse's death was the only loss. The loss of a spouse in this age-group commonly sets in train other losses (e.g., of income, home, or friends) and these may prove as traumatic as the bereavement itself.

There is also some evidence that older people may be more vulnerable to the effects of bereavement on physical health. This is evident in the increased mortality rate and the diminished nutrient intake that has been demonstrated in elderly widows after bereavement (Rosenbloom, 1993). There is also evidence that old people who are physically infirm are more vulnerable to depression after bereavement than those who are physically healthy (Richards and McCallum, 1979).

At the other extreme of age we have **children** who may also suffer bereavements. The subject is a complex one which would take us beyond the scope of this volume. The consequences have been reviewed by Raphael (1984), who concludes:

> There are, thus, many stresses to be faced by the child who loses someone with whom he has strong bonds of attachment. The

death itself is often bewildering and frightening for him. The threat to family life brings further insecurity. Yet with the sensitive support of his parent or parents he will master this trauma. His life and development within the family will go on.

Raphael agrees with Bowlby and Parkes (1970) that 'Provided their questions and recollections are not discouraged, the responses of children as young as two and a half years differ little from those of their elders'. Their grief, however, is often intermittent and there may be periods when they 'shut out' others and will not communicate about the bereavement. Boys, more than girls, commonly express their grief in aggressive ways, while girls, on the other hand, may become compulsive caregivers. Raphael comments on the common tendency of children to idealize the memory of a dead parent by comparison with the living who may be monsterized. Sadly the parents of a child who has died often do the same, denigrating their surviving children by comparison with the dead one. Older children often fear their own death and become over-protective to other members of the family fearing that they will lose them too. Often they become 'too grown up' and attempt to take over parental responsibilities; alternatively they may cling to a person who is identified in their minds with a lost parent.

Problems are particularly likely to occur if the family maintains a pattern of treating the death as a taboo subject that must not be mentioned, blames one of its members for the death, stops expressing warmth (on the grounds that if we don't care we can't be hurt), pretends that things can go on as if nothing had happened or, conversely, degenerates into chaos. In all of these cases the intervention of caring outsiders is needed.

10

DETERMINANTS OF GRIEF II

Mode of death

There is no comfort for those who are grieving
For faith is not enough
To assuage the tearing wound of sudden death.
O let me not drown in the flood of grief
For all young men who died before their time
And for this one so newly dead.
O let me catch the raft of life again
And not be swept away
In the darkest depths of grief and loss.

Marjorie Pizer, 'Lament for Glen
(killed in a motor-cycle accident, aged nineteen)'

Among the bereaved people who seek psychiatric help from me after bereavement *all* have been found to have suffered unusually traumatic forms of bereavement and/or to show evidence of prior vulnerability. Sudden unexpected deaths, multiple deaths, violent deaths, and deaths involving human agency (murders, suicides, etc.) represent a special risk to mental health even in the absence of other vulnerability. By comparison, natural deaths are relatively untraumatic (Weinberg, 1994).

Let us look first at **unexpected deaths**. The young widowers and widows in the Harvard Study were quite clearly more emotionally disturbed following deaths for which they had had little time to prepare, and their disturbance persisted throughout the first year of bereavement (see Appendix, section 13). 'Short duration of terminal illness' came first among fifty-five antecedent variables as a predictor of poor outcome thirteen months after bereavement. Other studies in Britain, the USA, and Sweden have come up with similar findings (Duke, 1980; Vachon *et al.*, 1980; and Lundin, 1984a). When Lundin followed up his group of 130 first-degree relatives eight years after bereavement he found that the unexpectedly bereaved were still more tearful, self-reproachful, and numb, and that they missed the dead person and mourned for them more than other people (Lundin, 1984b). A recent study by Smith (1990) has even shown that, in young widows and widowers, the increased mortality which follows bereavement is greater if the death was sudden and unexpected than if it was expected. This remains true to a lesser extent in older widowers but not in older widows, who show no difference in mortality after sudden as opposed to expected deaths.

Those studies which contain a substantial proportion of older widows (in whom even a sudden bereavement may not be totally unexpected) show no significant association between sudden death and poor outcome (Clayton et al., 1972; and Fulton and Gottesman, 1980). Furthermore, in one study of older men and women (Gerber et al., 1975), those whose spouse had suffered a very long illness had a poorer outcome after bereavement than did others with short histories. This suggests that very long illnesses in which the life of the spouse becomes centred on the partner may give rise to special problems after the partner dies.

Another category of sudden death which has received close examination in recent years is the sudden death of a newborn infant, or 'cot death'. Osterweis et al. (1984), reviewing the growing literature on this topic, state: 'The suddenness of SIDS (Sudden Infant Death Syndrome) in seemingly healthy babies may lead to extra difficulties in the bereavement process . . .' Misunderstandings commonly arise in the course of police inquiries, parents may blame each other, and some engage in a relentless search for a cause (Raphael, 1984). Peppers and Knapp (1980) suspect that 'shadow grief' may continue to plague some mothers from time to time for the rest of their lives.

Shanfield and his colleagues (1984a, 1984b, and 1985) found that deaths of adult children in road traffic accidents were associated with more intense grief in the surviving parents, more symptoms from a health check list, more depression, and more guilt than deaths of older adult children from cancer which had been treated in a hospice. Parents of children with cancer did not show more psychiatric symptoms than would have been expected in a normal population; in fact, over a half reported a sense of personal growth, increased spirituality, and a greater sense of closeness to their surviving family.

Among the parents who had lost a child in a road traffic accident, mothers had worse outcomes than fathers. The deaths of younger unmarried children who were still living at home and of children who died in single-car, single-driver accidents or who had alcohol or relationship problems were predictive of poor outcome in the parents.

But even if there is ample warning of an incipient death, it is not easy to prepare adequately for bereavement. Part of the difficulty resides in the fact that even though people may know that a person is dying they are likely to suppress their own anticipatory grief for fear of upsetting the dying person.

Typical was Mrs I, who said: 'My husband could read me like a book, so I couldn't show any sign of being upset. When the doctor told me it was cancer, I was upset for half a day, and pretended to him it was because he was likely to have to go into hospital. It was such a terrible thought I pushed it to the back of my mind.' The lack of communication got worse as his disease progressed: 'I seemed to go away from him. He wasn't the person I'd been married to. When I tried to share his pain it was so terrible I couldn't.' Her dissociation from the patient, her husband, was such that when he eventually died she felt 'It wasn't really him . . . I wondered where he was'. At the time I first saw her, three weeks later, she was still dazed and numb: 'I'm waiting for him to come back from somewhere,' she said.

Experience in hospices suggests that it is sometimes possible for a husband and wife to work together towards an acceptance of the approaching death of one of them. If the circumstances are right (as discussed in the next chapter), they can share some of the anticipatory grief which each needs to feel. The striking thing about such cases is that, despite the sadness which is an inevitable component of anticipatory grieving, couples who choose to face the future in this way often seem to win through to a period of contentment and calm which persists to the end. After bereavement has occurred, the surviving spouse is likely to look back on this period with a satisfaction that contrasts with the dissatisfaction expressed by many who have chosen to hide the truth.

In the Harvard Study unexpected and untimely deaths were found to give rise to a characteristic type of response to bereavement. The initial reactions of numbness and disbelief persisted for a considerable time and were associated with social withdrawal and a continuing sense of the presence of the dead person near at hand. This did not prevent the bereaved from becoming lonely, anxious and depressed, a reaction which was still present in over half the group two to four years later.

Those who have suffered unexpected and untimely bereavements are often preoccupied with memories of the lost person and, if the death was of a particularly painful type and was witnessed by the bereaved person, the memories themselves will be painful and meet the criteria for Post-Traumatic Stress Disorder. Indeed Schut *et al.* (1991) found higher rates of PTSD following unanticipated deaths than other types of bereavement. Intrusive and painful memories seem to prevent happier memories from emerging and in this way interfere with the work of grieving. It is not unreasonable to assume that this is one of the reasons for the long duration of some of these traumatic grief reactions.

Pynoos *et al.* (1987a and b), who have used their own check lists to measure both grief and PTSD in children who had been subjected to a sniper attack, found, as one would expect, that the magnitude of grief correlated with the intensity of attachment to a friend who had died while the magnitude of the symptoms of PTSD correlated with the extent to which the child had been in personal danger. When both grief and PTSD occurred together the PTSD tended to take priority.

Deaths by violence (Horowitz, 1976; Dillenberger, 1992), murder or manslaughter (Parkes, 1993a), suicide (Cain, 1966; Silverman *et al.*, 1994), civil disaster (Tyhurst, 1957; Raphael, 1986), and military action (Sanua, 1974) have been the topic of a number of studies. All show an increased risk to mental health. Thus Dillenberger, who used a variety of standard methods of assessing mental health to assess several groups of violently bereaved widows in Northern Ireland, showed high scores on most measures of psychological problems. In all of these cases grief is likely to be complicated by intense feelings of anger and guilt. If the danger persists, as in the case of an unsolved murder or a civil or military disaster, disillusionment with the power of the authorities to maintain a secure environment may generate a host of fears. Yet times of war are not associated with dramatic increases in neurosis and the social supports which focus on the families of those who have died 'for their country' may help to mitigate their grief. Thus Rubin (1992), who followed up parents who had lost a son in the Yom Kippur War, reports that thirteen years later bereaved parents had no more psychological symptoms than non-bereaved controls. On the other hand they continued to remember and to relate to vivid memories of the lost child who remained an important part of the family. Rubin refers to this as the second track in a 'two-track model of bereavement'.

Some, but not all, violent deaths are the result of human agency, in which case reactions of anger and guilt are very understandable. In an attempt to focus on the issue of blame, Weinberg (1994) carried out a postal study of 200 people who reported a bereavement as their most distressing experience. Of these, 47 per cent blamed someone else for the death, but blaming others was only associated with poor outcome if it was associated with a persisting desire for revenge. It seemed that a 'desire for revenge can keep survivors focused on the loss'.

This was certainly the case among many of the seventeen patients who were referred to my psychiatric clinic following bereavements by **murder** or manslaughter (Parkes, 1993b). Many of the risk factors associated with poor outcome after bereavement are to be found in such cases which must represent one of the most traumatic kinds of bereavement. Thus the combination of sudden, unexpected, horrific and untimely death, with all the rage and suspicions which followed, and the long-drawn-out legal proceedings, which often led to a sentence that seemed trivial by comparison with the magnitude of the loss, could be expected to overwhelm the family as a support for its members and lead to lasting psychological problems. It does this in several ways – by inducing PTSD, by evoking intense rage, by undermining trust in others including the police and legal systems that are expected to protect us and by evoking guilt at failing to protect the deceased. These consequences easily set in train vicious circles which perpetuate the problems. Avoidance of reminders and depressive withdrawal can lead to social isolation which aggravates the depression, lack of trust may cause people to turn away from sources of help, angry outbursts may further alienate others, and feelings of guilt may lead to self-punitive behaviour. It can be no surprise that most of the families bereaved by murder who attended my clinic saw themselves as stuck in a rut from which they could not escape. By the same token it was important for me not to be so drawn into this maelstrom that I too felt overwhelmed. By adopting a slow and gentle approach, by insisting on dealing with only one problem at a time, by maintaining a calm but caring attitude, and by allowing the bereaved to choose their own agenda, it was usually possible to create a safe place in which the bereaved could gradually begin the process of reviewing and rebuilding their lives. We shall return to further consideration of these issues in later chapters.

The families of **suicides** often blame themselves and may feel socially stigmatized. On the other hand, according to Cleiren (1992), 50 per cent of suicides have been anticipated so we should not expect all to be equally traumatic. His comparison of people bereaved by suicide, road traffic accidents and long illnesses indicates that road traffic accidents caused the most severe depression with suicide second and long-term illness third. Those bereaved by suicide were most likely to feel guilty and to wonder what more they could have done but this was seldom a major problem. On the whole parents of suicides suffered more than spouses (who tended to become depressed and to withdraw during the first four months but recovered sooner than the bereaved parents).

Psychiatrists and other health care staff are usually at hand when someone commits suicide but few take the opportunity to offer help to families bereaved by suicide. In a recent study by Brownstein (1992), eleven out of twelve families of psychiatric patients who had committed suicide said that they would have liked some contact with the psychiatrist who had cared for the person who died but only one psychiatrist had initiated any such contact. This may well be a reflection of the embarrassment which psychiatrists often feel when their patients commit suicide, but it tends to compound any problems that exist rather than to resolve them.

There is a large literature on civil and military **disasters** whose relevance to our understanding of bereavement has been examined by Raphael (1986). Multiple concurrent losses are more traumatic than single losses. In addition to the effects of multiple losses, disasters can also undermine the support networks on which we rely for our sense of security and even those who offer help in disaster situations may find themselves at risk. Those who have witnessed the disaster and survived are most at risk for PTSD which, as we have seen, can coexist with and complicate the course of grief. The scale, spread and character of disasters vary widely and influence the psycho-social damage which they cause and the type of response that is needed (Parkes, 1991b).

A category of loss which creates special problems has been termed by Doka (1989) **'disenfranchised grief'**. By this he means losses that cannot be openly acknowledged, socially validated or publicly mourned. The most obvious example is death from AIDS[1] but there are many others. Doka divides them thus:

1 Unrecognized Relationships (e.g., extramarital attachments, homosexual relationships, ex-spouses or lovers, true parents of adopted children and doctors or nurses who have become attached to their patients).

2 Unrecognized Losses (e.g., Perinatal deaths, abortions, returning foster children to their parents, giving up children for adoption, loss of a pet and social or psychological loss without death as when a partner develops Alzheimer's Disease).

3 Unrecognized Grievers (e.g., children who are thought to be too young to grieve, or adults who are too old or brain damaged as when a death occurs in an old people's home, mental hospital or an institution for those with learning difficulties).

In all of these groups problems can arise in the expression of grief which may be intensified by being ignored or repressed, anger and guilt which are very likely to arise and which then complicate the course of grieving, exclusion of the griever from helpful rituals of mourning and lack of social support or sanction for grieving.

AIDS is an example of a type of loss that is often concealed, unrecognized or ignored and Schneider *et al.* (1991) have shown that gay men who suffered the death of a partner (usually from AIDS) were more likely to express suicidal intentions than those who had not. Working in a hospital in which many HIV positive patients are seen, I have been struck by the number who have experienced multiple bereavements. Such patients are typically more distressed by the loss of friends and partners than they are by the threat to their own life. The hospital provides them with doctors, nurses and counsellors who can see them through the bad times and it is not surprising that they often turn to these staff for support at times of bereavement.

Unrecognized losses such as the death of a foetus also come to the attention of medical and nursing staff and it is important for staff to give sensitive support. A good account of the problems that can arise and their implications for the organization of support is given by Kowalski (1991).

When Joan's baby was born dead she asked the nurse what would become of the body. The nurse replied that, technically, this wasn't a baby but a foetus, an abortion. Its body would be consigned to the rubbish bin and incinerated along with the other detritus from the ward. Joan, who had grown attached to her unborn child, could not accept this; she asked to see the baby and, when the nurse demurred, became very upset. Eventually the nurse gave in and produced the foetus wrapped in a towel. Joan could see that it had fingers and toes and was very much a human being. She asked if she could see the hospital chaplain and was told, incorrectly, that there was nothing that the chaplain could do – there could be no funeral or other ritual for an abortion.

At this point Joan's distress became greater than ever. She discharged herself from the hospital and arrived home clutching her dead baby and in a distraught state. Her husband did not help by telling her that she had been very foolish and should return to the hospital. He refused to look at the baby.

Joan, on her own, took her baby to the crematorium where a surprised attendant showed her the first understanding that she had received. He provided her with a shoe box and accompanied her to the chapel where he turned on some recorded music and stayed with her while she prayed for her baby. Eventually he pressed the switch which transferred the shoe box with its sad contents to the cremation oven.

I saw Joan two years later in my psychiatric clinic. She was still seething with anger at what had happened and wanted to know if it was she or the world that was mad. I reassured her that she was certainly not mad and encouraged her to share her thoughts and feelings about what had happened. Her marriage was now threatened and it was important to see her husband and explain to him the normality of her reaction. A complaint to the hospital caused them to revise their instructions to staff regarding the handling of miscarriages and terminations of pregnancy.

Joan's case is not unusual and hospital chaplains are now recognizing the need for ritual and emotional support to mothers who need it. Peppers and Knapp (1980), who carried out a systematic study of eighty mothers who had abortions, found that most of the mothers complained that they had nobody to whom they could talk about what had happened. Most had suppressed or denied their grief but there were many exceptions. Persisting grief was most likely the later in the pregnancy the death had occurred. Roman Catholics were more likely to grieve than Protestants. In addition, the importance of the pregnancy in terms of the age and fertility of the mother, lack of education, and a history of previous miscarriages all contributed to aggravate grief.

Another type of unrecognized loss occurs when somebody develops Alzheimer's Disease or some other type of dementia. Here the spouse or other caregiver not only suffers grief in anticipation of the coming death of the patient but also grieves for the loss of the person they knew who is now radically changed by the disease. A systematic study of this phenomenon using an 'Anticipatory Grief Scale' has been conducted by Theut et al. (1991).

Grief can go unrecognized if the person who suffers it is unable to communicate or belongs to a group who are not expected to understand the loss. Recent studies of people with learning difficulties have shown that they have as much need to express grief as others. Sadly they are seldom invited to funerals or provided with opportunities to share their thoughts and feelings about the death of a friend or family member.

What **other events** occurring prior to bereavement can influence the nature of the reaction to it? Maddison and Walker (1967) have suggested that additional crises in close temporal relationship to a bereavement may be associated with a poor outcome, and in the London Study there was a significant association between the occurrence of major stresses during the two years preceding the bereavement and a poor overall adjustment afterwards (see Appendix, section 15). Stresses reported by the London widows were: losses of people (four), family discord (four), threats of loss (three), change of domicile (one), and poor housing conditions (one). When we add to these the secondary stresses that resulted from the bereavement itself – loss of income (for thirteen out of twenty-two widows), problems concerning work (twelve), worry about the future (five), and problems with children (uncounted but numerous) – the surprising thing is that nearly half of these widows seemed to have made a satisfactory adjustment a year after bereavement.

Although incidental stresses may contribute to a poorer outcome, their effect upon the intensity of the grief itself is by no means clear. In the London Study those widows who reported most stress prior to bereavement showed slightly (but not significantly) more grief symptoms than the rest.

An exception to the general rule that natural deaths give rise to less severe grief than unnatural can occur when survivors have centred their lives on caring for a sick person. One might have expected that the death of a person whose care the survivor had found stressful would lead to a relief of stress, but Bass and Bowman (1990) found that caregivers who had found their caring stressful suffered *more* difficulties in bereavement and more continuing strain than those who found their caring less stressful.

The effects of **extreme deprivation** are evident in studies of the Nazi holocaust. In Kval's study (1951) of life in Theresienstadt internment camp, where the Nazis kept 140,000 Jews, 'It was characteristic that serious matters like the death of relatives or close friends often met with only superficial sympathy, whereas trifles or small quarrels . . . would lead to severe temper outbursts'. In this situation unjust imprisonment, hopelessness, sexual segregation, lack of privacy, forced labour, semi-starvation, and the constant threat of being sent to an extermination camp were ever-present stresses. Grief and depression in such circumstances could well have tipped the scales against survival, and it may be that psychic defences come into operation to protect people in extreme conditions such as these. After the liberation a number of the survivors had severe depressive reactions: 'A strong feeling of guilt for having survived where relatives and friends succumbed was one of the outstanding features.' The grief was sometimes expressed in a prolonged search for the graves of beloved persons, as if it was possible in this way to get them back.

Kaminer and Lavie (1991), in a well-conducted study of concentration camp survivors, showed that those who were most successful in finding a balance between recalling and repressing their memories and emotions were better adjusted than those who continued to be preoccupied by them both waking and sleeping. This finding has been cited by Stroebe *et al.* (1994) in support of their Dual Process model of bereavement (see pp. 53 and 74).

11

DETERMINANTS OF GRIEF III

Personal vulnerability

Care draws on care, woe comforts woe again,
Sorrow breeds sorrow, one grief brings forth twain.
                                        Michael Drayton

If the magnitude and number of the stressors can influence the magnitude of the reaction to stress, what of the strength or weakness of the stressed person? The term 'weak ego-strength' is often applied as an indication of lack of resilience, of incapacity to withstand stress. Its usage is not satisfactory, since there is always circularity in the argument – they cannot cope with stress, therefore they have a weak ego. The next step is to assume that we have explained the inability to cope with stress by attributing it to a weak ego whereas all we have done is to define ego-strength in terms of coping ability. Unsatisfactory for the same reason were the obsolete terms 'lack of moral fibre' and 'psychopathic inferiority'. All these terms tended to be used as value judgements to imply a global incapacity to cope with stress. The exercise of such global judgements which ignore the nature of the stress, the situation in which it occurs, and the events that lead up to it can hardly be justified.

One indicator of vulnerability is, of course, a **prior history of mental illness** and this has been shown to be associated with increased risk after bereavement (Nuss and Zubenko, 1992).

PERSONALITY

Other major determinants of the magnitude of grief can be expected to be **personality factors** deriving from the genetic givens and previous life-experience of the individual. Unfortunately, attempts to measure personality factors after bereavement, such as the one conducted by

Vachon *et al.* (1982), tell us little about personality before bereavement. The high scores on emotional instability and anxiety which they report among widows showing 'high distress' tell us little about the causes of the distress. What constitutes a 'grief-prone' person? One can answer this question empirically by saying that it is anyone who tends to react strongly to separations, but this does not take us much further. We need also to discover the causes of such excessive reactions.

That a person may be **grief-prone** I do not doubt. There were five of the London widows who described excessively severe reactions to previous losses in their lives, and after their husband's death these were among the most disturbed widows interviewed. A year after bereavement there was not one who had recovered from her loss or whose psychological adjustment was rated as 'good'. Among the 121 bereaved psychiatric patients in the Case-note and Bethlem samples, a quarter (twenty-nine) had experienced periods of depression designated by the psychiatrist as 'affective disorders' at some earlier time in their lives, and though I have no comparable figures for normal populations this is obviously a larger proportion than one would expect by chance. It seems, then, that previous excessive grief and depression prognosticate a poor outcome following bereavement.

Horowitz *et al.* (1993) classify people as **'repressers'** or **'anxious'**. Repressers habitually avoid situations that will cause anxiety and deny that they feel anxious even when their bodily reactions suggest the opposite. Anxious people, on the other hand, are over-sensitive to danger and tend to seek it out and obsess about it. When faced with major traumas repressers avoid reminders of loss and minimize their distress while anxious people are haunted by intrusive thoughts and overtly fearful. Although these categories have not been fully investigated in bereaved people they certainly correspond to the two main categories of pathological grief, avoidance and chronic grieving.

This classification may describe two types of person but it does not explain them. Further research to be described below links these types of person to the types of insecure attachment patterns described by Ainsworth and Wittig (1969). They found that young children who cling to their mothers and cry a great deal during separation can be contrasted with others who take little notice when mother leaves and avoid or ignore her when she returns. The avoiders have recently been found to have surprisingly high heart rates throughout the period of separation and to have mothers who are insensitive to the child's needs and intolerant of bids for attention or closeness. The clingers also have mothers who are insensitive to their needs but in this instance the mothers are also inconsistent in their responses to the child, sometimes rewarding and at other times ignoring their bids for attention. This has the effect of causing the child to increase its demands (Main, 1991). The resemblance to the personality types described by Horowitz is striking. These attachment patterns have proved to be remarkably stable and to predict the child's relationships not only with their mothers but with other people too. Although children who were initially studied in their second year of life have only been followed up for ten years there are indications that the patterns observed are so strong that they will persist into adult life.

REPRESSION AND AVOIDANCE OF GRIEF

As indicated in Chapter 5, the mitigation of the overwhelming emotion of grief by **avoidance** of the full reality of the loss is a necessary part of 'distancing', of keeping the implications of disaster at a distance so that they can be dealt with little by little. Grief work is the process of learning by which each change resulting from the bereavement is progressively realized (made real) and a fresh set of assumptions about the world is established. Nobody can 'take in' at one blow the reality of so massive a psychic event as a major bereavement.

As I have explained there are many ways of avoiding the reality of loss. There is also wide variation in the duration and degree of avoidance. Some people express their feelings relatively freely and openly after the death of their spouse, whereas others attempt to inhibit their feelings but only succeed in postponing them: few get through the first three months of bereavement without expressing intense despair at some time.

In the London Study an attempt was made to assess, from self-reports and from observations, the severity of emotional upset during the early months (see Appendix, section 17). It was found that the widows showed three patterns in the expression of their grief.

One group became severely disturbed within a week of bereavement; they remained disturbed throughout the first and much of the second month; but by the third month most of them were only mildly disturbed. A second group showed moderate emotion within the first week; a week later most of them were severely disturbed, but their grief soon passed and they recovered more rapidly than the others. The remaining widows showed little or no emotion during the first week of bereavement, they succeeded in avoiding their grief; but by the fourth week most were moderately disturbed and at three months they were all moderately or severely disturbed and certainly more disturbed than either of the other two groups. It seems, then, that the widows in this last group were not able to avoid emotion but only to postpone it. After the third month they began to improve, but as the anniversary of the death approached they again became more disturbed than either of the other two groups.

Even during the first month this group of widows complained of more physical symptoms than those who had 'broken down' in the first week; headaches, insomnia, palpitations, and various aches and pains were common, and three of them suffered loss of hair (alopecia) in the first month. Thirteen months later the overall outcome was rated as good in only one of these cases and the rest all had psychological symptoms of one kind or another.

Why was it that this group failed to react emotionally to their bereavement? Several of the factors that have already been described seemed to play a part. Thus these widows were, on average, nine years younger than the other widows studied; only one of them was over the age of fifty. Also, their husbands tended to have died suddenly and unexpectedly. Moreover, a majority of them (five out of seven) had a history of previous psychiatric illness compared with only a third of the other widows. After bereavement it appeared that they had managed to avoid the early expression of their grief in a variety of ways: for instance, they engaged in little formal mourning (only one wore dark clothing) and none visited the grave or crematorium except on the occasion of the funeral.

Several deliberately kept themselves extremely busy in order to avoid feelings: 'I had so much to do I was geared at a tremendous tempo.' They found themselves unable to cry although a few expressed a wish to do so: 'I think that if I had a good outburst I might feel better.'

ANXIETY AND GRIEF

Among people seeking psychiatric help after bereavement anxiety is a very common symptom and often co-exists with chronic grief. In order to look more deeply at the reason why some people become more anxious than others, and to study the childhood influences on later bereavement in more detail, I developed a questionnaire aimed at measuring retrospectively the patterns of attachment between children and parents from the perspective of the child who has now grown up (Parkes, 1991a and 1995a). This questionnaire was completed by 60 bereaved people who were referred to me for psychiatric treatment and completed a second time some months after the end of treatment. It not only confirmed Bowlby's expectation that loss of a parent in childhood would be associated with grief-proneness and with increased symptoms after bereavements in adult life, it also showed that other negative parental influences contributed to the reaction to adult bereavement. In particular, parents whose behaviour could be expected to evoke fear in the child (e.g., because they were themselves unduly anxious) had children who described themselves as nervous and insecure and reacted to bereavement in adult life by becoming highly anxious and panicky. On the other hand, depression is more closely associated with parents who evoke feeling of helplessness, a finding which may indicate that both depression and cancers (as suggested by the research described in the Appendix, section 2) are most likely to occur in people with a predisposition to helplessness. Further details of this study are given in the Appendix, section 16.

DEPENDENCY

When one person greatly relies on, or has a strong insecure attachment to, another, the severance of the relationship is likely to give rise to difficulties. In the Case-note Study, bereaved psychiatric patients who still had grief symptoms at the time of their admission to hospital were significantly more likely to describe themselves as 'dependent' on their lost relative than those whose grief was not prominent. On the other hand, they were also more likely to describe the dead person as having been 'dependent' on them. This points to the reciprocal aspect of relationships. A is useful to B because he does things for her that she cannot or will not do for herself but B is useful to A in making him feel useful. In some senses people who lose a relative who relies on them are in a similar position to the mother who loses a child.

The Harvard Study found that intense yearning for the dead person in the early weeks of bereavement predicted chronic grieving later. We also found a strong association between the intensity of yearning three weeks after bereavement and assessments made by the coders (who listened to our tape-recorded interviews) of the extent to which the person had been 'dependent' on the dead person. An example of high involvement was Mrs J, who grieved intensely for several years after the death of her husband. Her description of her strong sense of identification with him has already been quoted (see p. 89). She had married at the age of thirty-five a man eighteen years older than herself. After his retirement twelve years later he became totally bound up with his home, his garden, and his wife. He hated it when she went out to work: 'He just sat at home worrying about me.' In the last ten years he had begun to show his age and she had nursed him at home for three years during his terminal illness (lung cancer). 'When we married he didn't seem like an older man, but ten years ago he got ill and ever since then he's shown his age and I've had to look after him . . . I felt I could preserve him . . . I gave in to his every whim, did everything for him . . . I waited on him hand and foot.'

Her devotion to her husband was such that, as his reliance on her increased, she spent more and more time at his bedside. She stopped visiting friends and relatives and if she left the home she was in a hurry to get back. In consequence her husband's death not only deprived her of her principal role in life but left her socially isolated and with a sense of failure.

The case of Mrs S illustrates another type of relationship, which has affinities with that of Mrs J, both bereavements being followed by unusually severe chronic grief. Mrs S, who had been brought up abroad, had been a sickly child, unhappy at school and tutored by her father for much of the time. Her mother dominated and fussed over her. She grew up nervous and timid, with the conviction that she was incompetent at any practical task. Leaving school at seventeen she remained at home with her mother, taking the dogs for a walk and (with great satisfaction) helping to care for a sick child. She left home at twenty, but continued to be supported by her mother. Her principal occupation at this time appears to have been that of professional child-minder and baby-sitter.

At the age of twenty-eight she met a man twenty years older than herself who was separated from his wife. He had been invalided out of the Navy and was having difficulty in settling down in civilian life. 'From the first our relationship was absolutely ideal – everything – was so right – he was so fine.' There was never any need for explanations, he accepted everything. She found she could do lots of things she'd never done before: 'I never feared anything with him. I could do new dishes. It was such a joy. I didn't get that feeling of incompetence . . . I'd absolutely found myself.' They lived together and she changed her name by deed poll to that of her *de facto* husband. To her great regret, she did not conceive a child, but despite this and despite the fact that they were very poor Mrs S described this period as the best in her life.

Mr S had a 'smoker's cough' which caused some anxiety to his wife, but she did not become seriously alarmed until 1959 when they had been together for eleven years. Then he had a haemorrhage from the lung and had to be admitted to hospital for six weeks. Shortly after returning home he lapsed into a coma. His doctor said that he had had a stroke and that his kidneys and lungs were failing. He was unable to move his limbs but made signs to her with his eyes. That same night the nurse roused her to tell her that he had died.

This woman's severe and lasting reaction to her bereavement was described on page 109. She was still grieving deeply nine and a half years later and had quite lost confidence in her ability to lead a worthwhile life in a world which she perceived as dangerous and insecure: 'I don't have much faith in the goodness of things,' she said.

The important thing about Mrs S's relationship with her husband would appear to be, not her reliance on him, but her relative competence in this setting. For the first time in her life she felt a useful, competent person. By her account he seems to have accepted her uncritically and, perhaps because she no longer felt criticized, she discovered new competencies she had not believed she possessed. She 'found herself' – that is to say, she found a new and more satisfactory self-model. But in another sense she relied on her husband for the maintenance of this new self and when he died she not only grieved deeply but also regressed to the earlier view of herself as incompetent, which had been implanted in her in childhood. All the problems of her childhood and early adult life returned, and her grief, instead of being a gradual relinquishment of one state of organization followed by disorganization and then the establishment of a fresh state, became stuck or 'fixated'.

The term 'fixation' refers to an arrest in the continuing series of changes in psychological organization and planning which are necessary if we are to meet the changing demands of a changing world. Fixation is, apparently, most likely to occur at times of major change and the term is used mainly to refer to 'hang-ups' occurring in childhood. As Bowlby (1963) has pointed out, however, it can appropriately be used to signify a 'hang-up' in the processes of change that follow any major change in adult life, including a loss. Thus a person who goes on grieving beyond the expected period, as did Mrs S, can be said to be 'fixated'.

Certain difficulties arise, however, which should lead us to employ the term with caution. In the first place, fixation is more a description than an explanation. To say that Mrs S suffers from chronic grief because she has a fixation at the second stage of grief adds little to the original assertion that the grief is chronic. Moreover, fixations are not necessarily as 'fixed' as the term might lead us to expect. It is sometimes possible to discern numbness or pining or depression as a prominent feature of chronic grief and therefore to describe sufferers as

...ixated in the first, second, or third phase of grief, but more often ...ey oscillate between phases (just as the typical bereaved person does) and there is no clear-cut fixation point. Also, a patient may be fixated at more than one point at the same time. Mrs S, for instance, could be said to be fixated at the second (yearning) phase of grief for her husband, but at the same time she exhibited behaviour which could be attributed to a much earlier fixation – a fixation to a phase of childish reliance upon her mother from which she had never fully escaped.

Does the evidence available allow us to speculate why Mrs S should have continued to grieve in this way? One possibility that must be considered is the secondary gain to be derived from mourning. Did she use her grief as an excuse to avoid facing up to the responsibilities and dangers of a new life? It would not be surprising if this were so, for her mother had long ago made it clear to her that her physical and mental weaknesses justified her attitude of reliance. Perpetual grief is a high price to pay for self-esteem, particularly as other people are seldom convinced by it for long. The friends and relatives of a bereaved person always start by being sympathetic, but their sympathy will pass if the grief does not abate, and before long the chronic griever is likely to be left alone, often complaining bitterly that 'nobody understands'. Mrs S had a lonely life, because she succeeded in alienating many of the people with whom she came into contact. Her grief did not, as far as I know, cause others to support her although she certainly gave it as the explanation, and, by implication, the justification, for her failure to cope. It may be that it was more important for her to justify her failure in her own eyes than in those of other people.

But such secondary gains do not, in my opinion, constitute a satisfactory explanation for more than a part of the pathological reaction to bereavement. In talking to patients such as Mrs S one is repeatedly impressed by the sheer intensity of feeling that is still bound up with the lost person; it seems to be the magnitude of the total psychological investment in the relationship that makes it hard for the survivor to realize the possibility of continued existence without the lost one. 'He was everything,' said Mrs S, and, by contrast, the rest of the world is 'nothing'. Another way of viewing this kind of problem has been put forward by Horowitz *et al.* (1980). They suggest that current relationships often hold in check earlier self-images and models of relationships which re-emerge when the subject is bereaved. Her marriage enabled Mrs S to believe in her own competence, but once the marriage came to an end her earlier image of herself as incompetent reasserted itself.

146

Previous experience of loss can be helpful or harmful depending on the success with which it has been handled. There is some evidence that people can learn from experience how to cope with loss (Bornstein *et al.*, 1973), but psychiatrists often see patients who have been referred after a loss which may be quite trivial but which has triggered off a reaction that properly belongs to an earlier loss. Thus Barnes (1987) found that 48 per cent of the 105 patients who sought help from his service for 'Bereaved in Trouble' had unresolved previous losses.

Bowlby (1963) has suggested that children who suffer the loss of a parent, particularly loss of mother, during childhood may be predisposed to **clinging** behaviour and excessive grief later in life. This is borne out by a comparative study of thirty adult psychiatric patients, fifteen of whom had lost a mother by death before they were four years old, and fifteen whose mother had died while they were in their teens. Thirteen of the early-bereaved groups (and only four of the late-bereaved) 'tended to cling desperately to a figure who represented security'. Sadly, this clinging often led to the rejection which it was intended to prevent (Barry *et al.*, 1965). Further confirmation comes from a similar study by Birtchnell (1975a), who found that female psychiatric patients who had lost a mother before the age of eleven had high scores on 'dependency'. Many of them had become chronic worriers and vulnerable to depression later in life.

AMBIVALENCE

Much has been written in the psychiatric literature about the effects of the dissolution of relationships in which feelings of love and hate were mixed. Fenichel (1948), for example, regards **ambivalence** as a cause of intense mourning. In such relationships the wish to drive out or hurt the other is often present and even the death of the other person may, from time to time, be consciously desired. When that death wish is gratified, it is claimed, survivors are left with a burden of guilt which is hard to bear. They may attempt to expiate their guilt by intense and prolonged mourning.

The study of bereaved psychiatric patients provides evidence to suggest that ambivalence does indeed contribute to pathological reactions, but research in this area is not easy. Retrospective distortion, particularly idealization of the dead person, is so common after bereavement that it is hard to know how much reliance to place on reports of the interpersonal relationship with that person. Also, if a woman who has had difficulty in relating to her husband also had difficulty making fresh relationships after his death, this is not in itself convincing evidence that one causes the other – both may result from a pre-existing difficulty in making relationships. Nevertheless, anyone who has worked clinically with bereaved psychiatric patients is likely to be impressed by the frequency with which ambivalence towards the dead person is seen by the patient as an important problem, and my evidence tends to confirm this impression.

As was shown in the last chapter, guilt is more commonly reported by women who develop a mental illness after bereavement than by unselected widows. Even so, it was reported by half the widows in the London Study, and it is hardly surprising that those who reported the largest amount of guilt over the course of the first year of bereavement also admitted the most quarrelling (see Appendix, section 14). Furthermore, they reported significantly more physical symptoms and showed more general tension than the other widows, and they were less likely to have a comforting sense of their dead husband's presence near at hand. A year after bereavement they tended to be socially isolated, to be seeing little of their friends and relatives, and to be less happy than those whose relationship with their husbands had been satisfactory.

In the Harvard Study, widows and widowers who reported two or more areas of conflict in their marriage were more likely to have poor scores on our outcome measures than those who had fewer or no areas of conflict. This was particularly the case when there had been warning of coming bereavement. In such cases the existence of a conflict-free relationship with the dying person seems to have allowed the partner to come to terms with the death. The death of a partner with whom the survivor had been in conflict gave rise to less distress during the first few weeks of bereavement than did unconflicted deaths. The survivors were laughing more and were more likely to be visiting others; on the surface they did not appear to be unduly upset by their bereavement. Yet this apparent recovery was short-lived. A year later this same group were showing signs of lasting tension and anxiety and, at follow-up two to four years after bereavement, 82 per cent of them were still anxious, 45 per cent depressed, and 61 per cent having difficulty in coping with their roles and responsibilities. More remarkable still, nearly two-thirds were yearning for the return of the partner with whom they had been in conflict (compared with less than a third of the rest).

One person who had great difficulty in coping with conflicted grief was Mrs Q. She was forty-five when her husband died. They had been married for twenty-six years, but their relationship had never been good. Mrs Q said that she had always been very fond of her husband but felt that he had never appreciated her or expressed very much real affection. This may have been due to his jealousy of her close relationship with the children but, according to a friend who knew them both well, her 'terrible temper' may also have contributed. At all events there were frequent quarrels. As Mrs Q put it, 'We were a passionate couple.'

Several years before his death Mr Q had a stroke. He had been an energetic, meticulous, and practical man and he found it particularly frustrating to be partially paralysed and dependent on his wife. He became querulous, complaining, and resentful, 'taking it out' on her and criticizing her unjustly. She 'pushed him' to do more and made plans for their future together but 'all he gave me was criticism and abuse'. Most painful of all, he frequently said that he hoped she would have a stroke too. She worried a great deal and complained of headaches which, she feared, might indicate that she had had a stroke. He died unexpectedly one night. When told that it was useless to continue mouth-to-mouth resuscitation since he was dead, Mrs Q would not believe it: 'I just couldn't take it in.'

Matters were made worse when the will was read and she discovered that most of his property had been left in trust. She became very bitter and resentful, saying, 'What have I done to deserve this?', and spent a great deal of time trying to persuade doctors and lawyers to contest the will on the grounds of her husband's mental incapacity. When they refused to support her in this she became angry with them and, when interviewed, recited a long list of the people who, she felt, had rejected her.

Alongside this deep anger were strong feelings of guilt, but she was unable to explain these and spent much time justifying every aspect of her conduct towards her husband. She was restless and fearful, fidgeting and going from one task to another, unable to concentrate on any. During the course of the following year she remained agitated and inclined to panic attacks. On several occasions she complained of symptoms resembling those her husband had suffered. She alienated friends and professional helpers by her aggressive attitude and demands for help.

She was given a variety of drugs by a psychiatrist and these helped a little, but thirteen months after bereavement she declared that she was no better than she had been a year previously. 'If only I was an ordinary widow – it's the bitterness and the will – the dreadful words. I go over it again and again thinking there must be a loophole.' Yet, 'if he could come back tomorrow I'd love him just the same'.

One gets the impression that if this woman had been able to write off her husband as a 'bad lot' or as 'mad' it would have been easier for her to forget him. But she was not able to do this. Her protestations served only to raise more doubts in her own mind. In condemning her during life and after death (in his will) her husband threatened to destroy her self-esteem. 'I feel,' she said, 'if I ever accepted what he has done to me I'd be destroyed – trampled underfoot.' Her attitude to the world betrayed her fear of just this eventuality, and because hostility provokes hostility she created a situation in which she was, in fact, repeatedly rejected by others. Thus her anger, instead of enabling her to overcome real external dangers, perpetuated the situation it was intended to relieve.

Why was it so difficult for this woman to allow herself to accept the guilt and loss of self-esteem that threatened to emerge? Some guesses can be made. Perhaps the newly bereaved need every bit of confidence in themselves that they can muster: the sense of internal desolation is so great following a major bereavement that a sense of personal worth must be maintained at all costs. Alternatively, the answer in this case may be found in the long-term attitudes of this woman. She seemed to lack trust in life and to regard others as bad and dangerous people from whom she could get nothing without a fight. If, as I suspect, this was a lifelong attitude, stemming, perhaps, from experiences in her early childhood, then it becomes easier to see why her self-esteem had to be maintained all the time. In such a world who else but yourself can you rely on?[1]

A contrast with Mrs Q is Mrs D, whose reaction to the death of her 'artistic' husband was described on pages 85 and 104. Whereas Mrs Q had tried to combat the real and implied criticisms her husband had made of her and in so doing had taken arms against the world, Mrs D accepted her husband's criticisms and attempted to make restitution to him and to tolerate the guilt she freely admitted. Nevertheless, a year after bereavement she was still socially isolated and preoccupied with self-reproachful ideas. 'I feel criminal,' she said, 'terribly guilty.'

Further confirmation of the effects of marital dysfunction on the bereaved family comes from a study by Shanfield (1979). Among the predictors of poor outcome were 'skewed decision making, constricted expression of affect, lack of resolution of conflict and insensitivity to feelings'.

SELF-ESTEEM

Low self-esteem is common in people who seek help after bereavement. For instance, in a study of 138 elderly widowers and widowers in Salt Lake City, Lund et al. (1985) found that it was the only variable observed at two to three weeks after bereavement that predicted who would be having 'significant difficulties in coping' two years later. It is not possible in this study to say for sure whether the loss of self-esteem preceded or followed the bereavement but it seems very likely that it was a reflection of lasting insecurity. Low self-esteem is particularly likely to be associated with depression.

The essence of low self-esteem is lack of confidence in one's ability to control one's world. This is sometimes referred to by psychologists as 'low internal locus of control' and methods for its measurement have been developed. Stroebe *et al.* (1988) found that a combination of unexpected death and low belief in internal controls were the two variables that were associated with an increased risk of depression and symptoms of Autonomic Disturbance (Somatic Anxiety) in a group of sixty German widows who were studied during a two-year period after bereavement. In other words lack of self-esteem makes people more vulnerable to unexpected bereavements.

SOCIAL AND CULTURAL INFLUENCES

Difficulty in expressing feeling sometimes seemed to reflect a family style. 'I've always been brought up to bottle up my feelings,' said one widow. Another described how her sister would not let her cry: 'At the funeral she said "People can hear you". The undertaker told her to leave me alone . . . My sister says, "He's gone and there's an end to it."'

Maddison (1968) reports a similar finding: the widows who suffered most deterioration in health regularly felt that they had not been permitted by those around them to talk about their husband's death and to express their feelings freely. Harari thinks that this may be a special problem for doctors' widows, who may consider it inappropriate for a doctor's wife to display negative feelings (1981).

Gorer concludes from his survey (1965) that 'the majority of contemporary Britons . . . have in effect neither help nor guidance in the crises of misery and loneliness which are likely to occur in every person's life'. He is of the opinion that the decline in formal religious belief and ritual has itself removed an important form of guidance. Whatever the personal inclinations of the widows in my studies who avoided grieving, it is clear that they did not engage in formal mourning, and it is hard to believe that this would have happened in a society that maintained definite expectations of the ritual expression of grief.

In sum, here were a group of insecure young women who were unprepared for bereavement, members of a society, and within that society of a generation, which has largely abandoned both the formal expression of mourning and belief in the efficacy of ritual. They came from families which either actively discouraged the open expression of negative feelings or were so widely dispersed that they conveyed no expectations at all. Urgent life tasks and the conviction that one must not 'break down'[2] in front of children seem to have contributed to cause these widows to restrain expression of their grief. The consequences of this for their physical and mental health have been described.

Mrs F was forty-five and her husband ten years older when he died suddenly and unexpectedly. He had worked for many years to build up his own business and this had absorbed much of his time and interest. With his wife he had maintained a somewhat distant relationship, but they had never quarrelled. Mrs F was an intelligent, socially ambitious woman of working-class extraction.

Her husband had died while at work in his garden in South London. Although it was known that he had a heart condition, it was a complete surprise to his wife to find him dead when she returned from shopping. She felt very 'shocked', but experienced no other emotion for three weeks. She had a large number of responsibilities in relation to her husband's business and these kept her fully occupied. She took drugs in order to sleep but even so found herself waking early; when this happened she occupied herself writing letters. Constantly restless and irritable, she complained of tension headaches, weakness, and loss of appetite. Towards the end of the third week she began to tire. She became increasingly anxious and depressed, missed her husband's guidance, and felt fearful of the future. For the first time and to her great annoyance she began to have episodes of uncontrollable crying.

During this time she lived at home with her three children aged seventeen, twelve, and ten. She found herself unable to discuss their father's death with them and her own irritability widened the gap she felt between herself and them. As an avowed atheist she felt that her beliefs could be of no help to them or to her and she found the burial service quite 'horrible'. The only relative with whom she had much contact was her mother, but, as Mrs F said, 'I'm fond of her but she worries about me so much that I'm afraid to tell her anything.'

She remained tense, anxious, and often depressed throughout the year. Her tension headaches continued and she developed chronic indigestion. In order to maintain her standard of living she took over the direction of her husband's business although she hated the work and the responsibility. Her relationship with one of her daughters deteriorated to the point where the daughter, whose standard of school work had dropped off, refused to do anything that her mother suggested. It was this girl's hostile attitude that was blamed for the break-up of an attachment between Mrs F and a man friend.

Although Mrs F expressed little need to grieve for her husband she did grieve intensely for the security of the life she had lost and for the hopes and expectations she could no longer entertain. She gave the impression of engaging in a continual battle to maintain her status and possessions. Although she was now financially very much poorer than she had been before her husband's death, she was quite unable to accept any change in her way of life and seemed to be placing all her hopes on the prospect of remarriage.

It would take too long to discuss all the nuances of this sad situation, but it is worth reiterating, at this point, the four principal factors that seem to explain why Mrs F avoided the expression of her distress after her husband's death. First, the fact that she had not had a close love relationship with her husband enabled her to pretend that she had nothing to grieve for and that life could go on in much the same way as it had before his death. Second, her view of herself as an intelligent, poised, sophisticated woman, well able to control her destiny, implied that she must suppress any signs of weakness. She hated crying because of the damage such behaviour inflicted upon her own self-image. Third, lacking any religious faith she was unable to take advantage of traditional mourning rituals which might have given social support to the expression of despair. Finally, she had no close relative with whom she could share her grief and her inability to communicate effectively with her own children served only to increase her sense of helplessness and isolation.

Enough has been said to indicate my own agreement with Gorer's hypothesis that the absence today of social expectations and rituals facilitating mourning is likely to contribute to the occurrence of pathological reactions to bereavement, although I would not go so far as he does in suggesting that this may be the chief cause of maladaptive behaviour.

Anthropological studies of funeral and mourning customs are too numerous to review in detail. They are of interest in showing both the universality of grief and the degree of variation from one society to another. Rosenblatt *et al.* (1976), comparing reports of a stratified sample of seventy-eight different societies, note that unrestrained aggression can sometimes be very damaging after bereavement. 'Large scale' societies deal with this by appointing 'ritual specialists' whose role it is to channel and redefine such feelings by providing alternative ritualized activities. Others mark or isolate the bereaved and thereby single them out for special consideration and appropriate distancing.

Support for the view that societies which encourage the expression of grief are likely to have fewer problems following bereavement comes from Burgoine's (1988) comparative study in which she made use of the interview schedule used in the London Study to interview a comparison group of newly bereaved widows in New Providence, Grand Bahama. New Providence widows, who live in a culture in which overt expressions of grief are expected and encouraged, had better health and fewer psychological problems than widows living in London. Similarly a comparison of Scottish and Swazi women who reported their reactions to the death of a close relative two weeks and a year after bereavement showed that, although the Swazis showed more initial tearfulness and distress, they were less troubled by feelings of guilt a year later than the Scottish widows (Lovell, Hemmings and Wear, 1993).

On the other hand Norbert Mintz, who worked in a mental health clinic serving the Navajo Indians in the USA, told me that Navajo regularly 'repress and suppress death and grief'. The names of the dead are no longer mentioned when three days have elapsed after a death and several elderly, traditional Navajos whom he interviewed, denied recalling the names of their dead parents. He found that 'about one third of all patients attending the mental health clinic had a history of the death of a close person within the past year'. He claims excellent results for psychotherapy aimed at helping these patients to express their grief and says that the results of therapy 'matched or exceeded the improvement in health for all [other] patients'.

The **social networks** that surround the bereaved person can be particularly influential in the case of the widow, when they may or may not provide her with support, with new roles, and with a start in her new career as a widow. Again, there are difficulties in studying these factors. For example, the widows in the London Study who saw the smallest number of friends and relatives during the thirteenth month of their bereavement had significantly more psychological disturbance than those who saw more friends and relatives, and it is tempting to conclude that social isolation is a cause of psychological disturbance. (Further confirmation of a link between social isolation and depression comes from a study of elderly bereaved people by Pasternak et al., 1994b, and a similar study by Harlow et al., 1991.) But we must beware of assuming that this necessarily means that the isolation causes the depression, psychological disturbance may equally well be a cause of social isolation: people who are depressed usually cut themselves off from friends and relatives. Thus no valid conclusions can be drawn from such evidence.

If we confine attention to the physical proximity of close adult relatives, two-thirds of those who made a good psychological adjustment to bereavement (nine out of fourteen) had close relatives living nearby, whereas this was the case with only one-third of those whose psychological adjustment was poor (three out of eight).

An interesting link between social support and self-esteem has been suggested by Dalgard *et al.* (1994). Following up on Brown, and Harris's (1978) claim that social support buffers people against the effects on mental health of negative life events (including bereavements), they showed that this effect only applies to people who have feelings of powerlessness and lack of control over their own lives.

Further evidence for the importance of family and neighbourhood supports comes from Ablon's (1973) study of the recovery of Samoan families from the death of children from severe burns. Practical assistance, emotional support, religious faith, and close involvement in an extended kinship system together seem likely to explain their rapid recovery from a type of loss which, in other circumstances, would have been very traumatic.

Clearly social supports vary greatly from one culture to another. Hence the difference between the American and Spanish university students studied by Catlin (1993) who found that whereas Spanish students who had suffered a bereavement liked and trusted other people, bereaved American students showed a diminution in their liking and trust of others.

The presence of **young children** in the home after a bereavement, whatever their age, tends in the short term to be associated with considerable psychological strain. One might think that their presence would be a godsend to the widow, providing her with roles and rewards she would otherwise lack. This may in the long run be true, but it is also true that the responsibility of providing for the physical and emotional needs of children at a time when, because of her own grief, the widow is least able to do so represents a considerable burden. The numerous practical tasks and unfamiliar responsibilities that face the family leader are onerous enough. When one considers that, in addition to the special tasks consequent upon the bereavement itself, including, frequently, the need to earn a living, the widow with children at home has to continue most of her household and maternal duties, it is not surprising that in this situation she often found it hard to cope.

Contrast the ways in which two widows, Mrs G and Mrs H, dealt with the problem of children at home.

Mrs G, an immigrant, aged twenty-seven at the time of her husband's death, was left with two pre-school children, Peter, aged two, and a baby, Mary, just a year old. Mrs G had herself been sent to an orphanage at the age of four, when her mother was killed. As a consequence of her own childhood experience she was determined on no account to be separated from her children: 'I always had the feeling that my mother was the only one who wanted us,' she said. She had been married for five years to a labourer who had brought her to England where jobs were easier to obtain. Three years after the marriage he had developed a tumour which resulted in severe headaches and irritability. He was in hospital for seven months before dying in a coma.

Because he had not worked in Britain very long and had failed to stamp his national insurance card, Mrs G was not entitled to a widow's pension. Her husband left no money and she had no job of her own that would have enabled her to earn a living. Consequently, she was totally dependent on National Assistance payments. She lived in a one-room flat in a decayed Victorian house in East London. Fuel, lighting, food, and clothing for herself and her family had to come out of the small allowance she received from the Assistance Board. It is hardly surprising that she was constantly depressed and anxious about her ability to survive and bring up her children in this situation.

Her family were all abroad and although they paid for her husband's body to be shipped home for burial, it was clear that her own financial situation would have been even more hazardous if she had decided to return home. During the first three weeks of bereavement she was so preoccupied with practical matters that she had little time to grieve. Towards the end of the first month, however, she became increasingly depressed and slept badly. Having little appetite she economized by living mainly on tea and giving the food to the children. She was one and a half stones under weight when seen six weeks after bereavement and was suffering fits of giddiness, dyspepsia, and loss of hair. Her GP prescribed a vitamin mixture but she was still in a very similar state five months later and had developed a skin condition which was probably caused by malnutrition. In the course of the year she had a host of problems: threats of eviction, sickness in the children, misunderstandings with the Assistance Board, and, greatest danger of all, sickness in herself. As a thoroughly partial investigator I found myself persuading landlords, jogging the Assistance Board, and consulting doctors on her behalf, and it was in this capacity that I discovered that she was far from helpless, and indeed talented in the arts of persuasion. The children were always clean, happy, and well looked after.

Nine months after her husband's death Mrs G spent a month with her family and returned looking better nourished and with none of the physical symptoms which had previously given rise to anxiety. When interviewed four months later it was clear that she was still preoccupied with her many problems; she had episodes of depression, and confined her attention solely to her children. She had only one friend and said that she had talked with no adult for over a week before the interview. She was planning to send the children to a day nursery school as soon as they were old enough, and said that she would then find herself a job. She had no intention of remarrying; nobody else could possibly match up to her husband, and he, being rather jealous, had made her promise, on his deathbed, never to take another husband.

My work took me overseas for a year at this point; by the time I returned Mrs G had left her flat and I was unable to trace her whereabouts. My guess would be that she continued to make ends meet and I would be very surprised if, after all she had been through, she did not continue to provide the love and most of the material things her children needed.

The situation of Mrs H was similar in many respects to that of Mrs G. She too was an immigrant with no relatives in Britain; she was the same age as Mrs G, and her husband had also died from cancer. Like Mrs G she was left with young children and had to choose whether to stay at home and look after them or to separate from them. She too lived in a decayed part of London and had difficulty in making ends meet. She had the same matter-of-fact approach to life and was not lacking in intelligence.

Here the resemblance ends. Mrs H had been brought up in a township in Africa. Her father had died when she was two years old and her mother had left her in the care of her aunt for long periods while she travelled about the country selling rugs. Despite these periods of separation Mrs H had a happy childhood. She developed close ties to her mother and her aunt and had numerous friends. At school she was an academic success and on leaving at the age of fifteen she spent a year at home and then took a job as a primary school teacher until her marriage two years later.

She accompanied her husband to England and they lived in a part of London where many of their childhood friends had come to live. Her husband worked in an office while taking evening classes with the aim of becoming a dental mechanic. He had been working hard for this qualification for two years when he developed a lump on his left leg which was found to be malignant. The disease progressed gradually, but Mrs H succeeded in nursing her husband at home until three weeks before his death. At this point he became confused and incontinent and it was clear that she could cope no longer. She was well prepared for his death but she still grieved severely over the first three weeks. She found herself preoccupied with her husband's memory and commonly misidentified people around her as being her husband.

Mrs H was left with four children ranging in age from nine to two. During her husband's last illness they had been a great burden to her and after his death she decided that the best plan was to find homes for them for long enough to enable her to learn a trade; she could then return to her home town with every prospect of earning a good living. She therefore sent the two eldest children to live with her mother in Africa, and the two youngest, aged four and two, were admitted to a children's home which was close enough for her to visit weekly.

It took six weeks to find places for the children but once her plans were made her anxiety about them and her grief diminished. She had numerous friends living in the same house and shared a communal kitchen. Also, she wrote weekly letters to her mother and her aunt and visited the children's home where she was relieved to find her youngest children happy and very fond of the house-mother. She took a job as a cook while taking evening classes as well. The work was hard and she suffered from insomnia and occasional troublesome headaches. In all other respects, however, she remained very well and when seen thirteen months after bereavement she was well and happy. She estimated that she had talked with twenty-four friends and one relative in the course of the previous week but, although she had gone out with men, she did not think she would remarry until she had finished her studies. She passed her first annual examination easily and expressed surprise and some pride at her own competence. It was this sense of increased competence, as much as anything else, that made her reluctant to remarry at once.

These two cases illustrate rather well the difference that dependent children can make to the life of a widow. On the one hand we have Mrs G, courageously struggling to retain her children at great cost to herself. Her adjustment could not be described as anything but tenuous, she had almost no social life, and her physical health was constantly threatened but her children were obviously thriving. Mrs H, on the other hand, was healthy and more successful than she had ever been before. It is not possible to determine the cost of her success, however, since we know little of the effect upon her young children of three years of separation from their mother. The observations of Bowlby and others indicate that such separations are potentially pathogenic, but much depends upon circumstances and upon the extent to which a satisfactory substitute for the missing mother can be found.

Economic factors are seldom a major problem in wealthy communities but they can be very important in poor communities. Thus Ide *et al.* (1992), comparing sixty-four Anglo-American widows with fifty-three Mexican-American widows at six-month intervals after the death of their husbands found that the Mexican-Americans were poorer and less educated than the Anglo-Americans, and that they also suffered worse health after bereavement.

RISK ASSESSMENT

Knowledge of the determinants of grief enables us to identify widows and other bereaved people who are at 'high risk' of getting into difficulties; that is to say, people to whom it may be appropriate to offer counselling or other forms of help after bereavement. This is already being done in many hospices where nurses and others who get to know a family before bereavement can ensure that relatives who are thought to be at risk get the help that they need. Some are using predictive questionnaires based on the findings of research in order to quantify the risk. Such screening methods not only enable us to focus help where it is most needed but they also tell us who will respond best to the help that is given.

Of course our ability to predict the course of grief will never be perfect. Too many unpredictable events and circumstances render such attempts very approximate. Even so the results already obtained indicate that systematic methods of prediction using a questionnaire are more reliable than an 'informed guess'. They also show that people who need and will benefit from counselling cannot be relied upon to seek help; it is necessary for helpers to offer their services. A detailed account of one such predictive measure is given in *Recovery from Bereavement* (Parkes and Weiss, 1983) and its value in a hospice setting is confirmed by Beckwith *et al.* (1990).

From the evidence available our high-risk family will contain a widow with young children living at home and no close relatives nearby. The widow will be a timid, clinging person who had reacted badly to separation in the past and had a previous history of depressive illness. Closely bound up with her husband in an over-reliant or ambivalent relationship she will not have prepared herself for his unexpected and untimely death. Cultural and familial tradition will prevent her from expressing the feelings that then threatened to emerge. Other stresses occurring before or after the bereavement – such as loss of income, changes of home, and difficulties with children – increase her burden. She will react to bereavement with intense pining, together with pronounced self-reproach and/or anger. These feelings, instead of declining as one might expect, will tend to persist. The children will have been told little about the seriousness of their father's illness and will be excluded from subsequent participation in family mourning. They will feel hurt by the barriers to communication about this important event in their lives and will react with fear and/or anger. Their work and behaviour at school and at home will be impaired and may lead to over-protective and/or punitive responses. The mother/child relationship may become inverted (with mother clinging to her children for succour), she may show excessive anxiety towards them, and/or react angrily to their anger. Vicious spirals of increasing insecurity and tension will be built up and become self-perpetuating. The end result is likely to be a 'breakdown' in the normal supportive function of the family and in the mental health of one or more of its members, with a risk that these problems will be passed on to future generations.

Having said this, we must remind ourselves that we are speaking only in terms of probabilities. A family may fit all of these predictors and still not break down after bereavement, or they may have none of them and yet break down. In an infinitely variable world there is infinite room for variation.

12

HELPING THE BEREAVED I

General principles

> Your logic, my friend, is perfect,
> Your moral most drearily true;
> But, since the earth clashed on her coffin,
> I keep hearing that, and not you.
>   James Russell Lowell

If bereavement can have detrimental effects upon physical and mental health, what can be done to prevent these effects from occurring and by whom should this help be given? The first source of help for most of us is, or should be, our family – that is, after all, what families are for. After them friends are likely to be the next source of support. Most doctors and clergy would regard it as one of their roles to give help and advice to the dying and the bereaved, but they have, in the past, received little formal training in this area of service. In recent years nurses of various kinds, social workers and other professional carers have begun to take an interest and bereavement counselling has become recognized as worthy of special attention by these professionals and by volunteers. Psychiatrists have always had a role to play in the care of the small minority of bereaved people who develop psychiatric disorders after bereavement but their training has also neglected the topic of grief and loss until relatively recently. Psychologists are late-comers to the field but are now beginning to show their worth.

Part of the reason for the increased interest shown by professional and volunteer counsellors arises from the failure of the existing family and other social supports to give the help that is needed. In a recent study of the difficulties experienced by fifty-seven adults in Minnesota in giving support to the bereaved (Rosenblatt *et al.*, 1991), many family members reported conflicts with other family members. These concerned lack of support, intrusion, accusations of grieving too little or too much, conflicting perceptions of the dead person, attitudes and behaviour towards the dead person when alive, and reassignment of family roles and responsibilities. Interpersonal difficulties also arose with friends. Many held back because they had no previous experience of loss and did not know what to do. They feared that they would make things worse for the grievers. This study confirms the observations of Vollmann's group in Colorado (1971). They are attached to a Coroner's Office where they find that they are often needed to help families who are emotionally unprepared for bereavement – 'Cultural norms are minimal, inefficient, contradictory or even non-existent.' Also in need are individuals who have become isolated, though they often refuse the help that is offered. By contrast less need exists in those subcultures where untimely deaths are still common and support systems intact.

Raphael (1977) has shown that, while the perception of one's family as unsupportive is one of the strongest predictors of poor outcome after bereavement, it is also one of the best predictors of *good* outcome after counselling.

In this chapter I shall examine some of the programmes that have been established and the research that has been carried out to test their efficacy.

PREPARING FOR BEREAVEMENT

From the data presented in the last chapter it would seem that a timely death is less likely to upset the psychological adjustment of those who survive than an untimely one. This may be because, when death is considered timely, the bereaved person is better prepared psychologically than when death is untimely. But how can one prepare for bereavement?

Even when a death occurs long before the age when it would normally be expected to occur there is usually some advance warning. This may take the form of an event, such as an attack of coronary thrombosis or a stroke, which increases the probability of premature death but gives no definite indication when it may occur; or it may comprise a progressive illness such as an inoperable cancer, which provides a definite expectation of death within a certain time span. It is, of course, extremely rare for anyone to know precisely the hour of death and the predictions of doctors and nurses are demonstrably unreliable (Parkes, 1972).

The difference between these two types of warning is that, while cancers allow fairly definite plans to be made, the outcome of coronary attacks and strokes is so uncertain that only contingency plans are possible. The woman whose husband has had a single coronary attack can only say, 'If he has another attack he may die.' In such circumstances two plans are necessary, a plan for survival and a plan for demise. In practice I suspect that it is very hard to make adequate psychological preparation in such uncertain circumstances and unless the husband insists on facing up to the danger himself and talking it through with his wife she is likely to brush the whole thing aside and act, as most of us do, on the assumption that there is no need to prepare for a future which is uncertain and which we would prefer not to think about.

Even when the death is confidently predicted by medical authorities there is, as was shown in Chapter 5, a tendency to disbelieve, ignore, or distort the truth. The extent to which this is done often depends on the extent to which it is thought necessary to hide the true situation from the dying patient, and it is rare for husband and wife to talk openly to each other about this subject. The tendency is for the healthy relative to hide the truth in an attempt to protect the dying person. That this pretence seldom succeeds completely has been shown by Hinton (1967) in his study of dying patients. Hinton visited patients in a general hospital at intervals throughout the course of their illness and took particular note of the comments they made about their expectation of recovery. Some were known to have fatal illnesses, others did not have such illnesses. His experience led him to two important conclusions. One was that, regardless of what they had been told, the majority of terminal patients realized that they were going to die at some time before the end. The other was that the opportunity to talk about such disturbing possibilities was viewed very positively by the patients. Far from stirring up discontent on the ward by upsetting the patients with his questions, Hinton found that most patients were glad to discuss their fears with a sympathetic listener who did not insist upon jollying them along.

This study is not isolated. Several other investigations have been carried out in this field and they tend to confirm the overall finding that nurses, doctors, and relatives often have great difficulty in communicating with dying patients. Their reticence reflects their own inability to cope with the whole concept of death: 'What can one say?'

During recent years hospices have been set up all over the world in which equal importance is attached to the physical, psychological, social, and spiritual needs of the dying patients and their families. The aim is to provide a setting in which it is 'safe' to die. This may sound like a paradox, but experience does seem to show that it is often possible to help patients and their relatives towards a calm acceptance of the true situation.

It is less a question of 'Should the doctor tell?' than of 'How much should the doctor tell, when should he tell it, and how should he tell it?' Patients on admission are often frightened and depressed. They have come through a long and sometimes painful illness and have seen themselves deteriorating in health despite the drastic operations and treatments to which they have been subjected. In such a situation the long-suspected truth can come as a relief: 'At last I know where I stand.' But only sometimes. There are other patients who, when they ask for the truth, are desperately asking for reassurance: 'It's not cancer, is it, doctor? If I thought it was cancer I'd kill myself.' Clearly, in a case like this, we need first to find out what this person means by the word 'cancer' for it is very likely that their image of the condition bears little resemblance to the illness they face.

In trying to help patients through their terminal illness, doctors and nurses are taking part in a process of psychological transition which requires time, empathy, and trust. A ward in which the spiritual and psychological resources of the medical staff enable them to accept death as a meaningful event, and in which the psychological as well as the physical needs of the patients are the central concern of everyone, can enable many patients, in time, to talk about the various fears and griefs that trouble them.

A busy surgical ward is not always a good place in which to die, because the staff are preoccupied with heroic efforts to save life and the patient who cannot be saved is a failure for all. If, however, the inevitable progression of a disease can be accepted, a hospital ward can become a peaceful place. In such a setting the disease is seen as one factor among many that influence the patient's peace of mind; attention is paid to the social climate of the ward, and physical and drug treatment is directed towards the relief of distressing symptoms. Measures for the prolongation of life are considered alongside the quality of the life that remains and in full awareness that fruitless attempts to prolong life can result in very bitter endings.

Here patients soon discover that the staff want to know them as people. 'The lung cancer in the end bed' has become 'Chris Jones who is depressed because his wife is on her own at home', and nurses know that they can sit and talk to patients without being told to get on with their work – talking to patients is work.

The wife who has shared her thoughts and plans with her dying husband and with others, who has begun to anticipate what life without him will be like, and who has made adequate preparation for managing practical affairs, is in a far better position to cope with bereavement than one who has pretended that her husband is going to survive until it is too late for her to prepare for anything. When both know that there are others around who will help her through the period of adjustment, it is easier for them to face the situation and, having faced it, to enjoy what remains of their time together.

Not that anticipatory grieving can ever be complete. No matter how well people may think they have prepared themselves for bereavement there are still things that cannot be anticipated. Partly this results from the similarity between a plan and a wish. The truth of this can be seen in our reluctance to buy a coffin before death has occurred. The very act would seem to be a dangerous thing to do.

Consideration was given on pages 15–16 to the distinction between grief work and worry work and there is no need to repeat the argument here. Suffice it to say that, if they are given time and support from those around, it is often possible for dying patients and their relatives to 'worry' to good effect. When the death occurs it is then seen as one more step in a process of psychosocial transition which all are prepared for and in which all the family have a share. Research (Cameron and Parkes, 1983; Ransford and Smith, 1991) has shown that relatives of patients dying in hospice-type settings are less distressed than relatives of patients who have died in other settings (see Appendix, section 18).

THE IMPACT OF BEREAVEMENT

Let us turn now to the newly bereaved person and consider what forms of help she needs at this time. (Because most of my own research has been with widows, I frequently refer to the bereaved person as a widow, but much of what is said here could apply equally to widowers, and to men and women after other types of bereavement.) While she is still in a dazed or numbed condition the bereaved person is likely to need help with the simplest decisions. She also needs time: time in which to sit back and begin to organize her ideas, to take in what has happened. The first task of close relatives and friends, therefore, is to help her with what must be done – e.g., the final visit to the hospital, the notification of other relatives – and then to bring her home and to look after her.

When she is ready to do so they should assist with the registration of the death and the funeral arrangements. They may need to protect a widow from the well-meaning attention of neighbours and friends, but even at this time they should not be too possessive – the widow needs her friends and it is important not to alienate them. It is a good idea to draw in friends and neighbours by asking for their help with practical matters while waiting until the initial shock of bereavement has passed before encouraging the widow to accept the sympathy they want to offer. This advice need not contradict the more general advice to do nothing that will inhibit the expression of appropriate grief, but it is particularly hard during the first few hours for those around to 'tune in' to the real psychological needs of the widow. Until she has 'taken in' the fact of her bereavement she seems, in the phase of numbness or shock, to be confused and disorganized. She has no plans that will enable her to cope with the situation and needs time and protection from intruders.

It was to protect them from excessive distress that Benjamin Rush, the famous American physician and signatory of the Declaration of Independence, wrote: 'Persons afflicted with grief should be carried from the room in which their relatives have died, nor should they ever see their bodies afterwards. They should by no means be permitted to follow them to the grave.' Few would agree that such over-protection is appropriate today; nor would we accept the advisability of prescribing Dr Rush's panacea for grief – 'liberal doses of opium'. But his statement does serve to emphasize the peculiar helplessness of the bereaved during the first day or so of a major bereavement. A little help given at this time is often recalled with special gratitude later.

One setting in which much can be done to minimize the impact of bereavement is the Emergency Room. Here medical and nursing staff have the unpleasant duty of informing families of sudden and unexpected death. If they do this in a sensitive and supportive way, taking time and trouble to make sure that people are not kept waiting for information and that the experience is as untraumatic as possible, they will have done much to mitigate the horror that can cause intrusive Post-Traumatic memories. A recent evaluation of the introduction of a special programme aimed at improving care came up with very positive results (Adamowski *et al.*, 1993).

THE RITUALS OF MOURNING

In the United States the funeral director plays a very much larger role in counselling the bereaved than he does in the United Kingdom. Most people take out life insurance to pay for their funeral and the funeral director normally attempts to assess the bereaved person's financial position before deciding what type of funeral to recommend. He is thus in a good position to advise the bereaved on financial matters. In recent years several books have been written criticizing the activities of unscrupulous American funeral directors who are said to take advantage of their position to persuade bereaved people to pay large sums of money for unnecessarily elaborate funerals. Expensive padded coffins, embalmment, special clothing, and facial restoration by means of cosmetics, have been lampooned in Evelyn Waugh's novel *The Loved One*, and more seriously criticized by Jessica Mitford (1963) and Leroy Bowman (1959). Much of this expenditure is attributable to the tradition of displaying the body for inspection in an elegantly furnished 'funeral parlour' prior to burial.

As a result of these criticisms a movement towards simpler funerals with closed coffins has sprung up, led by the Continental Association of Funeral and Memorial Societies. This organization recommends the pre-planning of funerals by husband and wife. It lists the names of funeral directors who are willing to provide a range of moderately priced funerals and gives advice on the legal aspects of the donation of body parts to hospitals and medical schools.

What is the cash value of a funeral? This is a question easier to ask than to answer. The funeral is usually regarded as a last gift to the dead and there is no doubt that many of those who come to 'pay their respects' are treating the dead person as if they were still alive and about to leave on a journey – they come in order to say 'Goodbye'. The funeral reformers point out the irrational component in such attitudes; they emphasize the fruitlessness of attempting to make a corpse look 'life-like' or to produce an illusion of sleep when death has nothing to do with sleep. By their matter-of-fact approach they make funeral directors look like tricksters and the public like gullible fools.

But even if we believe that the rituals attending bereavement can have no value to the dead, may they not have a value to the living? It has been repeatedly shown in previous chapters that physical death and social death do not take place simultaneously. Grief is a process of realization, of 'making real' the fact of loss. This process takes time and, while it can be assisted, anything that forces reality-testing in the early period of bereavement is likely to give rise to difficulties. Panic reactions, the massive shutting off of emotion, and/or the repetitious reliving of the traumatic experiences seem to be common consequences of premature confrontation. A painful death or a mutilated or distorted corpse may haunt the memory of the griever and shut out happier memories of the dead person. 'I keep seeing his mutilated face – as if someone suddenly puts a slide on,' said one woman after the death of her brother in a car smash. But this memory was somewhat mitigated by the memory of the funeral, which was 'awfully pretty'. She carried photographs of the cortege in her handbag which she showed to others as if to demonstrate how she had tried to repair the damage.

In the London Study eight widows spoke of viewing the corpse after bereavement. Three were horrified by what they saw and the horror remained with them as an unpleasant memory; four, on the other hand, were pleased and referred to the peaceful appearance of the body which seemed to imply that their spouse was at rest. 'He looked just like a little boy. I felt he'd died in a contented frame of mind.' 'I like to think of him like that. He was smiling and looked so peaceful. You could see he was all right. The last few weeks he was suffering and he'd showed it – but afterwards . . .'

A much larger proportion of the Boston widows and widowers had viewed the corpse of their spouse. Despite the efforts of the funeral directors feelings were mixed, and half the women and a quarter of the men were upset by the experience. Nevertheless there was very little criticism of the work of the funeral directors and most of the widows and widowers seemed grateful for the help they had been given.

The funeral itself is also likely to give rise to both positive and negative feelings. It is, of course, distressing to most bereaved people, but the overall attitude among about half the London widows and two-thirds of the Boston widows was favourable. 'It was such a lovely service.' 'I still like to think of the words.' 'Fifty of his workmates came; it was an ordeal, but I was very proud – they respected him.' 'It makes you feel you're not alone . . . You've got something to hang on to.' These remarks seem to imply that it is the beliefs expressed in the funeral service and the sense of social support that are viewed positively.

In contrast, negative or mixed feelings were expressed by some people who were clearly unprepared for the forceful way in which the funeral, and particularly the committal, brought home the reality of their bereavement. 'When the coffin went into the flames I thought, "Suppose he isn't dead?" It was as if I'd been hit or something.' 'I still can't get the memory [of the service] out of my head.' 'It was horrible – I don't want to talk about it.' 'It was terrible. We were the last cremation of the day. There didn't seem to be any meaning in it whatsoever. Seeing the coffin go through the door – for a few minutes it made me realize I'd never see him again.' Cremation, chosen by over half the London widows (but still rare in the USA), was more often seen as upsetting, mechanistic, and alienating than was burial. On the other hand it was praised on grounds of hygiene and simplicity: 'It's so much tidier. The grave doesn't get over-grown, they look after them so nicely.'

It is not possible, on the anecdotal evidence of the widows in the London Study who gave their opinion of the ritual aspects of bereavement, to make definitive judgements of the relative merits of burial and cremation. The preference of the spouse and cultural and personal expectations, which together determined the choice, also provided the frame of reference by which the decision was justified in retrospect. There is no confirmation of Gorer's (1965) finding that severe reactions of despair are more frequent after cremation than burial (seven of the nine bereaved people he found to be in a state of lasting despair had reacted in this way after a cremation).

Although some widows in the London Study subsequently visited the crematorium, entered their husband's name in the Book of Remembrance, and attended memorial services, there was less tendency to feel close to the dead person at the crematorium than there was at the cemetery. This was regarded by several widows as a distinct disadvantage of cremation.

On the whole I had the impression that for these young widows the funeral service took place too early after the death to be of great positive psychological value. It was too soon, in the first week of bereavement, for the service to constitute a successful *rite de passage*. Nevertheless the funeral did have the effect of drawing the family close to the widow, and the support that was offered was mentioned as a source of satisfaction and help by over half the widows in the London Study.

In many parts of the world, but particularly in Australia, funeral directors employ counsellors for the bereaved people whom they serve. I first became aware of this in Boston, Massachusetts, where the administrators of a Jewish cemetery employ the services of a public relations officer, herself a widow, who offers support and practical advice to the widows of men buried in the cemetery. She organizes annual conferences for these widows at which invited speakers give expert information on careers for women, the education of young people, the psychology of bereavement, and other relevant topics. A surprisingly large proportion of the widows who are invited to these conferences attend them, and they certainly seem to appreciate the service provided.

The unusual feature of this service is that it is part of the contract when a husband buys a grave in the cemetery. It thus gives him an opportunity to buy support for his wife during a period when she is likely to be in need of it. Like other forms of insurance this method can be expected to satisfy the dying man's wish to continue to 'look after' his wife after his death and can therefore help to remove one possible source of anxiety.

RELIGION AND RITUAL

A month after bereavement thirteen widows out of eighteen in the London Study who expressed belief in God said that their faith had helped them, and there is some evidence from a study by Austin and Lennings (1993) that those who express a belief in God experience less depression and hopelessness after bereavement than those who do not. The relationship between religion and adjustment, however, is not simple. There was some evidence in the London Study that those whose religious beliefs helped them to place the bereavement in a meaningful perspective coped better with bereavement than those who had no such faith, but it was also true that several of the regular church-attenders did not make out well and Austin and Lennings found no evidence that degree of knowledge or commitment to Christian beliefs moderated either depression or hopelessness. The view of God as a protecting, loving father is hard to maintain in the face of untimely bereavement, and the possibility of reunion in days to come does not help the widow to tolerate the absence of her husband now. On the other hand a study by Bohannon (1991) indicates that mothers, but not fathers, who have lost a child show less rumination, depersonalization, and loss of control if they are church-attenders than if they are not.

In general I have the impression, and it is no more than an impression, that several of the more religious widows were insecure women who tried to find, in their relationship to God, the same kind of support they had sought from their husbands. Since such women tend to do badly after bereavement it is not surprising that 'faith in God' and 'regular church attendance' were not necessarily related to good outcome following bereavement.

Three-quarters of the London widows claimed membership of the Church of England; the numbers representing other denominations were too few to make it possible to compare one sect with another. Some evidence for the value of religious faith comes from a study by Bornstein et al. (1973). They found that 40 per cent of widows who developed a depressive syndrome had never been to church. This compares with only 17 per cent of those who were not depressed.

Beliefs and rituals which provide an explanation for death and social support for the expression of grief should reduce the confusion felt by the newly bereaved and might even be of psychological value in helping them to express their grief. As noted earlier, Gorer has deplored the decline in the ritual observation of mourning today and believes it to be responsible for much mental ill health among bereaved people, and there is some support from my own work for the notion that those who fail to express their distress within the first week or two of bereavement are more likely than others to become disturbed later.

But it is not enough to prescribe a ritual; faith is also necessary. In his study of mourning customs in contemporary Britain Gorer (1965) praises the Orthodox Jewish shivah as an example of a custom that seems to provide ritual support for grief. The three Orthodox Jews he interviewed had found the 'very concentrated and overt mourning' that took place during the first seven days of bereavement to be of therapeutic value. During this period prayers are said for the dead and the mourners are expected to spend much of their time talking to visitors about the dead person. My impression, from talking to a number of intelligent middle-class Jews, is less favourable than Gorer's. They have pointed out that while it is true that the shivah still serves its traditional function of drawing the family together at a time of bereavement there is a tendency for it to be used as a distraction from grief rather than as an occasion for its expression. Conversation with the bereaved person often takes the form of neutral chat and the expression of overt emotion is avoided, as it is in other 'public' situations. The 'successful' mourner is thought to be the one who shows a proper control of his feelings on all occasions. In such circumstances the funeral, wake, or shivah becomes an ordeal which is likely to be viewed with mixed feelings.

After the rituals associated with the disposal of the body are at an end, there normally follows a period of mourning which gives social recognition to the fact that those most affected by the bereavement are in a state of depressive withdrawal. In Western culture the wearing of tokens of mourning, a black armband or a dark-coloured dress, provides an indication that certain individuals are to be treated differently from others. Such people are not expected to take part in 'light-hearted' activities. In so far as they feel heavy-hearted it may help them if society recognizes this. It also, presumably, encourages the mourner to accept depression rather than to avoid it.

But customs are changing. The black armband and the dark dress, themselves a diluted version of the black mourning and widow's weeds of the Victorian era, are now being abandoned altogether. Gorer found that: 'The customs of mourning dress, which were general when I was a boy, are now predominantly maintained by the old, the poor and the unskilled.'

When there is a prescribed period for mourning, a time is prescribed for its ending. (The term quarantine comes from quarantina, the Italian for 'forty', which was the number of days of sequestration expected of the widow.) Thus an accepted mourning period provides social sanction for beginning and ending grief, and it is clearly likely to have psychological value for the bereaved. While it is true that social expectations concerning the duration of mourning cannot correspond closely to all individual psychological needs to express grief, which vary considerably, the absence of any social expectations, as is common in Western cultures today, leaves bereaved people confused and insecure in their grief. A clear lead from the churches in this matter would be psychologically helpful to many bereaved people.[1]

While ritual is generally assumed to be the province of the church there is no reason why it cannot be used in other settings. In fact many of the procedures performed by doctors have the character of rituals – they are often rites of passage or ordeals through which a person must pass on their way to the next passage of their life. And some of their beneficial effects may well result from their ritual qualities.

One person who makes deliberate use of ritual in therapy with the bereaved is Van der Hart (1988). The aim of such rituals is to help the bereaved to take leave of the dead. He regards preparation for the ritual as an important part of the process and spends time helping the bereaved to undertake tasks which will allow them to review the implications of the death. Tasks are set to stimulate the working through of grief by writing poems or stories for the dead person. Only 'when it is clear that reorganization has come to an end' can the final leave-taking ritual begin. This enables the bereaved to bid a 'solemn and stately farewell' to the dead, to bury or otherwise dispose of symbols of the dead person, and finally to take a cleansing bath followed by a meal or other ritual which includes the person's family and symbolizes the relationships that will continue to matter in the next phase of the person's life.

AFTER THE FUNERAL

The funeral often precedes the peak of the pangs of grief, which tends to be reached during the second week of bereavement. The 'bold face' put on for the funeral can then no longer be maintained and there is a need for some close relative or friend to take over many of the accustomed roles and responsibilities of the bereaved person, thereby setting him or her free to grieve. The person who is most valued at this time is not the one who expresses the most sympathy but the person who 'sticks around', quietly gets on with day-to-day household tasks and makes few demands upon the bereaved. Such a person must be prepared to accept without reproach the tendency of the bereaved person to pour out feelings of anguish and anger, some of which may be directed against the helper. In fact it may be necessary for the helper to indicate to the bereaved that he or she expects such feelings to emerge and that there is no need for them to be 'bottled up'. The helper should not 'pluck at the heartstrings' of the bereaved person until breakdown occurs, any more than he or she should connive with the bereaved in endless attempts to avoid the grief work. Both probing and 'jollying along' are unhelpful. The bereaved person has a painful and difficult task to perform which cannot be avoided and cannot be rushed. True help consists in recognizing this fact and in helping the bereaved person to arrange things in whatever way is necessary to set him or her free for the task of grieving.

To what extent can the helper or counsellor 'share' grief? 'Dry your eyes,' says Shakespeare's Richard II. 'Tears show their love, but want their remedies.' Nevertheless it is often seen as reassuring by a bereaved person when those who are nearest show that they are not afraid to allow feelings of sadness to emerge. Such communal expressions of sorrow make the bereaved person feel understood and reduce the sense of isolation he or she is likely to experience. This was clearly illustrated to me by a widower in the Boston study who said that he had succeeded in rigorously suppressing his own feelings until he saw his father weeping at the funeral. He had always regarded his father as 'tough' and his first reaction was one of shocked surprise. Then it dawned on him that perhaps there was nothing wrong with weeping at a funeral and he too began to cry. Subsequently he viewed this event as a valuable lesson which had helped him over a difficult hurdle.

People need to express both feelings and thoughts about their loss. This was demonstrated in an elegant and important experiment by Pennebaker *et al.* (1988). They assigned college students to four groups: Group 1 were told to write about neutral topics on four consecutive days; Group 2 were told to write about events that had upset them but not to write about their feelings about these events; Group 3 were told to write about their feelings about such events but not about the facts; and group 4 were told to write about both feelings *and* facts. Subsequently it was found that the members of group 4, who had expressed both feelings and facts about traumatic events in their lives, consulted the College Health Centre less frequently than members of the other three groups. A second study confirmed these findings and showed that the 'disclosers' had less evidence of physiological disturbance (measures of congruity between left and right brains, lower skin conductance, and improved T cell immune response), and that these differences were most pronounced in students who had disclosed information about traumas in their lives *for the first time.*

The authors conclude that active inhibition of thoughts and feelings about a trauma requires physical work and, over time, acts as an accumulative stress increasing the risk of illness and stress-related problems. In order to suppress a thought the thought must be recognized at some level and an active process undertaken. On the other hand the expression of thoughts and feelings can interrupt this sequence and have a therapeutic benefit.

There is an optimal 'level of grieving', which varies from one person to another. Some will cry and sob, others will betray their feelings in other ways. The important thing is for thoughts and feelings to be permitted to emerge into consciousness. How they appear on the surface may be of secondary importance.

Helpers should show, by their willingness to reveal their own feelings, that they are not ashamed of them or rendered useless by them. If they are ashamed or feel destroyed by them, they will not help the newly bereaved and had better stay out of the way.[2]

In a similar way the widow or widower who is succeeding in coping with his or her own grief can help his or her children to cope with theirs. But if, as is likely in early days, the parent feels overwhelmed by grief, it may be advisable to draw upon the support of others to help with the children. Conversely, adult or near-adult children can give a great deal of support to a grieving parent. Who is the caregiver and who the cared for in this situation is an open question, but in most cases the sharing of grief is more likely to do good than harm.

People entering a household that contains a newly bereaved person are often enjoined not to say anything that will 'upset' the bereaved. Since conversation about trivialities is irrelevant at such a time, this makes communication difficult. Usually such an attitude reflects a mistaken notion that grief can somehow be avoided. Even when no explicit prohibition is made the visitor may have the impression that his presence is embarrassing – others do not know how to react to him any more than he knows how to react to them. While a conventional expression of sympathy can probably not be avoided, pity is the last thing the bereaved wants. Pity turns one into an object; somehow, in being pitied, the bereaved person becomes pitiful. Pity puts the bereaved person at a distance from, and in an inferior position to, the would-be comforter. So it is best to get conventional verbal expressions of sympathy over as quickly as possible and to speak from the heart or not at all. This is not a situation in which there is a proper thing to say: trite formulae serve only to widen the gap between bereaved and non-bereaved.

Pain is inevitable in such a case and cannot be avoided. It stems from the awareness of both parties that neither can give the other what they want. The helper cannot bring back the person who is dead and the bereaved person cannot gratify the helper by seeming helped. No wonder that both feel dissatisfied with the encounter.

And yet bereaved people do appreciate the visits and expressions of sympathy paid to them by others. These are seen as a tribute to the dead, thereby confirming the mourner in the belief that the dead person is worth all the pain. They also reassure the bereaved that they are not alone in the world and so reduce feelings of insecurity. The world may seem dangerous and alien but they have some allies.

Since pain is inevitable, helpers must be prepared to share the pain, to accept it as their contribution to friendship, while assisting the bereaved quietly with the small tasks and responsibilities that still have to be carried out even though they may have lost much of their value. Help derives, therefore, from the quiet communication of affectionate understanding and this can be conveyed as well by a squeeze of the hand as by speech. Into such a warm silence the bereaved may choose to pour the worries and fears that are preoccupying them. It is not necessarily a bad thing if they become upset, for they may be glad of an opportunity to express their feelings. 'Give sorrow words,' says Malcolm to Macduff. 'The grief that does not speak, knits up the o'erwrought heart and bids it break.'

A person from outside the family who offers help at this early stage of grief may find himself or herself occupying a role which is not open to family members. The family are seen as 'too involved', too easily hurt by each other's grief. Also, they may be in competition with each other to show a brave face or retain a position of respect in the family. All families have their own hierarchy, and elements of rivalry and competition frequently distort the natural expression of feeling. If one member cries more, or less, than another, this is noticed and conclusions are drawn about the nature of their relationship with the dead member. Several widows have told me how they felt obliged to curtail the expression of their own feelings after witnessing what they took to be insincere grief in in-laws. Others put on a bold face for the sake of children or elderly relatives who were seen as weaker than themselves. It may, therefore, be easier to talk to outsiders about problems which threaten self-esteem, and those families whose traditions provide no acceptable means of expressing grief are in particular need of an outsider who is not ruled by such inhibitions.

Many bereaved people are surprised and frightened by the sheer intensity of their emotions and imaginings after bereavement. Reassurance that they are not going mad, that such feelings are perfectly natural, and that crying does not mean a 'nervous breakdown' can be given explicitly, and especially by an attitude that shows that the helper is not alarmed, frightened, or even surprised.

It is important for those who attempt to help the bereaved to know what is normal, and the reader will, I hope, already have a good idea of this from what has been said in foregoing chapters. Bereaved people are so surprised by the unaccustomed feelings of grief that they often ask, 'Am I going mad?', or 'Is it normal to be like this?' Such fears are particularly felt when intense feelings of anger or bitterness erupt, but they may also arise in relation to disturbances of perception. Hallucinations are so well known as a sign of madness that it can be most alarming to experience the hypnagogic hallucination of a dead husband. Fortunately it is easy to reassure people of the normality of such phenomena. Vivid nightmares are another occasional source of alarm, as are nocturnal orgasms occurring during sleep or in a half-waking state. Distractibility, difficulty in remembering everyday matters, and a slight sense of unreality are other features of the typical reaction to bereavement which may worry the bereaved. There is no reason to regard any of these as signs of mental illness.

On the other hand, absence of grief in a situation in which it would have been expected, episodes of panic, lasting physical symptoms, excessive consumption of alcohol or drugs, excessive guilt feelings, excessive anger, or the persistence of intense grief beyond the normally expected period – these should be taken as signs that all is not going as it should. Not that the bereaved person is going mad, since psychosis as such seems to be a very rare consequence of bereavement; but bereaved people who show these features may require special help. When, despite our efforts, it is clear that the bereaved person is 'stuck', or if,

176

for any reason, the caregiver is uncertain about the course of events, he or she should not hesitate to advise the bereaved person to get additional help.

LATER BEREAVEMENT

Our discussion so far has focused upon the early stage of bereavement, which is the time when most people first seek help. Let us go on, now, to consider what kinds of assistance and support are most appropriate at a later stage.

If the early stage of bereavement is a time when family, friends, and others should rally round and relieve newly bereaved people of some of their roles and obligations, the later stage is one when bereaved people should be helped to establish their own autonomy. It may be important for bereaved people to grieve. It is also important for them to stop grieving, to give up their withdrawal from life, and to start building a new life for themselves.

In a situation in which well-established norms are absent, the expectations of those around are potent determinants of behaviour. Thus friends or relatives can indicate, implicitly or explicitly, that grief is expected and permitted, but they can also indicate that it has gone on long enough. To some extent grieving is seen as a duty to the dead and it may take an outsider to point out that that duty is now done, or at least that the mourner can be permitted to let up a little. Not that this is usually a major problem nowadays. It is more likely that the bereaved person will get little encouragement to mourn at any time – but when grief has broken through it may take a special circumstance to get the mourner out of a state of habitual mourning.

Although there is no clear ending to grief, it is common for widows to describe one or several 'turning-points' – that is, events associated with a major revision of their feelings, attitudes, and behaviour. Such turning-points may occur, for instance, when a widow goes away on holiday, takes a job of work, goes out with a man for the first time since her bereavement, or redecorates the house. They both reflect and engender an abandonment of the old modes of thinking and living. The widow shows that she is no longer doomed to centre her life upon the search for the dead husband, and in proving this to herself as well as to others, she seems to open up the possibility of numerous other changes. Returning to the old home after a week with her sister, one widow said to herself: 'I'm not going to let all that start again.' She moved the furniture around, started redecorating the house, and found herself a job of work outside the home – all within a short space of time. Similar turning-points occur in the lives of widowers.

The timing of such turning-points is important. They tend to occur at the expiry of a set period of time, for instance at an anniversary. A memorial service or a visit to the cemetery carried out at this time can have the significance of a *rite de passage*, setting the bereaved people free from the past and allowing them to undertake fresh commitments. Friends, relatives, and others can often help to initiate such turning-points and to enhance the change in attitude that should accompany them. Problems can be talked through and practical arrangements made.

Frances Beck in her *Diary of a Widow* (1966) describes a series of turning-points. The first occurred two months after bereavement, when she started attending evening classes: 'Perhaps I am coming out of my shell,' she writes, 'I won't cry tonight.' Nevertheless she continued to grieve deeply until six months after her husband's death, when she wrote a long 'letter' to him reviewing both positive and negative aspects of their relationship. From here on she referred to herself as a widow and took seriously the process of her own re-education. Jobs, homes, and children became major issues and she moved to a different city. But she was lonely and friendless, and after a while her 'letters' to her dead husband again became more frequent and pathetic.

Another turning-point occurred when she went on vacation eleven months after the death: 'For the first time I have the feeling that I can make it,' she writes. The anniversary itself was painful, but within three weeks she went to a dance for the first time.

It was the second new year after her husband's death, however, that constituted the decisive turning-point. Here she met, at a party, a fellow 'orphan of the storm' and henceforth she saw him regularly. A year later she became formally engaged, but only on the eve of her second wedding did she start to refer, in her diary, to her first husband in the past tense.

Frances Beck's diary illustrates clearly the point that 'full realization comes in steps'. Other people are involved in these steps and without others it is hard to give up habits of withdrawal and mourning. Part of the function of counselling services and clubs that provide special help for bereaved people must be to act as a bridge between the socially withdrawn widow and the community. Social activities with other widows should be seen as steps towards other forms of activity rather than as ends in themselves. Otherwise there is a danger that inward-looking cliques will develop whose members succeed only in reinforcing one another's fears of the outside world as a hostile and dangerous place.

It is to be hoped that the growth of organizations for bereaved people will help to prevent some of the pathological effects of bereavement that have been discussed in previous chapters of this book. Increased awareness of 'danger signals', such as those described in Chapter 9, should enable efforts to be made to support those families and individuals who are at special risk. It is a principle of crisis intervention that help given at a time when pathological patterns of thought and behaviour are developing is likely to be more acceptable and more effective than help given a long time after these pathological patterns have become established.

13

HELPING THE
BEREAVED II
Types of help

> Without any warning, the tears rose up and broke out of her, and
> Potter sat on his chair saying nothing, and yet being a comfort to
> her, taking some of her grief on to himself. She wept as she had
> never wept before in front of another human being, and it was a
> good thing to do; it was more value than all the months of solitary
> mourning. It brought something to an end.
>
> Susan Hill, In the Springtime of the Year

The bereaved are faced with many possible sources of help. In this
chapter we shall look at the types of help that are likely to be available
and a few that are very unlikely to be available at the present time but
which may become so in the future. Choices lie between: specialist or
non-specialist help; individual or group help; help from professionals or
volunteers; medical or non-medical help and religious or secular help.

Specialist help is now available to bereaved people from many
sources ranging from organizations for the bereaved to trained
professionals but we should not decry the help that can be given by
people without special training. These are often the most easily and
immediately available. If social support is all that is needed a social
club or church group may have more to offer than a bereavement
counselling service.

Newly bereaved people and those who are shy seldom feel brave
enough to join groups and will prefer someone they can meet on their
own or with a family member. Clergy, GPs, and many bereavement
counselling services; such as Cruse – Bereavement Care, offer such
support. On the other hand group support is a good way to meet others
who are 'in the same boat' and groups have particular value to bereaved
people who are in danger of becoming socially isolated.

We should not assume that, just because someone has a medical degree or a training in social work, they are necessarily well trained in the care of the bereaved and there are many professionals who refer bereaved people to volunteer bereavement counsellors because they feel that the latter have more understanding of bereavement than they. In recent years professional counsellors who charge fees for their service have become more numerous and many of them provide excellent care but, again, unless they have had special training in working with the bereaved they may prove less helpful than a volunteer counsellor who has been carefully selected and trained for this one job and whose services may be free. The important thing is not to be afraid to ask for information on such matters. The services available vary widely from one district to another.

Medical care is obviously needed if people think that they are sick and, in Britain, it is the GP who is the first person to consult. They are often able to provide reassurance about the normality of many of the physical symptoms that can worry bereaved people. They are also in a good position to decide when or if the help of a psychiatrist or psychologist is needed and they are aware of the strengths and weaknesses of the existing services.

Psychiatric referral is particularly important if there is thought to be a risk of suicide. Caregivers should never be afraid to ask direct questions about suicide. It is common enough for a bereaved person to say 'I wouldn't care if I died tomorrow', and such remarks need not cause alarm, but a person who has thought seriously of killing himself or herself should always see a psychiatrist. If the bereaved person refuses to agree to a consultation, the helper should at least take advice. It is rare for anyone to commit suicide without telling somebody of the intention and a direct question will usually evoke a direct answer from those who have seriously contemplated it. People are often afraid to mention suicide as if, by doing so, they could bring it about. But a simple question, 'Has it been so bad that you have thought of killing yourself?', is more likely to save a life than to take one.

An actual suicidal attempt must, of course, be taken seriously. Even if it is thought that it was only a gesture, the plea for help that the gesture implies should not be ignored. Once again close collaboration between the family, GP, psychiatrist, and anyone else in a position to help is desirable if further danger is to be averted.

Clergy are, of course, the traditional source of support for the bereaved, and those who have made a religious commitment will usually find their religious community a good source of spiritual and social support, but there are few people today who seek their help. This is a pity because many clergy are well able to provide support and advice without putting pressure on people to 'return to the fold'. Again, in selecting a clergyman to confide in it may be wise to ask around, since so much will depend on the interest and training of the particular cleric.

Let us now examine, in more detail, the main alternatives.

MUTUAL HELP

People who have themselves experienced a major bereavement may be particularly well qualified to help the bereaved. They really do understand what the other person is going through and know that bereavement is not the end of life. In the Laboratory of Community Psychiatry in Boston, Massachusetts, a research social worker, Dr Phyllis Silverman (1967), started a Widow-to-Widow programme which has been widely copied. Mature widows routinely call upon newly bereaved women living in their area. They offer friendship, help, and advice, but they do not present themselves as 'professionals' and in fact have no professional qualification although they are paid for the work. The one qualification they all have is to have grieved effectively. My impression from talking with these widows' aides was of great enthusiasm for the work and a strong positive conviction of its usefulness, but no adequate evaluations of its efficacy have been published and those few well-conducted studies of mutual help that have been undertaken have had equivocal results.

Thus Tudiver *et al.* (1992) assigned 113 widowers in their first year of bereavement, at random, to a mutual help group or to a waiting list. After the mutual help group had received nine semi-structured sessions, which focused on 'grief process, diet, new relationships, exercise and lifestyle issues', the two groups were compared but no significant differences were found between them.

A similar programme involving widows rather than widowers has been evaluated by Vachon *et al.* (1980). They compared a group of sixty-eight widows who had received support from 'Widow Contacts' with another ninety-four who had no such support. Only a few results reached statistical levels of significance but there were consistent trends in favour of the supported group. As in my own studies, those widows who showed the greatest distress at the time of bereavement benefited most from counselling.

A mutual help organization for the bereaved which has spread rapidly across the English-speaking world since its inception is the

Compassionate Friends (founder: Rev. Simon Stephens). This is run by parents who have lost a child to provide comfort and support to others who are about to suffer or who have already suffered such a loss. The organization enables parents in such a situation to feel less isolated and to meet others who understand their feelings because they have experienced them themselves.

In the United States another mutual-help organization that has made a great difference to the lives of many widows and widowers is Parents without Partners. It is open to widowed, separated and divorced people, who themselves organize a wide range of recreational and educational activities. Participation in the numerous committees that organize these activities helps to re-establish feelings of self-reliance and esteem. Other bodies that provide a range of counselling and group activities for bereaved people in the USA are THEO, Inc in Pennsylvania, NAIM in Chicago and Post-Cana in Washington, DC.

One group in special need are the surviving partners of homosexual relationships. In Britain 'Gay Switchboard' has taken a special interest in this group and similar organizations exist in the USA (Siegal and Hoefer, 1981).

AIDS aggravates problems that already exist within the communities in which it is likely to arise. Homosexuals, intravenous drug abusers, immigrants from lands with a high incidence of AIDS, prostitutes and even sufferers from blood diseases such as haemophilia are all members of minority groups who are likely to be misunderstood and whose psychological needs are ignored by society. The fact that the disease itself causes fear and rejection gives rise to a fresh lot of problems. Small wonder that members of these communities form their own support groups on the assumption that fellow sufferers are the only people who will understand. This may create new difficulties for, within such groups, there may be so many afflicted by the disease that, before long, everyone is bereaved and there is a danger that they will 'burn out'.

Other problems that arise in mutual-help groups include the way in which some groups become dominated by their most disturbed members. Unless they have the leadership of a well-trained group leader they are in danger of becoming anti-therapeutic. But it is often seen as contrary to the principle of self-help to accept leaders from outside the index group and there may be no suitably qualified or motivated person within the organization.

The assumption that only someone with AIDS can understand someone with AIDS is fallacious and those who offer their support to such people regularly find that they have much to offer. The very act of persuading the bereaved person to explain their situation to an ignorant outsider can be very therapeutic for, while the other person is explaining themselves to us, they are also explaining themselves to themselves and getting the situation into perspective.

BEREAVEMENT COUNSELLING

More sophisticated forms of bereavement counselling are offered by professional psychiatrists, psychologists, or social workers, and by counselling services which make use of carefully selected and trained volunteer counsellors. These are aimed at the minority of bereaved people who are at special risk following bereavement, and they range from individual or family support in the client's home to office consultation or group meetings. Several of them have passed the test of scientific evaluation. Thus Raphael (1977) showed that 'high risk' widows whom she counselled had better health and adjustment a year after bereavement than a similar control group who were not counselled (see Appendix, section 19), while De Veber (1977) showed that the inclusion of a counsellor in a haematology/oncology team substantially reduced the number of marriages that broke up among the parents of children who had died from cancer.

Most hospices across the world now provide support for the families of patients who have died under their care. The first of these to have been set up, and still a good example, is the Family Service at St Christopher's Hospice, Sydenham, which makes use of volunteer counsellors who have been subjected to a rigorous programme of selection and training. Anyone who has worked with hospital volunteers will have been impressed by the potential of the people who offer help to the dying and the bereaved, and there is no doubt that they rival professionals in the talents which they bring. Busy doctors and social workers often lack the time to become good at bereavement counselling, whereas volunteers who choose to learn the necessary skills of this one field of care soon achieve a high standard.

My own evaluation by random assignment of 'high risk' bereaved to the service at St Christopher's or to a control group showed that the provision of counselling can reduce the risk of 'high risk' widows and widowers to that of the 'low risk' group. The control 'high risk' group who received no special counselling were found to have more persisting symptoms of anxiety and tension twenty months after bereavement and to be consuming more drugs, alcohol, and tobacco (see Appendix, section 20). It is also worth noting that, whereas six successful suicides are known to have occurred within two years of bereavement among relatives of patients who died in the hospice during the two years before the Bereavement Service was started, only one further suicide is known in the ten years which followed.

A more recent evaluation by Relf (1994) of a similar service in Oxford has shown that the provision of the help of bereavement volunteers to those at risk can substantially reduce levels of anxiety and the need for medical care from GPs.

SUPPORT GROUPS

During the first few weeks or months of bereavement it is difficult to persuade bereaved people to join a group, but there are some who may benefit from group counselling when the first pangs of grief are over. This can range from the mutual support of a social group for widows who get together to help each other, to structured groups such as Weiss's programme in which formal seminar/discussions focus on specific topics of importance to bereaved people (Parkes and Weiss, 1983). Many of those who have run such groups have used models of 'therapy' derived from psychiatric settings and may be in danger of treating the bereaved as if they were sick. This may explain the modest results of the few attempts that have been made to evaluate such groups. Thus, Jones (unpublished dissertation, 1979) randomly assigned thirty-six widows and widowers to two groups, one of which received three hours of 'group therapy' per week for eight weeks 'aimed at helping them to adjust to bereavement'. The group were regarded as 'normal grievers' and had been bereaved for six to eight months when they entered the group. At the end of therapy, although the groups as a whole did not differ greatly, those in the therapy group who were thought to be 'at risk' of poor outcome were significantly better than the 'at risk' controls on four out of five measures of outcome. Similarly inconclusive results were obtained by Lieberman and Yallom (1992) who assigned widows and widowers in mid- and late life to brief 'group psychotherapy' or no treatment. On follow-up a year later both groups had improved but the treated group reported only modest improvement in role functioning and psychological state by comparison with the untreated group.

There are, of course, numerous other organizations available to widows, but without the disadvantage of being limited to widows only, which can serve as a bridge to the wider community. However, the newly bereaved are not readily clubbable, and the organizations which offer personal help on an individual basis may be required to enable them to take the first step. A list of UK national organizations for the bereaved is given at the end of this book and more detailed information about local services for the bereaved is available from the National Association of Bereavement Services, which also runs training courses for the many small bereavement services that lack the facilities to run their own programmes. The Hospice Information Service publishes regular lists of training courses relating to death and bereavement.

Help for bereaved children is obtainable from many sources and it is not possible to review them here. Information about such services in Britain is given in *The Widow's Child*, a pamphlet produced by Cruse. In the USA assistance can be obtained in some areas from the organizations known as 'Big Brother' and 'Big Sister' as well as from the other organizations mentioned above.

Times of war and disaster often evoke considerable sympathy and support for the bereaved. In Israel the Five-Day War and the Yom Kippur War both took their toll of young men and gave rise to some impressive support groups for widows.

SUPPORT FOR FAMILIES

Programmes of support aimed at entire families have a lot to commend them. Examples range from home-based family meetings to weekend camps for parents and children (Birnbaum, 1994). Two evaluations of family support have been published. Sandler *et al.* (1992) assigned families at random to either support group or control and both were then followed up. In this case intervention was associated with markedly less depression and conduct disorder in the children, parental ratings of increased warmth in their relationships with their children, and increased satisfaction with social support. A similar study by Black and Urbanowicz (1987) showed that family support can halve the number of problems of bereaved children.

CRUSE – BEREAVEMENT CARE

With so many different approaches to the problems of the bereaved to choose from it has been Cruse – Bereavement Care, the organization for all bereaved people, which has attempted to provide a range of services across the whole of the United Kingdom. Although it originated as an organization for widows its branches now offer help to all bereaved people regardless of the type of bereavement. A quarter of a century of experience in caring for the bereaved and nearly 200 branches makes Cruse the most impressive bereavement counselling service which I have discovered. Cruse aims to provide individual and group counselling as well as social support to all bereaved people who seek its help. It also provides training in bereavement counselling for members of the caring professions and for its own volunteer counsellors, and it publishes a range of literature including the 'Cruse Chronicle', for bereaved people, and 'Bereavement Care', for all who care for the bereaved.

Cruse is aware of the danger of 'in-breeding'. Although it is open to widows and widowers no matter how long they have been bereaved, its services are particularly suited to helping sufferers in the first few years of bereavement. Cruse therefore constitutes an organization for transition rather than a perpetual refuge, and it is perfectly appropriate for widows and widowers who have been coming to social or counselling meetings for a year or two to begin to feel that they no longer need the type of help that is offered.

This organization has grown steadily in recent years, thanks to a government grant and the leadership of a succession of excellent directors. In 1984 Her Majesty The Queen became the first monarch to grant her patronage to an organization for bereavement counselling. Cruse is already the main source of bereavement counselling in the United Kingdom. Sadly, it has not yet received the attention which it deserves in other parts of the world.

Organizations for the bereaved obviously have a great deal to offer, and in the United Kingdom, given their current rate of growth, they will soon be accessible everywhere. Even so, it is extremely unlikely that such organizations will ever help more than a fraction of those who need them, and the day-to-day counselling of the bereaved will remain the responsibility of those members of the care-giving professions whose work brings them into close contact with bereaved people: clergy, doctors, district nurses, social workers, health visitors, and the like.

What special contributions can members of these care-giving professions give to the bereaved? Let us consider first the clergy.

THE CLERGY

It has been traditional in most churches for clergy to visit the sick and the bereaved, but the opportunity thus given to the clergy to become key figures in supporting the bereaved and in aiding the transition from married person to widow or widower is seldom realized. Clergy, like everyone else, are often embarrassed and ineffectual when face-to-face with those who have been or are about to be bereaved. Many have now abandoned the tradition of routinely visiting bereaved parishioners they may never have met.

Among the twenty-two London widows only seven had been visited by a clergyman at the time of my first interview a month after bereavement, yet five of those seven had enjoyed the visit and found it helpful. Several, who had an ongoing relationship with their local vicar, found him a 'tower of strength' and spoke very warmly of the encouragement and support he had given. The two exceptions were both lapsed Catholics who were seen within the first twenty-four hours after their husband's death by a priest who was unknown to them. In both cases they felt that he did not understand their needs.

Clearly, parishioners who are already on friendly terms with their priest will be more likely to accept him than those who are complete strangers, or who believe that his only reason for calling is to take advantage of their bereaved state to get them back to church. And yet the majority of widows did express belief in God, albeit only a minority accepted, in full, the doctrines of a particular church. I had the impression that a visit from the right clergyman at the right time would have been valued by all of them.

In general, the first twenty-four hours is too soon for strangers to call. The bereaved person is still in a state of numbness or shock and is not yet ready to come to grips with his or her confusion. At a guess I would say that the best time for clergy to visit is during the week that follows the funeral and again at intervals throughout the first year of bereavement. It is when the funeral is over and the family have begun to disperse that the bereaved are likely to be left alone. At this time their grief is at its height, as they begin to try to deal with the painful, perplexing thoughts that beset them.

The role of the visiting clergyman is similar to that of any other friendly person who wishes the bereaved person well and would like to be of help. He too should be prepared to show by his manner acceptance of grief and particularly acceptance of the bitter anger against God and human beings that is likely to be expressed. He will not help matters by returning the anger, by meeting emotion with dogma or agony with glib assurance. He will help best by listening and, if invited to do so, by trying to collaborate with the bereaved person in an honest attempt to 'get things straight'. The clergyman who is 'in tune' with his parishioners may be able to find the right prayer or a helpful biblical quotation, but it is tempting to hide behind such 'easy' answers and avoid involvement by too readily prescribing 'magical' solutions to grief. Nobody can provide the one thing the bereaved person seeks – the lost person back again. But an honest acknowledgement of helplessness in this respect may make the visitor more acceptable than a spurious omniscience.

A person who goes to a clergyman probably expects to find a religious answer to problems. A person who goes to a doctor expects a medical answer. Because people are 'open' to the types of answer they seek, it is appropriate that doctors and clergy should attempt to provide the answers they feel qualified to give and not minimize the value of these answers. But members of both these professions must be sufficiently flexible to redefine their own roles so that they can act more effectively. The clergyman or doctor who can find the time to allow a bereaved person to talk about his or her feelings and fears will add a fresh dimension to counselling and a greater depth to their relationship with their parishioner or patient.

THE PRIMARY MEDICAL CARE TEAM

Although the clergyman is traditionally the person whose role it is to help those that mourn, it is more likely, in Britain today, that the widow or widower will turn to the family doctor for professional help. Thus in my study of the case records of forty-four unselected London widows (see page 21) it was found that three-quarters (thirty-three) had consulted their GP at some time during the first six months of bereavement. Fifteen of these widows complained of symptoms that were clearly psychological, and thirteen of these were treated with sedatives or tranquillizers. In general, physical treatments of this kind were all that the GP gave or was expected to give. This finding seems to reflect a change in attitude towards grief which is coming to be seen as an illness to be treated rather than a time of spiritual or emotional need. The doctor can somehow abolish grief; the clergyman can only sympathize.

There is, of course, no scientific evidence that enables us to compare the therapeutic efficacy of clergyman and doctor after bereavement. Doctors tend to use drugs[1] and the amount of drugs prescribed for the forty-four London widows did not fall off much over the first eighteen months of bereavement. This indicates that, since most of those who were prescribed drugs early in bereavement stopped taking them after six months or so, others had started to take them later in their bereavement. In this way nearly half (twenty-one) of the widows obtained a drug from their GP at some time during the first eighteen months, compared with only a fifth (nine) during a similar period before bereavement.

Drug-taking was most common among the younger widows even though, during the period preceding bereavement, it was the older women who took rather more than the younger. But in our society the commonest drugs taken are not those prescribed by doctors but those we choose for ourselves – alcohol and tobacco. I have no details of the smoking and drinking habits of London widows, but 41 per cent of the young widows and 37 per cent of the young widowers in the Harvard Study were smoking more a year after bereavement than they had before it and 38 and 31 per cent, respectively, were drinking more alcohol.

These findings suggest that widespread use is made of drugs to alleviate the stress of bereavement. Were their popularity any indication of their value, drugs would be counted the principal treatment for grief. But few systematic attempts have been made to assess their effects. Drugs are, of course, taken for various reasons. Night sedatives are popular (and alcohol is commonly taken for sleep), but tranquillizers are often given for anxiety by day and a great deal of use is now made of anti-depressive drugs.

Many widows and widowers complain of insomnia and subsequent tiredness during the day which adds to the difficulty of coping with life. Night sedatives are prescribed in the hope that adequate sleep will help them to deal more effectively with their problems in the daytime. Some use alcohol as a sedative, but the level in the blood wears off rapidly during the night and may cause the drinker to wake up three to four hours later. Medical prescriptions provide better drugs and control. Both forms of therapy are potentially habit-forming and it is wiser not to take them regularly every night but to make use of them only intermittently. If a bereaved person has had one bad night and fears that the next will be equally bad, it makes sense to take something at bedtime. A dozen Nitrazepam tablets can be made to last for two or three months if used judiciously, and they are handier and less likely to be abused than a bottle of whisky.

Society permits the bereaved a greater measure of control over their alcohol intake than it does over other drugs, but it also provides a system whereby they can obtain some of the time of a highly trained professional, whose skills should include a greater understanding of psychosocial problems than is to be expected from the average barman. They are likely, therefore, to feel safer if their drugs are being prescribed by a doctor, who will tell them when they have had enough and who can supply a variety of medications to suit their special needs. If alcohol is chosen they may repeatedly have to choose between a hangover and a restless night.

Apart from their use as night sedatives, tranquillizers (including alcohol) are taken to reduce anxiety and tension by day. There is now a wide range of the so-called benzo-diazepines on the market which can be expected to take the edge off feelings of panic and excessive anxiety. While I do not doubt the efficacy of these drugs in reducing the intensity of these unpleasant features of grief, the appropriateness of their use after bereavement is questionable. The biggest problem is that of the development of a drug habit. In one clinic which was set up to help people who had an undue dependence on such drugs one-fifth had been prescribed the medication after a bereavement (Hamlin and Hammersley, 1988). Tranquillizers have also been accused of interfering with the process of grieving. If, as we suppose, grief is a process of 'learning' and if it is necessary for the bereaved person to go through the pain of grief in order to learn, then anything that continually allows a person to avoid or suppress this pain can be expected to prolong the course of mourning. Admittedly, we have little empirical evidence that drugs have this effect and their use is so widespread that any serious consequences would probably have become apparent already if they were at all frequent. But the fact remains that until the effects of tranquillizing drugs have been properly assessed, they should be used with caution following bereavement.

Anti-depressants are a different category. There are certain types of depression (particularly those in which there is a general slowing down of thought and movement, early morning waking, and a tendency for the depression to be at its worst early in the day) which do respond to anti-depressant drugs. In these cases it would be cruel and sometimes dangerous to withhold treatment. Pasternak *et al.* (1994a) measured the sleep patterns of elderly bereaved people with depression and showed that an anti-depressant (Nor-triptyline) relieved both depression and insomnia. The newer anti-depressants such as Fluoxetine (Prozac) have also been used successfully for the treatment of panic syndrome and anxiety states both of which commonly occur following bereavement. Their efficacy as a remedy for normal grief has not, at this time, been demonstrated and it would be rash to recommend them until proper trials have been conducted but they are relatively safe and may even, in my experience, help people who cannot grieve to do so. Certainly there is no reason to believe that they inhibit grieving. Lynn and Racy (1969) have reported successful relief of major depression following bereavement by means of electro-convulsive therapy and this remains an alternative if other methods fail.

Dependence on alcohol is a real danger after bereavement, and thirteen of the 115 bereaved psychiatric patients in the combined Bethlem and Case-note Studies had become chronic alcoholics. In the case of tobacco the dangers to health are, of course, now well established, and smoking may even account for a part of the increased mortality from coronary thrombosis that has been found following bereavement.

Drugs aside, family doctors, because they are likely to have cared for the dead person during the last illness and to have helped the relatives to prepare for bereavement, are in a very advantageous position to give psychological support after this event has occurred. Many widows have spoken of the great help given by GPs, who have come to be regarded as friends, and they are often thought of as the wisest and most understanding people available. Through their profession they are acquainted with the reality of death, and this should make it possible for the bereaved to talk to them about this taboo topic.

Although their time is often assumed by humbler people to be 'too valuable to waste on the likes of us', their advice is treated with respect and their attitude to the situation is taken seriously. Unfortunately, it is all too easy for them to convey to the relatives their own sense of defeat when one of their patients dies. For example, they may see the widow as a survivor rather than as a person with a life of her own to lead, and this view will colour their attitude to her.

The GP who can recognize grief as the painful process through which a family must pass in becoming another kind of family is aware that the symptoms to which it gives rise must be seen in perspective. By showing willingness to accept their need to mourn, GPs may help them more positively than they would by taking the easier course of prescribing anti-depressives and tranquillizers. It may be important, for instance, that they reassure a distressed woman that her feelings of anger and guilt or her hallucinations of her dead husband are a normal reaction to loss, and that physical symptoms resembling those suffered by her husband do not mean that she is dying of the same disease. They may need to remind her that she is not a bad mother if she finds that it is hard to cope with the demands of her children, and to assure her that it is right for her to call upon the support of others to help them and herself. And they may also need to sit patiently through outbursts of hostility towards themselves as one of the people who might have saved her husband and to show, by their attitude, that they understand such feelings and are not going to allow them to spoil their relationship with their patient.

In like manner community nurses, health visitors, and social workers who are in a position to help bereaved people will be able to find many opportunities to do so, and there is no need for me to reiterate, for each of them, the general principles that will have emerged from consideration of the roles of the clergy and the family doctor.

TREATING PATHOLOGICAL GRIEF

The treatment of pathological reactions to bereavement follows the same principles as those that have been indicated for the support of bereaved people in general. Thus the appropriate treatment for delayed or inhibited grief would seem to be a form of psychotherapy in which patients are encouraged to express their grief and to overcome the fixations or blocks to realization which have prevented them from relearning their world. Similar situations are commonplace in psychiatric practice, and most current techniques of psychotherapy provide non-judgemental, benign interaction with the therapist in a manner that can be expected to help patients to begin to express the feelings they have inhibited. The therapist, by accepting, without criticism, the anger, guilt, despair, or anxiety that patients express, implicitly reassures them that such feelings, however painful, are not going to overwhelm the therapist or destroy the relationship with the patient. Having discovered that it is safe to express feelings the patient is now free to carry out the grief work and, as Lindemann (1944) puts it, pathological grief is transformed into 'normal grief' and follows the usual course towards resolution.

Approaches which derive from 'Learning Theory' have been developed by Gauthier and Marshall (1977) and by Ramsey (1979). Comparing avoidance of grief with phobic behaviour, Ramsey treats it by confronting the sufferer with reminders of the lost person, in much the same way that phobics can be treated by confronting them with the situation which they fear ('flooding'). Thus the bereaved are pressed to handle and smell clothing, to look at photographs, read letters, and listen to music associated with the dead person.

Initially, this approach often required Ramsey's patients to be admitted to a psychiatric unit for intensive therapy, but more recently he has treated patients as out-patients and his methods seem to have become gentler. Likewise, Gauthier (1979) has developed a method of graduated exposure to distressing stimuli, which is said to be particularly suitable for patients for whom 'flooding' would be too drastic a treatment (e.g., in the event of heart disease). These authors claim excellent results, as does Lieberman (1978), who used a similar kind of 'forced mourning', but the results of a systematic evaluation of a similar method of treatment which was conducted at the Maudsley Hospital gave less satisfactory results (Mawson et al., 1981). In this study patients who had been referred for the treatment of pathological grief were assigned at random to two groups. One received 'Guided Mourning' along the lines laid down by Ramsey; the other was encouraged to avoid thoughts of loss and to get on with living. At the end of treatment and on follow-up ten to twenty-eight weeks later, the 'Guided Mourning' group were able to talk and think more easily about their loss than those who had been instructed to avoid it, but their mental health was only slightly better than that of the comparison group.

A fundamental error which seems to have crept into most of this work is the assumption that there is only one kind of pathological grief and one appropriate treatment. My own studies suggest, however, that there are several types of pathological grief and that these may require quite different methods of treatment. Lindemann's and Ramsey's methods may work quite well when grief is being avoided, but they may be quite inappropriate in cases of chronic grief when the problem is not to start grieving but to stop. I have come across many patients with chronic grief who, it seemed to me, would have gone on expressing their grief in therapy indefinitely without improvement. These were people who were socially isolated and unable to find anything in life to look forward to. They had usually had difficulty in coping with responsibility before their marriage and were now unable to face the prospect of life without their loving protector. Clearly, rehabilitation is difficult and success may depend upon whether people are available in the family and community who can be drawn in to help the patient to find a new place in society. An approach which is sometimes successful in such cases is to set targets which the bereaved person can achieve along the way to restore their self-confidence and find new directions in life. These need to be carefully negotiated with the patient and written down so that progress can be monitored at each visit. Successes are rewarded with enthusiastic approval, failures subjected to careful reappraisal to determine why they occurred and with the implication that therapy is a waste of time unless something is achieved. The therapist must explicitly reject the idea that 'As long as you remain sick, I will look after you', and substitute the idea that 'You are not a sick or inferior person. I have faith that you can survive and find a worthwhile life for yourself.'

In some senses the designation of such people as sick militates against their rehabilitation by providing them with an identity as a sick person. This can only reinforce their existing tendency to give up competing in a world which they already see as complex or too dangerous to face. While they are glad to accept any amount of psychotherapy, their dependency is such that this easily becomes interminable.

Support for the view that, while some need help in expressing grief others may need help in relearning their world, comes from recent work by the research team at the Department of Clinical and Health Psychology at the University of Utrecht. Their Dual Process Model allows for the fact that both expression and inhibition of grief may be appropriate at various times and that problems can arise if either becomes excessive (Stroebe *et al.*, 1994).

In an important study Schut *et al.* (1991) assigned people with pathological grief reactions to two types of therapy: one a problem-focused type of behaviour therapy, and the other an emotion-focused, client-centred therapy aimed at facilitating grief. Both groups were followed up 11, 18, and 25 months after bereavement. The most important finding of this study was that widows benefited most from the problem-focused and widowers from the emotion-focused therapy. This confirms our contention that it is men rather than women who have difficulty in expressing their emotions and can be expected to benefit from therapy aimed at helping them to do this, whereas women in our society grieve relatively easily but may need help in finding new roles and meanings in their lives. Of course people do not always know what is good for them and Hopmeyer and Werk (1994), who followed up and compared a variety of groups for bereaved people, found that women ranked 'sharing feelings and emotions' as the things most worth spending time on in groups while the men preferred 'learning how to solve problems like mine'. Perhaps the ideal solution is to provide both.

This conclusion is borne out by another study by Schut's group in Utrecht (1994). They compared two types of service for bereaved people who had accepted in-patient care for the treatment of 'complicated bereavement' in a Dutch Health Care Centre. One group received individual psychotherapy with group relaxation, social skills training, and 'rational emotive therapy'. The other received a combination of behaviour and art therapy. The behaviour therapy aimed to help the bereaved to order their problems and to undergo a process of progressive desensitization to traumatic memories and images. The art therapy used music and art to evoke and express emotions and to visualize and portray 'disasters and jewels'. After a period of personal focus, therapy changed to a more social focus with an emphasis on social skills training and active tackling of problems. The three-month programme finished with rituals of farewell and present giving. On follow-up four months after discharge the combined art and behaviour therapy group had improved more than the comparison group on all of the outcome measures employed. Daily functioning and anxiety were particularly good with depression rather less improved.

This impressive study shows what can be done but it was evidently a very expensive programme and I understand that it has now been discontinued for lack of funds. It is to be hoped that the authors will go on to find less expensive ways of achieving their results.

Art therapy with the dying and the bereaved has also been advocated by Simon (1982). She points out that art created by most Westerners tends to be intellectual and self-conscious. By contrast 'primitive' art is archaic and evocative of powerful symbols. In therapy she tries to offer the security which will enable people to move from controlled and self-conscious representations to more archaic styles. When this happens people often find themselves compelled to create images which reflect the conflicts they face. This, she says, enables them to move from expression of the conflict to containment and eventual resolution. Bright (1986) adopts a comparable approach in her work as a music therapist. Music is an art form that goes straight to the heart. Bright uses improvised music and musical reminiscence to 'bring to the surface many and perhaps most of the hidden feelings which people have in situations of grief and loss'.

PSYCHIATRIC AND PSYCHOLOGICAL SERVICES

Since psychiatrists have, or should have, experience in recognizing the indirect ways of expressing conflict which are employed when grief becomes distorted, it may be easier for them than for others to help the bereaved person to deal with these problems; and since they are also likely to be well acquainted with the uses and side-effects of the wide range of drugs that are available today, they can employ these, where appropriate, to tide the bereaved patient over a difficult period. Furthermore, they have access to a variety of forms of therapeutic community currently available – day hospitals, night hostels, in-patient psychiatric units – which can, in certain cases, provide the patient with a temporary retreat.

It should be emphasized, nevertheless, that the care of the bereaved is a communal responsibility, and family members and others should not withdraw their support simply because a person has been referred to a psychiatrist.

Under the National Health Service in Britain, community psychiatric nurses and psychiatric social workers play a part in the care of those who are referred for psychiatric treatment; they also liaise with the primary care team. Often they are the people who work most closely with the family and they constitute valuable additions to the therapeutic team. The way in which they are used varies greatly from one area of the country to another, but since they often have more time and more opportunity than psychiatrists to visit patients' homes, they are uniquely placed to participate in family-centred service; they are, moreover, well placed to assist voluntary organizations.

In recent years psychologists have begun to take an interest in the field and this welcome development holds out much hope for the future. Psychologists, more than social workers and counsellors, have the scientific training which will encourage research and, as has been shown, they are already beginning to make an impact. It may well be that it is to this profession that we should look in the future for a lead in the establishment of well-founded services for the bereaved.

Claims have been made for a wide variety of other 'therapies' for bereavement. These include Gestalt therapy (Smith, 1985), hypnosis (Savage, 1993), imagery (Cerney, 1985), rational emotive therapy (Van den Bout, 1994), logotherapy (Giovinco and Monahan, 1994), and, when PTSD is present, eye movement desensitization (Shapiro, 1989 and Solomon, 1994), but in the absence of well-conducted comparative studies it is not possible to evaluate their effectiveness.

PROGNOSIS

Although it was not possible to follow up the bereaved psychiatric patients in the Bethlem Study in order to find out what subsequently became of them, a recent systematic follow-up of sixty people who had all been referred to me for treatment of psychiatric problems after bereavement found significant improvement in the number of people who said that they are very depressed or miserable, finding it hard to cope, tearful, wishing they could cry more than they do, using alcohol to control their feelings or drinking more alcohol than they should. They were also less likely to say that they had recently got to the end of their tether and more likely to say that they now never cry. In other words these people were less depressed and coping better than they had been at the outset of therapy. On the other hand there was little or no change in the number who said that they lacked confidence, and general feelings of anxiety and tension were not improved (Parkes, 1995a).

14

REACTIONS TO OTHER
TYPES OF LOSS

> Departure from this happy place, our sweet
> Recess, and onely consolation left
> Familiar to our eyes, all places else
> Inhospitable appeer and desolate,
> Nor knowing us nor known . . .
>
> John Milton, *Paradise Lost*

To conclude this book on the reaction to bereavement, let us consider to what extent grief at the loss of a loved person resembles reactions to other types of loss. Can the lessons we have learnt in our studies of widowhood be of help, for instance, to the sick or the physically disabled? This is the theme of a series of papers currently awaiting publication in the British Medical Journal which look at the many losses and changes which are met by members of the health care professions. Other types of loss which have been studied using the same frame of reference include divorce (Kitson, 1982), unemployment (Fagin and Little, 1984), forced migration (Munoz, 1980), death of a domestic pet (Keddie, 1977; Rynearson, 1978), childlessness (Houghton and Houghton, 1977), and the losses involved in, of all things, recovery from cancer (Maker, 1982).

For the purposes of this chapter I draw on studies of the reactions to two types of loss: loss of a limb and loss of a home. (These are described in more detail in Parkes 1972b, 1973 and 1976.) The former is the topic of my own research for the Department of Health and Social Security in Britain and the latter has been studied by Marc Fried in the United States. The field is a broad one, and these subjects have been chosen to illustrate it rather than to represent it.

We shall look, in turn, at the principal components of grief as they have emerged in bereavement studies and see what comparable features are discernible in the reactions to these other two types of loss. Each of the main components of grief has had a chapter to itself in the present work, and it is not possible, in the space that remains, to give as thorough an appraisal of similar phenomena as they appear after loss of a limb or a home.

The features that seem to me to be major aspects of many bereavement reactions are:

I The Trauma Response

1 An alarm reaction – anxiety, restlessness, and the physiological accompaniments of fear.
2 Anger and guilt, including outbursts directed against those who press the bereaved person towards premature acceptance of the loss.
3 Post-Traumatic Stress Disorder, the specific pathological response, and the less specific anxiety states and panic syndromes.

II The Grief Response

4 An urge to search for and to find the lost person in some form.
5 Relocating the lost person, including identification phenomena – the adoption of traits, mannerisms, or symptoms of the lost person, with or without a sense of that person's presence within the self.
6 Pathological variants of grief, i.e., the reaction may be excessive and prolonged or inhibited and inclined to emerge in distorted form.

III The Psychosocial Transition

7 A sense of dislocation between the world that is and the world that should be, often expressed as a sense of mutilation or emptiness which reflects the individual's need to relearn their internal model of the world.
8 A process of realization, i.e., the way in which the bereaved moves from denial or avoidance of recognition of the loss towards acceptance and the adoption of a new model of the world.
9 This process may be impaired by the feelings of helplessness and hopelessness which characterize depression.

LOSS OF A LIMB

The amputation study comprises information obtained from thirty-seven men and nine women under the age of seventy who were interviewed one month and thirteen months after the amputation of an arm or a leg. Loss of the limb was the main disability from which the majority of the subjects suffered. All were well enough to be fitted with an artificial limb. The interviews were all carried out by me and followed a similar pattern to those of the London Study.

Loss of a limb does not, on the face of it, seem to bear much resemblance to loss of a wife. I don't love my left leg, at least not in the same way that I love my wife. Society does not expect me to mourn for my leg, and the soldier who insisted on placing an amputated leg in his tomb, to await the coming of the rest of his mortal frame, is clearly atypical. But those who have studied the psychological reaction to amputation repeatedly refer to the 'grief' they encounter. Thus Wittkower (1947) says: 'Mourning is the normal emotional reaction.' Kessler (1951): 'The emotion most persons feel when told that they must lose a limb has been well compared with the emotion of grief at the death of a loved one.' Dembo *et al.* (1952): 'A person may mourn his loss.' And Fisher (1960): 'The reaction to loss of a limb, and for that matter to loss of function of a vital part, is grief and depression.' In none of these studies, however, is it clearly indicated just what it is that the amputee is mourning for or even just what is meant by 'mourning'.

Perhaps consideration of the seven aspects of the reaction to bereavement will help to clarify the issues.

The Trauma Response

1   The first component of the bereavement reaction, alarm, is to be expected in any situation of danger and it does, of course, occur in many people who are about to undergo or have just undergone major surgery. Feelings of anxiety, tension, and restlessness were common among the amputees and, during the year after amputation, 30 per cent complained of three or more symptoms that are attributable to the types of disturbance of the autonomic nervous system described in Chapter 3. Loss of appetite and weight were the rule during the immediate post-operative period, and 35 per cent of the amputees still required sedatives to help them to sleep at night a month after the operation. As pointed out in Chapter 3, there is nothing specific about the alarm reaction, but it is worth noting that amputees, because of their physical helplessness during and after the operation, are more reliant on others during the period of transition than are widows. They may, however, feel protected during this period. Only later do they have to become more independent and give up the safety of the role of 'patient'.

2　Feelings of bitterness or anger are commonly expressed by amputees. Just as the widow says, 'I can't see a married couple without thinking – why should it happen to me?', so 35 per cent of the amputees admitted feelings of envy towards healthy, intact people. Intense anger may be directed towards doctors or others whose actions might have helped to bring about the amputation, and, like the widow or widower, amputees often blame themselves.

3　Severe anxiety and panic syndromes were not uncommon among amputees and a number of them, who had suffered physical injuries when losing their limb, undoubtedly suffered from Post-Traumatic Stress Disorder in which they were haunted by memories of the trauma.

II The Grief Response

4　The urge to search for the lost object is less obvious in reactions to amputation than it is in bereavement reactions. Obviously, amputees are not going to search the hospital for their missing leg. An important question here seems to be 'What is it that has been lost?' All the amputees I interviewed answered 'Yes' to the question 'Do you miss your limb?', but when questioned further on this point it was clear that what they missed most was the functions that had formerly been performed by means of the limb. Leg-amputees described how they would lie in bed pining to go swimming or run through fields. The more athletic and active they had been in the past the more they seemed to suffer.

Some amputees did admit to missing the limb itself and 63 per cent admitted some concern over the disposal of the limb after it had been cut off. 'Outside the ward there's a great chimney stack. I used to look at the smoke and think "They're having a burn-up" but I comforted myself by thinking that they might have kept my leg for medical research. I didn't ask them.'

Whereas the maintenance of contact with loved persons requires the use of scanning, searching, and following behaviour from early childhood, there is no need to develop such behaviour in relation to parts of the body. Nevertheless, like the widow or widower, amputees do tend to be preoccupied with thoughts of loss. They mourn for their lost intactness, particularly at times when this is forced on their attention.

Provided they are physically fit there is little that younger amputees cannot do with one leg or one arm, once they have learnt how. But many amputees are physically frail or old, and even in the case of a younger person, it may take a long time for a well-fitting prosthesis to be made. In the meanwhile they must get about as best they can. For the new leg-amputee, going up and down stairs, carrying a cup of coffee across a room, or going to the toilet are difficult and dangerous manoeuvres. If it is an arm that has been lost, getting dressed, cutting up food, buying a bus ticket, or opening a letter are very hard. And either type of amputee is likely to be self-conscious about being seen in public in a mutilated state: 'Kids look at you – it's like the Lord Mayor's Show when I go out.'

Although 67 per cent of the amputees attempted to take their mind off their loss, they were constantly being reminded of it, and each frustration brought back a feeling of painful pining for the world that was no longer theirs.

5   What of the identification phenomena that were apparent after bereavement? Do they too have their equivalent in the amputee?

From these figures it appears that amputees do experience a sense of the presence of the lost object, which is referred to in the medical literature as the 'phantom limb' – indeed this is reported much more frequently than the 'phantom husband'. A possible explanation for this may be that the phantom limb and the phantom husband are not strictly analogous. A wife, however close she may be to her husband, is not connected to him by nervous pathways which must be severed when he dies. It is reasonable to suppose that the phantom limb is, to some extent at any rate, attributable to the fact that a part of the nervous system, including nerves of the limb and all of their central connections, remains in existence after the removal of the limb.

Nevertheless, the phantom limb is influenced by psychological factors. Thus one amputee described how, after the first weeks, his phantom limb seemed to grow shorter so that it was now a little foot situated where his shin would formerly have been. 'As soon as I put my artificial leg on it zips down to the foot again.' Clearly the location of the phantom in space was governed partially by this patient's psychological need to identify the residue of the lost limb with the substitute which had now been provided for it.

A phantom limb does seem to be treated as a part of the self. For example, one amputee described how he would lift his stump in the air if his wife was vacuuming the floor for fear that she would hurt his phantom foot.

Just as the widow may have symptoms resembling those of her husband, so the phantom limb may be perceived as suffering from the same disease that brought about the limb's removal. An ulcer on the heel, for instance, may still be felt to be present and even the pain that was suffered prior to surgery may persist.

Thus among twelve patients who had experienced severe pain in a limb for eight weeks or more prior to amputation, nine continued to have severe pain in their phantom limb afterwards. Severe pain in the phantom limb was much less frequently reported by amputees whose pre-operative pain (and most had had some pre-operative pain) had been present for less than eight weeks (six out of thirty-four).

Like the identification symptoms of the bereaved, these pains tended to disappear, but it is well recognized that in a minority of such cases pains persist or recur at some later date. The problem of the painful phantom limb has long been a matter of concern to surgeons and it is not possible here to review the literature on this subject. A wide variety of physical methods of treatment have been undertaken, but it seems that, whatever the treatment, there is a small minority of amputees who continue to complain. No physical cause is known for the majority of these pains but several studies have revealed their susceptibility to psychological influence: thus they have sometimes been aggravated by anger, tiredness, and frustration, and relieved by hypnosis and other forms of suggestion. Complaints of pain are commoner in compulsively self-reliant individuals who find it difficult to accept helplessness and in the face of unsettled or inadequate settlement of compensation claims. It may be, then, that persistence of phantom pains sometimes represents one type of difficulty in accepting the loss of the limb.

6 Many of the pathological reactions to amputation resemble those to bereavement. They commonly reflect distortion or prolongation of the process of realizing the loss and, although additional research is needed to clarify the picture, it does appear that one of the main types of reaction found among disturbed widows and widowers is also found in amputees – chronic grief.

By contrast there were sixteen patients who showed little or no emotional reaction to the loss of their limb. 'I had a feeling that I could kick the world about for quite a long time,' said one patient; 'they told me they were going to write me up as their prize patient.' Later, however, he realized how restricted he was: 'I wept bitterly – the helplessness, being dependent on people, the humiliation.' Several amputees said that they had been told that the prosthesis would be a perfectly good substitute for the part that was being removed and they did not allow themselves to consider the possibility that they would be disabled in any way. This view of the situation was less easy to maintain when they left hospital and started trying to compete with intact others in the outside world.

III The Psychosocial Transition

7   Feelings of internal loss of self or mutilation, the fifth component, were also common and were well expressed by one man: 'You sometimes feel you've had part of your body taken away and you're no longer part of the world – they've taken part of your life away.' Another said: 'You feel mutilated, you know you'll never be the same again . . . Underneath I feel badly damaged' – the 'underneath' reflects the injury to the self which lies within the body whose intactness has been shattered.

8   Do amputees go through a process of realization in which they move from denial of the full meaning of amputation towards an acceptance of the true situation? I think they do. Just as the widow finds it hard at first to believe that her husband is dead and often has a strong sense of his presence nearby, so the amputee has difficulty in accepting the loss of a limb and continues to feel that it is still present. Thus 39 per cent of the amputees described an initial period of 'numbness'; all forty-six had a feeling of the persisting presence of the lost limb; and 87 per cent related how they often forgot that the limb was missing and went to use it. The sense of numbness passed within a few days, but a year later 80 per cent still had some sense of the presence of the limb, 35 per cent still forgot it had gone from time to time, and 46 per cent said that they still found it hard to believe what had happened.

The modern prosthesis, despite intensive research and modification over the years, is a poor, cumbersome, and uncomfortable thing by comparison with a real limb. Lacking any sensation or muscle power of its own, it must be fitted to a stump of bone and tissue which was never meant to bear weight in the first place and which has an infuriating habit of shrinking or expanding whenever a decent fit has been obtained. The limb-fitters, who are great craftsmen in metal and leather, spend their lives patching, modifying, and remodelling the socket into which the stump must fit, and the amputees spend a lot of their time waiting hopefully for the perfect fit, which may never come. Patience and the acceptance of a modicum of discomfort are essential if the amputee is to make a good adjustment to the realities of a new life.

9   Among the forty-six amputees I have interviewed there were twelve who were still depressed and withdrawn a year after amputation. Most of them were making much less use of their artificial limb than their doctors had expected (bearing in mind their physical powers) and people were inclined to accuse them of 'giving up'. In fact several of these men and women seemed to believe that

they were crippled for life and, because they believed it, they may well in fact be crippled for life.

Without placing too fine a point on it, it does seem that the psychosocial transition from being an intact person to being an amputee is a painful and time-consuming process which is, in many ways, similar to the transition from married person to widow or widower. It would seem justifiable, therefore, to regard these two situations as parts of the same field of study. Just what this implies for the organizations of health care is spelled out elsewhere (Parkes, 1996b), and there is no space to repeat it here. Instead, let us take a brief look at the findings of Fried's study concerning the effects of relocating 789 Boston slum-dwellers. They were interviewed before compulsory rehousing took place and again two years later.

RELOCATION

Fried's investigation was carried out at the Center for Community Studies at Harvard Medical School, with Erich Lindemann as principal investigator. It is not surprising, therefore, that Fried should have attempted to find the same 'symptoms' in relocated slum-dwellers that Lindemann had previously found in the bereaved. The surprise, if surprise there be, is in the extent to which he succeeded. He writes:

> While there are wide variations in the success of post-relocation adjustment and considerable variability in the depth and quality of the loss experience, it seems quite precise to refer to the reactions of the majority as grief: These are manifest in the feelings of painful loss, the continued longing, the general depressive tone, frequent symptoms of psychological or social or dramatic distress, the active work required in adapting to the altered situation, the sense of helplessness, the occasional expressions of both direct and displaced anger, and tendencies to idealize the lost place . . . 46% gave evidence of a fairly severe grief reaction or worse.

As in amputation reactions, each of the components of grief is present. Thus Fried describes the way in which the relocated slum-dweller attempts to minimize and postpone the realization of his loss by trying to avoid thinking about it, but, as in other forms of grief, the painful memories break through. Thus one woman who had been brought up in the West End of Boston said: 'Home is where you hang your hat . . . Don't look back – try to go ahead.' But when asked how she felt when her old home was demolished she replied: 'It's just like a plant . . . when you tear up its roots, it dies. I didn't die, but I felt kind of bad. It was home . . .'

Fried makes several references to 'somatic distress' and the physical accompaniments of the alarm reaction, but he gives rather more evidence for the urge to search. In this connection it is again relevant to ask 'What is it that has been lost?' – for the answer to this question will determine what is missed. In the interviews carried out before relocation, an attempt was made to ascertain the 'focus of commitment' expressed by each respondent with regard to the neighbourhood. Their replies were grouped into 'Accessibility and financial', 'Interpersonal', 'Places', 'Interpersonal and Places', and 'Nothing'. When the respondents were re-interviewed after relocation, those who had expressed a commitment to people, places, or both showed much more grief than those who had valued the neighbourhood for its accessibility or financial aspects or those who had expressed no commitment at all. Intensity of grief was also found to be related to the amount of the surrounding neighbourhood that had been known to the respondent; in other words, intensity of grief correlated with the measured area of physical life-space that had been lost (in other types of loss we can seldom find so clear a measure of the magnitude of the loss).

Among respondents whose commitment was primarily to places it would seem to be places that were missed most, and we can see the urge to recover the lost object reflected in the wish expressed by some to return to the West End. For example, one person said: 'I always felt I had to go home to the West End and even now I feel like crying when I pass by.' And another: 'I used to stare at the spot where the building stood.' Those whose commitment was primarily to friends and neighbours were more likely to stress interpersonal loss: 'I lost all the friends I knew.' Attempts to retain as much as possible of the lost world were made by families who 'tried to remain physically close to the area they knew even though most of their close interpersonal relationships remained disrupted'.

Feelings of anger were expressed as denigration of the new environment by comparison with the idealized memory of the old – 'I felt cheated,' said one respondent.

Most striking of all Fried's findings, however, is that many of his respondents expressed feelings of personal mutilation in a vivid way. 'I felt like my heart was taken out of me,' said one. 'Something of me went with the West End.' 'It was like a piece being taken from me.' Like the widows described in Chapter 7 these people seem to have experienced a loss of self, a psychological mutilation which was subjectively just as real as the mutilation experienced by the amputee. Once again we are forced to realize that the skin is not the only boundary around the self and that the home we live in and the people to whom we are attached are, in some sense, ours – they are parts of ourselves. Although Fried does not mention this point, there are several published accounts of the way in which people who have lost a home often try to build another in the same place and manner. Similarly, immigrants in an alien culture commonly attempt to re-create around them the culture they have lost. It is clearly not possible for a person to identify with a lost home in the same way that one can identify with a lost person. But the identification symptoms of widows and the efforts of relocated persons to re-create their lost environment seem to be two different ways of attempting to retain, in some measure, the world that has been lost.

Fried's assessments of the health and psychosocial adjustment of his respondents revealed two patterns of reaction that were associated with a high incidence of 'problems'. There were some individuals who over-reacted to relocation: although they did not seem to be strongly committed to the neighbourhood before relocation they showed severe grief afterwards and required a lot of help from social and legal agencies. There were others who seemed strongly committed to the neighbourhood prior to relocation but who showed minimal grief afterwards: they were found to have a disproportionate frequency of physical and psychosomatic problems. It seems quite likely that these two patterns of 'over-reaction' and 'denial' correspond to the 'excessive' and 'inhibited' forms of grief which have been found following bereavement.

CONCLUSIONS

I have tried to show, in this chapter, how some of the phenomena that have emerged in studies of the reaction to bereavement are found in similar form following other types of loss. Like stress, which was discussed in Chapter 3, loss can have many meanings and there is no reason to believe that all types and degrees of loss give rise to identical reactions. But, like stress, a loss tends to be a *post hoc* attribution. That is to say, we may not know, until after it has occurred, whether a given life-event is to be construed as a loss or a gain. 'You are not losing a daughter but gaining a son,' says the optimistic wedding guest, but the truth of the matter is that the bride's mother is undergoing a major change in her life which, from her point of view, may be regarded as a net profit or a net loss. She may grieve or she may rejoice, or, with the typical human ability to split herself, she may oscillate between tears and delight. The hard-headed research worker may well find it hard to classify such life-events as the marriage of a daughter as losses or gains.

Similarly, there were a few amputees who were glad to lose a troublesome leg, and some of the slum-dwellers interviewed by Fried regarded relocation as an unqualified blessing. Fried takes pains to point out that the grief that was expressed by the majority of his respondents might not be found among other populations in other places undergoing other experiences of relocation: the degree of attachment to a particular physical and social environment shown by the Boston working class, for instance, might not be found among nomads, or among ambitious young business executives for whom a change of city may be part of a desired pattern of adventurous progress.

Nevertheless, the similarities between bereavement, amputation, and relocation reactions must lead us to consider whether the methods of preventing pathology outlined in Chapter 10 might not also be applied to help amputees to adjust to the loss of a limb and slum-dwellers to cope with the transition to new housing. Anticipatory preparation, to enable a realistic picture of the new world to be built up before the destruction of the old, can be useful, as can provision of support through the period of transition of such a kind that the necessary grief work is facilitated with eventual acceptance of the loss. Also, help can be given where necessary to introduce the individuals undergoing the transition to the new opportunities open to them, and to facilitate changes in their attitude by means of appropriate events (e.g., anniversary celebrations, holidays, training courses, or other 'rituals' which have the significance of a *rite de passage* and act as turning-points in the process of realization).

The establishment of such methods of education and support on a sound scientific basis must be an important task of professionals in the field of community mental health in the years to come. I use the term 'community mental health' because I believe that 'preventive psychiatry' is too narrow a term for this field. We should not be concerned solely with attempting to reduce the prevalence of mental illness but should be seeking to improve the quality of living, the mental health of the community.

Times of transition are times of opportunity and any confrontation with an unfamiliar world is both an opportunity for autonomous mastery and a threat to one's established adjustment to life. Taken overall the effect of such experiences is more likely to be beneficial than harmful. Education and upbringing have as their chief aim increased mastery of the unfamiliar, and mature people are the ones who have achieved a degree of autonomy which enables them to approach the unfamiliar with confidence. But there are some life changes which, because of their magnitude or because of a particular characteristic, carry a special risk of producing, not maturation, but dislocation.

This book, in focusing on bereavement, has attempted to illustrate and explain the consequences of one such change, and in this last chapter brief reference has been made to two other types of change. No doubt, in time, the whole range of reactions to life changes (or PSTs) will be mapped out and we shall have a body of knowledge with implications for child care, education, medicine, and welfare services of all kinds.

But it is not enough to institute new ways of housing the homeless, rehabilitating the crippled, or counselling the bereaved. Any plan for change should include an attempt to anticipate and provide for the psychosocial effects of the change. Thus the decision to remove a leg should be made in full awareness of the patient's prospects of making a successful adjustment to life as an amputee; plans for slum clearance should be made in full awareness of the probable effects of relocation upon the population to be resettled; the decision to send a man to prison should be made only after there has been an attempt to predict the probable effects of this action upon the man and his family.

We can extend this reasoning to include decisions in many areas: decisions concerning the admission of young children to nursery schools, and of old people to institutions; the introduction of new methods in industry and the redeployment of labour; the bombing of a city or the closure of a factory. Each of these situations imposes upon the planner the obligation to take full account of how the decisions taken will affect the populations or individuals concerned, and to do all that is possible to ensure that any planned change leads to growth and maturation rather than dislocation and dysfunction.

I recently returned from a visit to Rwanda where I advised on the development of a programme of psychological rehabilitation for the victims of the genocide which had swept that sad country only a year previously. The saddest aspect of my experience was the realization that the people who are most in need of help are the ones who are least likely to ask for or to get it – the refugees, soldiers, and politicians who are themselves traumatized and who are in danger of reacting to their trauma by repeating the pattern of violence. The harm caused by such cycles of violence across the world is incalculable and close study of the ways in which such cycles could be interrupted should be high on our list of priorities in the years to come.

In our present state of knowledge sociologists and psychologists are beginning to be able to meet the challenge of advising the planners and to help those whose lives are most affected by change. We can no longer ignore the fact that research into the effects of change is an essential area of study. Willingness to look at the problems of grief and grieving instead of turning away from them is the key to successful grief work in the sufferer, the helper, the planner, and the research worker. Prisoners who remind us of the precariousness of our freedom, cancer patients who remind us of our own mortality, immigrants who encroach upon our territory, and widows and widowers who prove to us that at any moment we too may lose the people we love are a source of anxiety and threat. We choose to deal with our fear by turning away from its source, by rejecting the prisoner, jollying the cancer patient along, excluding the immigrant, or avoiding contact with the widow and widower. But each time we do this we only add to the fear, perpetuate the problems, and miss an opportunity to prepare ourselves for the changes that are inevitable in a changing world.

APPENDIX

Many of the assertions made in the foregoing chapters are based on evidence that was referred to only briefly in the text. The detailed findings that constitute this evidence are presented and discussed below.

1. Let us consider first the assertion made in Chapter 2 that bereavement can increase the mortality rate, especially from heart disease. Evidence for the increased death rate was given by Young, Benjamin and Wallis (1963), whose work was supplemented by Parkes, Benjamin and Fitzgerald (1969). These papers contain data relating to all males over the age of fifty-four in England and Wales whose wives died during two months of 1957.

The National Health Service central register was tagged so that all deaths occurring in the sample of 4,486 widowers would be reported. As Figure 1 shows, the mortality rate during the first six months of

Figure 1 Mortality rate of widowers aged over fifty-four as a percentage of the rate for married men of the same age

bereavement was found to be 40 per cent higher than the expected rate based on national figures for married men of the same age.

The greatest proportional increase was in deaths from coronary thrombosis and other arteriosclerotic and degenerative heart disease, which group was 67 per cent above expectation ($p < 0.01$).

2. The findings of Schmale and Iker (1966) concerning the diagnosis of cervical cancer by psychiatric interview can best be illustrated by reproducing one of their tables. Table 1 shows that when the psychiatrist predicted the diagnosis of cancer on the basis of the patient's report of having responded to a life event prior to the first cervical smear with feelings of hopelessness, he was more likely to be right than wrong. To be precise, he was right in thirty-six cases and wrong in fifteen, a finding that is significant at the 0.02 level. (The life events that preceded the illness were usually construed by the patient as being irrevocable losses.)

Table 1 *Psychiatrist's predictions of cervical cancer and biopsy diagnosis in fifty-one women admitted for investigation of suspicious smear test (Schmale and Iker, 1966)*

Biopsy diagnosis	Psychiatrist's prediction	
	Cancer	Not cancer
Cancer	11 (61%)	8 (24%)
Not cancer	7 (39%)	25 (76%)

$x^2 = 5.29 p$ (two-tailed) = 0.02

3. In the London Study (Parkes, 1970) twenty-two London widows were interviewed five times during the course of their first year of bereavement. The data collected at each interview included a subjective assessment by the widow of her 'general health' (scored as 'good', 'indifferent', or 'bad'), a count of the number of physical symptoms she had experienced since the previous interview (from a check-list), a count of the number of consultations she had had with her GP since the last interview, and an assessment of irritability or anger as observed at the current interview (scored as 'very marked', 'marked', 'moderate', 'mild', or 'absent').

Correlation coefficients between the mean scores on each of these variables are shown in Table 2. Only the correlation between general health and irritability and anger was statistically significant ($r = 0.70$, $t = 4.28$, $p < 0.001$).

Table 2 *London Study: intercorrelation of health assessments and anger in twenty-two London widows*

	Subjective assessment of general health	No. of symptoms from check-list over one year	No. of GP consultations in course of year	Irritability and anger observed at interviews
Subjective assessment of general health		0.00	0.23	0.70*
No. of symptoms from check-list over one year	0.00		0.08	−0.15
No. of GP consultations in course of year	0.23	0.08		0.27
Irritability and anger observed at interviews	0.70*	−0.15	0.27	

Note: Assessments represent sums of assessments made at five interviews during the course of the first year of bereavement.
* $p < 0.001$ (using t test)

4. My study of the case records of forty-four widows (Parkes, 1964b) showed that the consultation rate with the GP rose from a mean of 2.2 consultations per patient per six months during the eighteen months prior to the terminal illness of the husband to a mean of 3.6 during the first six months of bereavement; and for the second and third six-month periods of bereavement the mean consultation rates were 2.6 and 3.0 respectively. The increase is highly significant ($Z = 5.7$, $p < 0.001$, Wilcoxon matched-pairs signed-ranks test).

In the under-sixty-five age-group during the first six months there was a 200 per cent increase in consultations for psychological symptoms (i.e., the case notes indicated either a specifically psychological complaint such as depression or insomnia, or the prescription of a sedative, hypnotic, or tranquillizer). This increase was also highly significant ($\chi^2 = 200$, d.f. 3, $p < 0.001$, Friedman two-way analysis of variance by ranks).

As shown in Figure 2, sedative consumption in the younger age-group increased from a mean of 0.7 weeks on sedation per patient per six months prior to bereavement to a mean of 5.0 in the first six months afterwards ($\chi^2 = 10.7$, 3 d.f., $p < 0.02$, Friedman two-way analysis of variance by ranks).

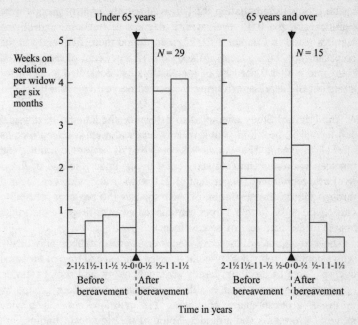

Figure 2 Sedative consumption, before and after bereavement, of forty-four widows in two age-groups

The small increase (25 per cent) in consultations for psychological symptoms in the sixty-five-and-over age-group did not approach statistical significance, and there was no significant change in sedative consumption in this group. However, there was an overall increase in consultations for non-psychiatric complaints ($z = 3.96$, $p < 0.00005$, Wilcoxon test) and this remained significant when the older age-group was considered alone ($p < 0.05$, Wilcoxon test).

When the consultations were broken down by diagnosis the numbers in each diagnostic group were too small for statistical analysis. The exception was consultations for muscle and joint conditions which, in the under-sixty-five age-group, increased from a mean of 0.11 consultations per six months prior to bereavement to a mean of 0.52 during the eighteen months after bereavement ($p < 0.05$, Wilcoxon test).

5. Maddison and Viola (1968) record that questionnaires were completed by 50 per cent of the bereaved women approached. Total

health scores differentiating the bereaved and the control groups were significant at the 0.01 level, with 2 degrees of freedom, and all the features listed in Chapter 2 (p. 22) were found more frequently in the bereaved ($p < 0.05$, χ^2 test). In addition, 12.8 per cent of the bereaved compared with 1.0 per cent of the controls had consulted a doctor for treatment of 'depression' during the preceding year ($p < 0.001$).

6. The Harvard Study attempted to determine the amount of physical and mental ill health in young widows and widowers fourteen months after bereavement. The sample was composed of forty-nine widows and nineteen widowers (making sixty-eight in all) under the age of forty-five, who represented 34 per cent of 231 widows and widowers located through the death registration of their spouses (50 per cent refused to participate and a further 17 per cent moved away or dropped out in the course of the first year of bereavement).

The sixty-eight widows and widowers were matched individually with a control group of sixty-eight married women and men of the same age, sex, area of dwelling, family size, nationality, and social class.

Information about their health was obtained from both groups by means of a questionnaire containing 218 questions covering a wide range of symptoms and attitudes. Some of the significant findings are presented in Table 3. The table shows that the bereaved differed from the controls in having more hospital admissions and consulted more people about emotional problems. They reported more disturbance of sleep, appetite, and weight, and had increased their consumption of alcohol, tobacco, and tranquillizers. Psychological symptoms more frequently found in the bereaved included depression, strain, loneliness, restlessness, difficulty in making decisions, and poor memory.

Scores were obtained by combining the answers to a number of questions on the same topic (the intercorrelation of these scores was confirmed by factor analysis). A comparison of the bereaved and non-bereaved on these scores is given in Table 4. It is clear that, while the bereaved subjects were more depressed than the controls and manifested some disturbance of the autonomic nervous system (revealed by such symptoms as dizziness, trembling, chest pains, palpitations, sweating, and lump in the throat), there was no evidence that any real personality change had followed the bereavement (the full meaning of the terms used in the table are given in Parkes and Weiss, 1983).

When a score of 1 was given for each physical symptom said to have occurred for the first time in the previous year, a significant increase in

Table 3 *Harvard Study: bereaved men and women under forty-five years of age compared, fourteen months after bereavement, with non-bereaved subjects of the same age*

	No. reporting feature		
	Bereaved N = 68	Non-bereaved N = 68	p
Admitted to hospital in past year	12	4	<.05
Trouble falling asleep in past year	19	8	<.02
Awakening during night in past year	27	8	<.001
Changes in appetite in past year	34	20	<.05
Big ups and downs in weight in past year	18	7	<.05
Increased smoking in past year	19	6	<.01
Increased alcohol consumption in past year	19	2	<.001
Taking tranquillizers in past year	18	3	<.001
Sought help for emotional problems in past year	23	5	<.001
Wonder anything worth while	34	18	<.01
Not too happy (multi-choice question)	13	4	<.05
Worried by loneliness (multi-choice)	44	17	<.001
Wish to change many parts of life (multi-choice)	15	5	<.05
Depressed or very unhappy in past few weeks	33	20	<.05
Restlessness in past year	33	15	<.01
Memory not all right in past year	20	6	<.01
Hard to make up mind in past year	36	22	<.05
Life often a strain	25	12	<.05
Judgement not too good	28	14	<.02
Feel somewhat apart or remote even among friends	23	10	<.01
It's safer not to fall in love	13	2	<.02

symptoms was found among the widowers, but not the widows, in comparison with the controls (see Table 5). There was no evidence, however, in the bereaved group, of any worsening of chronic physical symptoms (Parkes and Brown, 1972).

7. Of the ninety-four patients who had been admitted to the Bethlem Royal and Maudsley Hospitals during 1949–51 with a mental illness that had come on within six months of the death of a parent, spouse,

Table 4 *Harvard Study: psychological symptoms and personality scores in bereaved and non-bereaved subjects over the fourteen-month period*

	Mean scores		
	Bereaved N = 68	Non-bereaved N = 68	p
Depression	6.10	4.13	<.01
Autonomic disturbance	1.53	0.88	<.02
External anxiety (worry)	5.42	6.46	n.s.
Interpersonal fear (shyness)	3.28	2.94	n.s.
Compulsive self-reliance	4.09	4.12	n.s.
Stimulus-seeking	2.79	2.85	n.s.
General irritability	1.50	1.77	n.s
Paranoid attitude	2.47	2.43	n.s.
Self-esteem	5.51	5.63	n.s.
Authoritarianism	5.34	5.52	n.s.
Rigidity	1.77	1.66	n.s.
Emotionality	1.81	2.35	n.s.
Psychosocial functioning	8.28	8.86	n.s.

n.s. = not significant

Table 5 *Harvard Study: acute physical symptoms in bereaved and non-bereaved subjects*

	N	mean no. symptoms		p
		Bereaved	Non-bereaved	
Men	19	2.36	1.10	< 0.05
Women	49	3.28	3.00	n.s.

sibling, or child, thirty had lost a spouse. Calculations from mortality tables showed that only five spouse-bereaved patients would have been expected by chance alone. This difference is statistically significant ($\chi^2 = 19.2$, 1 d.f., $p < 0.001$).

When the diagnoses of the bereaved patients were compared with those of non-bereaved patients admitted during the same triennium, a diagnosis of affective disorder was found to have been made in respect of 65 per cent of the bereaved and 47 per cent of the non-bereaved (χ^2 = 11.98, 1 d.f., $p < 0.01$). When this category was further subdivided, the subgroup 'reactive or neurotic depression' (ICD number 314) was found in 28 per cent of the bereaved and in only 15 per cent of the non-bereaved cases (χ^2 = 10.19, 1 d.f., $p < 0.01$) (see Table 6 and Parkes, 1964a).

8. Clayton *et al.* (1972) describe their operational definition of the 'depressive symptom complex': '. . . low mood characterized by feeling depressed, sad, despondent, discouraged, blue . . . plus 5 of the following 8 symptoms for definite depression and 4 of the 8 symptoms for probable depression:

Table 6 *Case-note Study: psychiatrists' diagnoses of bereaved and non-bereaved psychiatric in-patients*

ICD[a]		Bereaved patients		Non-bereaved patients	
		N 94	% 100	N 3151	% 100
300	Schizophrenia	8	8	481	15
301	Manic-depressive psychosis	19	20	551	18
302	Involutional melancholia	4	4	191	6
304 & 306	Senile and arteriosclerotic psychoses	3	3	73	2
305, 307, 308 & 309	Other organic psychoses	5	5	76	2
310	Anxiety reaction	12	13	233	7
311	Hysteria	8	8	166	5
313	Obsessive-compulsive neuroses	0	0	99	3
314	Reactive depression	26*	28	481*	15
312 & 315–18	Phobic and other neuroses	2	2	135	4
320–1	Other personality disorders	3	3	215	7
322–3	Drug addictions (inc. alcoholism)	3	3	74	2
	Other diagnoses	1	1	376	12
301, 302, 310 314	All affective disorders	61*	65	1456*	47

[a] Code numbers of principal diagnoses after *Manual of Diseases* (1947).
* $p < 0.01$

1 Loss of appetite and/or weight.
2 Sleep difficulties including hypersomnia.
3 Fatigue.
4 Feeling restless.
5 Loss of interest.
6 Difficulty in concentrating.
7 Feelings of guilt.
8 Wishing to be dead, or thoughts of suicide.

This cluster had to be present since the death of the spouse.'

Depressed widows had significantly ($p < 0.05$) fewer adult children whom they considered close than the non-depressed widows.

9. In the London Study the twenty-two young and middle-aged widows were assessed at each of the five interviews on a number of psychological measures. Assessments were based on information from the widow combined with my own direct observation at the interview, and each feature was rated on a five-point scale as 'very marked', 'marked', 'moderate', 'mild', or 'absent'. The meaning of the terms is usually self-evident, but note particularly: 'numbness' = reports of feeling 'numb', 'blunted', or 'cloudy'; 'difficulty in accepting the fact of loss' = difficulty in believing fully in the reality of the husband's death, statements such as 'I still can't believe it's true'; 'restlessness' = observable hyperactivity; 'tension' = observable increase in muscle tension.

The mean year scores (the mean of each measure over the whole year) were intercorrelated and the significance of all correlations was tested. This revealed certain clusters of associated variables. Table 7 shows the correlation coefficients for each variable with each other variable (only those variables that intercorrelated are included), and it will be seen that the main clusters of variables are:

1 Preoccupation with thoughts of the deceased
  Clear visual memory of him
  Sense of his continued presence
  Tearfulness
  Illusions of the deceased (assessed only at the first interview)
2 Irritability and anger
  Restlessness
  Tension
  Social withdrawal (assessed only at the first interview)

These results indicate, then, that there are two main types of variable

Table 7 London Study: correlations (r) between mean year scores on psychological measures among twenty-two London widows

	Pre-occupation with thoughts of deceased	Clear visual memory	Sense of his presence	Tearfulness	Illusions of deceased	Irritability and anger	Restlessness	Tension	Social withdrawal	Numbness	Difficulty in accepting
Clear visual memory of him	0.73‡										
Sense of his continued presence	0.58†	0.56†									
Tearfulness	0.54†	0.38	0.42*								
Illusions of the deceased	−0.13	0.38	0.52*	0.34							
Irritability and anger	−0.05	−0.18	0.02	0.41	0.04						
Restlessness	0.18	−0.04	0.08	0.32	0.03	0.65‡					
Tension	0.15	0.18	0.10	0.43*	0.09	0.58†	0.83‡				
Social withdrawal	0.05	0.17	−0.13	0.20	−0.19	0.44*	0.10	0.12			
Numbness	−0.11	0.32	−0.14	−0.06	−0.15	−0.14	−0.03	−0.12	0.35		
Difficulty in accepting fact of loss	0.24	0.21	0.08	0.29	0.22	0.42*	0.42*	0.43*	0.36	−0.09	
Avoidance of reminders	0.44*	0.46*	0.29	0.07	0.24	−0.16	0.14	0.23	0.21	0.29	0.40

* Assessed only at first interview.   *p < 0.05   †p < 0.01   ‡p < 0.001 (using t test)

that go together and create two general trends of reaction to bereavement. The implications are: (a) that these variables are meaningfully related to one another; and (b) that individuals who show a feature of either cluster are also likely to show the other features of that cluster.

On the face of it, the mode of response represented by the features in the first list is passive and oriented towards the dead husband. Preoccupation with thoughts of reunion alternate with painful pining and tearfulness. One can characterize this as a reaction of yearning for the past (see Chapter 4). The second mode of response is more active and more self-oriented. Here the survivor, instead of calling to the lost person to return, angrily turns to face a potentially hostile world. This type of response is described in Chapter 6.

Despite what has been said it should be remembered that components of both these modes of reaction are found in most bereaved people; the passive and active styles represent tendencies rather than discrete types of response. It should be noted, further, that defensive reactions such as 'numbness', 'difficulty in accepting the fact of loss', and 'avoidance of reminders' were not significantly intercorrelated, hence there is no support from this study for the notion of a general factor of 'defensiveness'.

10. Figure 3 is based upon findings in successive interviews of the London Study. It will be seen that, whereas there is a gradual decline, throughout the year, in the number of widows who were tearful at interview and in the number who reported or showed marked preoccupation with thoughts of the dead spouse, there is an increase in the number who said that they had clear visual memories of their dead husband (Parkes, 1970).

11. The Bethlem Study was carried out on twenty-one patients (eighteen in-patients and three out-patients) brought to my attention by staff of the Bethlem Royal and Maudsley Hospitals and interviewed by me during 1958–60. They had all developed a mental illness within six months of the death of a spouse, child, parent, or sibling. A further six bereaved patients were excluded because they did not wish to participate or were too ill to give an account of their reaction to bereavement.

At the interview the patient was encouraged to talk freely about the dead person and the bereavement, and questions were asked, when necessary, to supplement the information given. The presence or

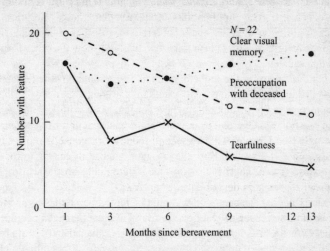

Figure 3 Widows under sixty-five years of age showing or reporting preoccupation with the deceased, clear visual memory of him, and tearfulness, over the first thirteen months of bereavement

absence of some common features of grief was assessed by means of a check-list.

For purposes of comparison, Table 8 shows the incidence of these features as found in some studies of 'normal' (unselected) widows and in fourteen of the Bethlem Study patients. (These fourteen were women under sixty years of age. The remaining seven patients – three men under sixty and three women and one man over sixty – were not included in the comparative sample because of the problem of matching.) The most striking finding is that ideas of guilt or self-reproach were reported by 79 per cent of the psychiatric population but by only 0–18 per cent of the unselected widows. Although the psychiatric sample is small, the incidence of guilt or self-reproach in this group was significantly greater than that reported by Marris ($\chi^2 =$ 13.7, 1 d.f., $p < 0.001$). The disturbed patients also showed a greater tendency towards social withdrawal (Parkes, 1965).

12. The tape-recorded interviews in the Harvard Study were rated independently by two coders who made quantitative assessments of psychological and social indices of adjustment. Only assessments that were reliably coded were used in the analysis of data.

Table 8 *Incidence of some common features of grief in five studies of young and middle-aged bereaved women*

Features of grief	Hobson (1964) Unselected UK widows aged < 60 N = 40	Yamamoto et al. (1969) Japanese Motor accident widows aged < 55 N = 20	Marris (1958) Unselected UK widows aged < 60 N = 72	Parkes (1970) (London Study)[a] Unselected UK widows aged < 65 N = 22	Parkes (1965) (Bethlem Study) Bereaved psychiatric patients (women) aged < 60 N = 14
Depression/ anxiety	–	85	100	85	100
Apathy	73	55	61	–	50
Insomnia	88	70	79	45	71
Sense of presence of the deceased	80	90	50	55	50
Attempts to avoid reminders	30	55	18	–	36
Difficulty in accepting fact of loss	50	60	23	59	79
Ideas of guilt or self-reproach	–	0	11	18	79
Blames others	35	60	15	45	43
Social withdrawal	48	–	38	36	64

[a] The figures given here for the London Study relate to the presence of these features a year after bereavement; they differ, therefore, from the figures given in Chapter 3 (pp. 35–6), which refer to the first month of bereavement.

The outcome measure was a combination of scores on psychological, social, and physical adjustment fourteen months after bereavement. The variables shown in Table 9 each correlated at the stated level with outcome.

The principal conclusions to be drawn from this study are that intense grief, anger, or self-reproach expressed shortly after bereavement, particularly if it is not declining in intensity within six weeks, predicts poor outcome a year later; and that poverty, low social class, a sudden or unexpected death, and other life crises, especially if they are associated with difficulties in the marital relationship, also predict a poor outcome.

In general, these findings confirm those of other studies carried out in the United States and Britain.

Table 9 *Harvard Study: variables that predicted poor outcome among sixty-eight young American widows and widowers*

	r	p
DEMOGRAPHIC AND OTHER ANTECEDENT VARIABLES		
Low weekly income	0.44	< 0.01
Low social class	0.28	< 0.05
Number of sisters	0.26	< 0.05
Cause of death not cancer	0.27	< 0.05
Short duration of terminal illness	0.29	< 0.05
No opportunity to discuss death with spouse	0.25	< 0.05
Life crises affecting respondent:		
Pregnancy	0.25	< 0.05
Divorce	0.27	< 0.05
Infidelity	0.44	< 0.01
Job loss	0.25	< 0.05
PSYCHOLOGICAL FACTORS ASSESSED THREE WEEKS AFTER BEREAVEMENT		
Overall anxiety	0.38	< 0.01
Yearning for the deceased	0.32	< 0.01
Respondent feels isolated, nobody understands or cares	0.32	< 0.01
Respondent would welcome own death	0.32	< 0.01
Respondent agrees with the following feelings:		
'I feel empty'	0.30	< 0.01
'I spend a lot of time thinking about him/her'	0.30	< 0.05
'What will I do now?'	0.30	< 0.05
'I'm worried I might have a nervous breakdown'	0.28	< 0.05
'It's not real'	0.25	< 0.05
'I still act at times as though he/she were alive'	0.25	< 0.05
'I wouldn't care if I died tomorrow'	0.29	< 0.05
'I can't get myself to do things'	0.30	< 0.05
Disturbance score	0.40	< 0.01
Overall negative affect	0.45	< 0.01

	r	p
PSYCHOLOGICAL FACTORS ASSESSED SIX WEEKS AFTER BEREAVEMENT		
Overall anxiety	0.51	< 0.01
External anxiety (worry)	0.35	< 0.01
Overall hostility	0.27	< 0.05
Death still not fully accepted	0.33	< 0.01
Respondent would welcome own death	0.36	< 0.01
Negative attitude to remarriage	0.30	< 0.05
Respondent agrees with the following feelings:		
'I can't stand being alone'	0.35	< 0.01
'I have no interest in anything'	0.32	< 0.01
'Underneath I guess I'm depressed'	0.30	< 0.05
'I think you never get over it'	0.33	< 0.05
'I think about him/her almost all the time'	0.25	< 0.05
'I feel so scared'	0.29	< 0.05
'I have to fight the feeling of being useless'	0.25	< 0.05
Respondent disagrees that:		
'I'm beginning to feel like myself again'	0.31	< 0.05
Drinking more alcohol than before bereavement	0.26	< 0.05
Overall negative affect	0.47	< 0.01

The above results were obtained from forty-nine widows and nineteen widowers. Differences were observed, however, between the responses of the two sexes in the early interviews. Women expressed much more overt anger and bitterness than men ($p < 0.0001$ at one month and $p = 0.018$ at three months after bereavement) and they cried more at interview (at one month $p = 0.17$, at three months $p = 0.03$). By the third month, men were more likely to say that the pain of grief had diminished ($p = 0.005$), they were generally less anxious ($p = 0.036$), and they were more willing than women to consider the possibility of remarriage ($p = 0.006$).

There were no significant differences between the sexes, however, on any of eight outcome scores a year after bereavement, and when subgroups were followed up two to four years after bereavement, it was the women who had returned to levels of adjustment equivalent to married women of the same age, whereas the men were still significantly worse adjusted than married male controls. It seems, therefore, that while overt manifestations of grief were more pronounced in women than men during the first year of bereavement, it was the women who were the first to recover from bereavement (Parkes and Weiss, 1983).

13. The Harvard Study was confined to a young age-group (widows and widowers under forty-five). Respondents were subdivided into those who had only a short time in which to prepare themselves for the death (less than two weeks' warning coupled with a terminal incapacity in the spouse of less than three days) and those who had a longer time (a terminal incapacity of more than three days, whatever the period of warning).

During the first month of bereavement short preparation for death was significantly related to an immediate reaction of disbelief, feelings of anxiety, self-reproach, and depression, as revealed by the fact that 46 per cent of those who had had little time to prepare (compared with 15 per cent of those who had had some time) said that they did not care whether they lived or died, or expressed some positive wish for death.

A year later, the twenty-three who had had the least opportunity to prepare for bereavement continued to be more pessimistic about the future, more inclined to tearfulness, and more anxious and depressed than the forty-five who had had a longer time to prepare themselves. Only three (13 per cent) of the group who had had little opportunity to prepare themselves were rated as having a good overall outcome compared with twenty-six (59 per cent) of the group who had had time to prepare ($p < 0.001$) (Parkes, 1972).

14. Widows in the London Study were asked to rate the frequency of quarrels with their spouse on a four-point scale ('usually', 'frequently', 'occasionally', 'never'). Half admitted that they did quarrel, and a score of quarrelling derived from this scale was significantly related to three of the mean year scores:

tension as observed at interview : $rr = 0.54, p < 0.02$
ideas of guilt or self-reproach   : $rr = 0.51, p < 0.05$
number of physical symptoms
   from check-list   : $rr = 0.60, p < 0.01$

and also to:

few illusions of the dead person
   during the first month   : $rr = 0.48, p < 0.05$
social isolation a year after
   bereavement   : $rr = 0.59, p < 0.01$

The assessment of social isolation differed from that of social withdrawal (included in Tables 7 and 8) in that there was no attempt to discriminate as to the agency – the widow herself or other people – that brought it about. Likewise, no attempt was made to establish who was to blame for quarrels.

15. A score based on the number of major stresses that the London widows reported they had undergone during the two years prior to bereavement was correlated with the mean year scores and outcome scores as in section 9 above. Two significant correlations were obtained:

ideas of guilt or self-reproach : $rr = 0.42$, $p < 0.05$
overall outcome : $rr = 0.46$, $p < 0.05$

This would suggest that those who report a large number of stressors get on less well after bereavement than those who do not. However, since we had no means of checking the reliability of the retrospective information given, a causal connection between stress and poor outcome was not proved in these cases.

16. Previous studies had shown that patients referred to me for the treatment of psychiatric problems after bereavement had either suffered traumatic types of loss (multiple or sudden deaths) or were vulnerable people in terms of lack of trust in themselves and/or others. In order to learn more about the vulnerable group I developed a questionnaire which, over several years, was sent to all patients referred to my psychiatric clinic at the Royal London Hospital. They were requested to fill it in and bring it with them to their first appointment with me. In this way I hoped to obtain information that would be unbiased by any preconceptions that I might have. Sixty bereaved patients completed the questionnaire a second time several months after the end of treatment. This enabled me to check the reliability of questions about the past and to obtain follow-up data concerning any changes that might have occurred in their current problems and symptoms.

The questionnaire comprised 31 questions about each parent (62 in all), 7 about events and circumstances occurring during the patient's childhood, 28 about the patient's view of themselves as a child, 22 about events and circumstances in adult life, 6 about recent losses and the reaction to these, and 19 about current problems and symptoms.

Adding together the answers to the 62 questions about parents it was possible to obtain a measure of negative parental influences likely to affect the child. When these were plotted against the answers to the 28 questions about childhood vulnerability a clear association emerged. This was not particularly surprising. Bearing in mind the fact that only a few of these patients had suffered the death of a parent, what came as more of a surprise was the association between parental influences and the intensity of emotional disturbance, particularly anxiety, panic and depression, reported at the current time. This is shown in Figure 4.

Looking more closely at the group of patients who had suffered separation from their parents during childhood it was clear that they had been unhappy children, timid, insecure, and intolerant of separation throughout their childhood. A score reflecting the number and duration of separations predicted their current problem score, as seen in Figure 5.

Focusing on parental influences likely to evoke fear in the child (e.g., anxious parents, rejection or over-protection by parents, parental conflict, and alcohol abuse), these were associated with self-reports of fear in childhood which, in turn, was associated with current symptoms of high anxiety and tendency to panic, as shown in Figure 6.

These influences did not predict depression but another constellation that did was a group of questions thought likely to indicate parental influences which would evoke feelings of helplessness in the child (e.g., the death of a parent before the patient reached seventeen years of age,

Figure 4 Negative parental influences and number of problems/symptoms after bereavement in adult life

Figure 5 Separation from parents in childhood and number of problems/ symptoms after bereavement in adult life

Figure 6 Childhood fears and types of symptom/problem arising after bereavement in adult life

mother inconsistently available or responsive, parents repeatedly rebuffed or scoffed at the child). A majority of those with one or more predictors of helplessness said that they were now 'very depressed' (see Table 10).

These findings confirm the theory of learned helplessness and depression propounded by Seligman (1975). Further details of these studies have been published in Parkes, 1991a and 1995a.

Table 10 *Predictors of helplessness and depression*

	Very depressed n	Not depressed n
One or more predictors of helplessness	15	8
None	10	21

Chi-squared with Yates' Correction = 5.8. 1 d.f., *p* less than 0.05

17. Figure 7. shows changes in the expression of overall emotional disturbance (anxiety/depression) during the first three months of bereavement in twenty-five London widows. (Note that three of these widows – a, b, and c – were not included in the final analysis of the study, whose findings have been reported and discussed elsewhere in the book, because they moved away and I was not able to obtain all the interviews necessary for the full investigation.)

Intensity of emotional disturbance was scored on a five-point scale during interviews at the end of the first and third months of bereavement. Retrospective estimates were then made of the amount of overall upset week by week during the first month and monthly thereafter, based on the widows' own accounts of changes in their feelings.

Emotional upset during the first week of bereavement correlated -0.8 with emotional upset three months later ($p < 0.01$) (Parkes, 1970).

Similar findings come from a study by Levy *et al.* (1994) who found that, although there was a general decline in the mean scores of distress over the first eighteen months after bereavement, 22 per cent of their sample of widow(er)s of patients who died from cancer in the Baltimore area experienced initial low levels of distress followed by an *increase* across the eighteen months. This applied to both subjective stress (as measured by the Impact of Events Intrusion Scale) and depression (as measured by the Center for Epidemiological Studies Depression Scale – CES-D).

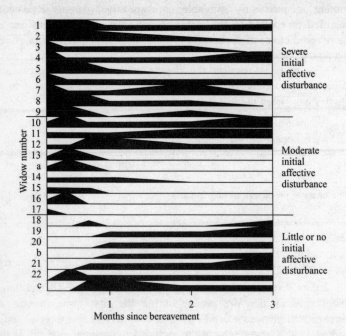

Figure 7 Severity of emotional disturbance in twenty-five widows during the first three months of bereavement

18. Cameron and Parkes (1983) compared the reactions to bereavement of relatives of cancer patients who had died in two different types of ward in the same hospital in Montreal. One ward, the Palliative Care Unit (PCU), provides hospice-type care to patients and their families on the ward and in their homes; one or two visits and a similar number of telephone calls are made after bereavement. The comparison group were relatives of patients who had died on other wards in the Royal Victoria Hospital. They were matched for relationship to the dead person, sex, and whether living alone or with others.

Twenty people in each group were interviewed by telephone one year and two weeks after bereavement, using a standard series of questions. The PCU group reported a mean of 4.5 symptoms and the comparison group fourteen symptoms each ($p < 0.002$).

Table 11 shows the incidence of eighteen symptoms and features of grief in the two groups of relatives. It will be seen that the largest

Table 11 *Incidence of eighteen symptoms and features of grief in twenty Palliative Care Unit (PCU) relatives and twenty control relatives*

	PCU	Controls
1. Stress symptoms		
Has not recovered lost appetite	1	5
Sleep worse since bereavement	13*	19*
Using sleeping pills since bereavement	4	10
Using tranquillizers since bereavement	1**	9**
Health, deteriorated at bereavement and not improved	8	15
2. Psychological stress reactions		
Is hyperactive	2	5
Is unable to carry out everyday responsibilities	0	3
Experiences panic attacks	0	1
Death wish and suicidal ideation	2	4
Is socially withdrawn	3	7
Tearfulness	8	11
3. Persisting features of grief		
Pining and seeking	5	10
Sense of presence of dead person	5	9
Irritability and anger	1*	17*
Is hostile towards others	0**	10**
Guilt	2	7
Feels uncomfortable with reminders	1	4
Believes to have developed symptoms of the dead person	0	2

*$p < 0.05$ **$p < 0.01$

difference between the two groups lay in the high incidence of irritability, anger, and hostility to others reported by the comparison group. This group also consumed more tranquillizers and suffered more disturbances of sleep than the PCU group. Half of the comparison group (and none of the PCU group) referred to distressing memories of the dead person's unrelieved pain as the worst thing they had to bear. They had often received little warning that death was imminent and one gets the impression that communication between the relative and the staff was poor.

Overall, this study provides ample confirmation of the value of 'hospice' care and some evidence that it was the adequacy of pain relief for the patient and communication and support to the family which explains this.

19. Raphael (1977) compared a 'low risk' group with two groups of 'high risk' widows who had been assigned at random into intervention and control groups. Her methods of risk assessment were similar to my own but with the addition of measures of concurrent life crises and assessments of the extent to which family and friends were perceived as unsupportive. Counselling was provided by Raphael herself, an experienced psychiatrist with considerable knowledge of bereavement. She set out to encourage the expression of grief, to help the respondent to review aspects of the lost relationship and to deal with any specific problems which were special to each person. This took place in the client's home and was limited to the first three months of bereavement. Outcome was measured by means of a postal check-list of symptoms thirteen months after death. 91 per cent of these were returned.

The overall outcome in the three groups is shown in Figure 8. Results are very similar to my own and there is a significant difference between helped and unhelped groups ($p < 0.02$). The subgroup which benefited

Figure 8 Proportion in each group with poor outcome (Raphael, 1977)

most from counselling were the widows and widowers who had perceived their families and friends as unsupportive ($p < 0.001$).

20. Widows and widowers of 164 patients who died in St. Christopher's Hospice were divided into three:

a a low risk group of eighty-five;
b a high risk intervention group of twenty-eight;
c a high risk control group of twenty-nine.

(There were also twenty-two patients whom the staff regarded as being in urgent need; they are not included.)

The intervention group were visited in their homes by volunteer counsellors under my supervision. The help given varied from case to case but seldom involved more than three to four visits. These visits, though few in number, were often very lengthy. It was not unusual for them to last for one or two hours.

The control group were not offered help and in fact none of them asked for help from the Hospice.

About twenty months after bereavement all three groups were followed up by a research interviewer who administered a shortened version of the Health Questionnaire which had been used in the Harvard Bereavement Study.

Figure 9 gives the overall outcome in the three groups. It shows first that the predictive questionnaire did, in fact, predict outcome, since the high risk control group did have a poorer outcome than the low risk group ($p < 0.02$); second, that the intervention was successful in that the intervention group had a better outcome than the control group ($p < 0.03$). In fact it appears that counselling had the effect of improving the adjustment of the high risk group to about the same level as that of the low risk group. It is worth noting that no differences between supported and unsupported groups were found during the first few months of the project when our counsellors were still very inexperienced. The above figures refer to results obtained from experienced counsellors (Parkes, 1981).

Figure 9 Mean outcome scores of each group (Parkes, 1981)

SOME NATIONAL UK ORGANIZATIONS OFFERING HELP TO THE BEREAVED

The Compassionate Friends, 53 North Street, Bristol BS3 1EN. Tel. 01179 539 639.

Cot Death Help Line 0171 235 1721.

Cruse – Bereavement Care, Cruse House, 126 Sheen Road, Richmond, Surrey TW9 1UR. Tel. 0181 940 4818 (Fax 7638). Help line 0181 332 7227.

The Foundation for the Study of Infant Deaths, 14 Halkin Street, London SW1X 7DP. Tel. 0171 235 0965.

The Lesbian and Gay Bereavement Project, Vaughan M. Williams Centre, Colindale Hospital, London NW9 5HG. Tel. 0181 200 0511 or 0181 455 8894 (evenings).

The London Association of Bereavement Services, 356 Holloway Road, London N7 6PN. Tel. 0171 700 8134 (Fax 8146).

The Miscarriages Association, c/o Clayton Hospital, Northgate, Wakefield, West Yorkshire WF1 3JS. Tel. 0192 420 0799.

The National Association of Bereavement Services, 122 Whitechapel High Street, London E1 7PT. Tel. 0171 247 0617 Referrals 0171 247 1080.

The Samaritans, 10 The Grove, Slough SL1 1QP. Tel. 0345 909090 or 0171 734 2800 (London).

Support after Murder and Manslaughter, Cranmer House, 39 Brixton Road, London SW9 6DZ. Tel. 0171 735 3838 (Fax 3900).

NOTES

1 THE COST OF COMMITMENT

1 The following account of the nature of the child's tie to its mother derives from the work of Bowlby, whose book *Attachment* (1969) gives a fuller exposition of the origins of love ties.

2 THE BROKEN HEART

1 Under the National Health Service each member of the British population is registered with a general practitioner who keeps a medical record on an envelope-card designed for the purpose. Most wives are registered with the same GP as their husbands.

3 ALARM

No notes.

4 SEARCHING

1 The term was coined by Meyer-Holzapel (1940) to emphasize that attachment figures evoke many of the same behavioural responses as does 'home'. In fact, the process by which a young child returns to its mother whenever she moves away could well be termed 'homing'.
2 I am indebted to Professor John Romano for permission to include this case.
3 Another reason for staying close to home was implied earlier in this chapter, namely the characteristic of home valency. Individuals who have lost one source of emotional security are likely to remain near or return to other havens of safety, be they people or places to which they are attached.
4 It obviously helps if the animal knows what its 'goal' is, but it is not necessarily the case. The robin who feels impelled to collect pieces of dead grass and fly with them to a tree may have no idea that it is building a nest.
5 The term 'frustration' can be used to indicate both the situation of a person or animal whose appetitive behaviour is balked and the subjective discomfort to which this characteristically gives rise.

5 MITIGATION

No notes.

6 ANGER AND GUILT

1 Adulation seemed to be a means of appeasing these powerful people and was, if anything, commoner than its opposite – punishment by denigration.

7 GAINING A NEW IDENTITY

1 Gardner Murphy (1958) has described the several boundaries that exist between the person and the world. Even the physical boundary between the body and its environment is not as clear cut as it seems to be: 'Oxygen in the red cells can be regarded either as part of us or of our environment', and those aspects of a response which are properly called personal and 'those aspects which are properly anchored in the environment come to meet one another in one organized field dynamic'. Self-awareness, says Murphy, is the way in which individuals experience the barriers around them, but 'the contours of the self are often blurred, and the distinction between the self and the non-self made indistinct'.

2 Carl Rogers (1961) makes it the aim of psychotherapy to help the patient to discover his 'real self' by stripping away the masks that hide it. His account of this psychological fiction, however, suggests that for him the 'real' person is that identity which is most appropriate to the potentialities of the individual. The awareness of a 'fit' between form and function reassures people and strengthens them in their belief that they have discovered the authentic, the 'real' self. Conversely, a lack of 'fit' is experienced as 'unreal' or false.

3 To some extent we choose where we place the boundaries around ourselves. In a similar way we choose where to place our territorial boundaries and how permeable we make them. It is in accord with the view presented here to regard territory as an extension of the self. It is easier to share territory, however, than it is to share more intimate parts of the self.

4 Doctors, aware of the psychological injury they are inflicting, normally disclose bad news in hushed tones as if they can thereby minimize the mutilation.

8 ATYPICAL GRIEF

1 'Grief' is taken to imply the experience of deep or violent sorrow whereas 'mourning' implies the expression of sorrow.

2 I use the term 'identification phenomena' for those features of the reaction to bereavement which, rightly or wrongly, seem to indicate identification with the deceased. 'Identification symptoms' I reserve for hypochondriacal symptoms such as are described above. Thus 'identification symptoms' are a type of 'identification phenomenon'.

9 RELATIONSHIP, GENDER AND AGE

No notes.

10 MODE OF DEATH

1 For a review of fifty-four papers on this complex topic see Bergeron and Handley (1992).

11 PERSONAL VULNERABILITY

1 Psychoanalysts such as Rochlin (1965) and Erikson (1950) have written at length about the roots of trust and self-esteem, but it would take us beyond the scope of this book to attempt a comprehensive review of this field.

2 The assumed link between the 'breakdown' of emotional control and mental illness – the nervous 'breakdown' – reflects the contemporary fear of strong emotion. Because of their previous history this group had special grounds for fearing such an outcome. It seems reasonable to suppose that inability to handle emotion was responsible for the illnesses these widows reported.

12 HELPING THE BEREAVED I: GENERAL PRINCIPLES

1 The encyclical of Pope Pius XII delivered in September 1957 to the World Federation of Family Organizations points out that there is nothing ignoble in tears and that the widow should withdraw from the activities of the world for a 'reasonable period of mourning'. A note on this encyclical is given by Miller (1961).

2 It is not unknown for people who have been unable to master feelings of grief after a loss to attempt to do so by offering help to other bereaved people. Clearly these helpers are not to blame for their own difficulties, but it seems unlikely that they will succeed in reassuring the newly bereaved that it is 'safe' to grieve.

13 HELPING THE BEREAVED II: TYPES OF HEALTH

1 I use the term 'drugs' here to mean any substance taken for the relief of psychological symptoms. There was no indication that dangerous drugs such as heroin or morphine were taken by the widows or widowers in any of my studies; nor were marijuana or hashish a problem.

14 REACTIONS TO OTHER TYPES OF LOSS

No notes.

REFERENCES

ABLON, J. (1973). 'Reactions of Samoan Burns Patients and Families to Severe Burns'. *Social Science and Medicine*, 7: 167–78

ABRAHAM, K. (1924). 'A Short Study of the Development of the Libido'. In Abraham, *Selected Papers on Psychoanalysis*. London: Hogarth, 1927, new edition, 1949; New York: Basic Books, 1953

ADAMOWSKI, K., DICKINSON, G., WIETZMAN, B., ROESSLER, C., and CARTER-SNELL, C. (1993). 'Sudden Unexpected Death in the Emergency Department: Caring for the Survivors'. *Canadian Medical Association Journal*, 149(10): 1445–51

AINSWORTH, M. D. and WITTIG, B. A. (1969). 'Attachment and Exploratory Behaviour of One-year-olds in a Strange Situation'. In B. Foss (ed.), *Determinants of Infant Behaviour*, vol. 4. London: Methuen

ALDRICH, C. K. and MENDKOFF, E. (1963). 'Relocation of the Aged and Disabled: A Mortality Study'. *Journal of the American Geriatrics Society*, 11: 185

ANDERSON, C. (1949). 'Aspects of Pathological Grief and Mourning'. *International Journal of Psycho-Analysis*, 30: 48

AUSTIN, D. and LENNINGS, C. J. (1993). 'Grief and Religious Belief. Does Belief Moderate Depression?' *Death Studies*, 17: 487–96

BARNES, D. (1988). 'Previous Losses: Forgotten but not Resolved'. In J. Morgan (ed.), *Bereavement: Helping the Survivors*. Ontario: King's College.

BARRY, H. JR., JARRY, H. III, and LINDEMANN, E. (1965). 'Dependency in Adult Patients Following Early Maternal Bereavement'. *Journal of Nervous and Mental Disease*, 140(3): 196

BARTROP, R., LUCKHURST, E., LAZARUS, L., KILOH, L. G., and PERRY, R. (1977). 'Depressed Lymphocyte Function after Bereavement'. *Lancet*, 1: 834–6

BASS, D. M. and BOWMAN, K. (1990) 'The Transition from Caring to Bereavement: the Relationship of Care-related Strain and Adjustment to Death'. *Gerontologist*, 30(1): 35–42

241

BECK, F. (1966). *The Diary of a Widow: Rebuilding a Family after the Funeral*. Boston: Beacon

BECKWITH, B. E., BECKWITH, S. K., GRAY, T. L., MICSKO, M. M., HOLM, J. E., PLUMMER, V. H., and FLAA, S. L. (1990). 'Identification of Spouses at High Risk during Bereavement: A Preliminary Assessment of Parkes and Weiss' Risk Index'. *Hospice Journal*, 6(3): 35–46

BERGERON, J. P. and HANDLEY, P. R. (1992). 'Bibliography on AIDS-related Bereavement and Grief'. *Death Studies*, 16(3): 247–67

BIRNBAUM, A. (1994). 'Haven, Hugs and Bugs: An Innovative Multiple-family Weekend Intervention for Bereaved Children Adolescents and Adults'. Paper read at 4th International Conference on Grief and Bereavement in Contemporary Society, Stockholm, 12–16 June. Abstract from Swedish Association for Mental Health

BIRTCHNELL, J. (1975a). 'The Personality Characteristics of Early-Bereaved Psychiatric Patients'. *Social Psychiatry*, 10: 97–103

—— (1975b). 'Psychiatric Breakdown Following Recent Parent Death'. *British Journal of Medical Psychology*, 48: 379–90

BLACK, D. and URBANOWICZ, M. A. (1987). 'Family Intervention with Bereaved Children'. In J. E. Stevenson (ed.), *Recent Research in Developmental Psychology* Oxford: Pergamon.

BOHANNON, J. R. (1991). 'Religiosity Related to Grief Levels of bereaved Mothers and Fathers'. *Omega* 23(2): 153

BOJANOVSKY, J. (1980). 'Wann droht der Selbstmord bei Verwitweten?' *Schweitzer Archiv. Neurologische Neurochirurgie und Psvchiatrie*, 127: 99–103

BONNANO, G. A. (1994). 'The Consequences of Emotional Avoidance and Emotional Inhibition during Bereavement'. Paper read at the 4th International Conference on Grief and Bereavement in Contemporary Society, Stockholm, 12–16 June

BORNSTEIN, P. E., CLAYTON, P. J., HALIKAS, J. A., MAURICE, W. L., and ROBINS, E. (1973). 'The depression of widowhood at three months'. *British Journal of Psychiatry*, 122: 561–6

BOWLBY, J. (1951). *Maternal Care and Mental Health*. WHO Monograph 2

—— (1953) *Child Care and the Growth of Love*. London: Pelican

—— (1961). 'Processes of Mourning'. *International Journal of Psycho-Analysis*, 44: 317

—— (1963). 'Pathological Mourning and Childhood Mourning'. *Journal of the American Psychoanalytic Association*, 11: 500

—— (1969). *Attachment and Loss*. Vol. 1, *Attachment*; vol. 2, *Separation: Anxiety and Anger* (1973); vol. 3, *Loss: Sadness and Depression* (1980). London: Hogarth; New York: Basic Books

BOWLBY, J. and PARKES, C. M. (1970). 'Separation and Loss within the Family'. In *The Child in his Family*, (ed.) E. J. Anthony. New York: Wiley

REFERENCES

BOWLING, A. (1988). 'Who dies after Widow(er)hood? A Discriminant Analysis.' *Omega*, 19: 135

BOWMAN, L. (1959). *The American Funeral*. Washington DC: Public Affairs Press

BRABANT, S., FORSYTH, C. J. and MELANCON, C. (1992). 'Grieving Men: Thoughts, Feelings and Behaviour following the Death of Wives'. *Hospital Journal*, 8(4): 33–47

BREUER, J. and FREUD, S. (1893). 'On the Psychical Mechanisms of Hysterical Phenomena: A Preliminary Communication'. Standard Edition of *The Complete Psychological Works of Sigmund Freud*, vol. 2. London: Hogarth

BRIGHT, R. (1986). 'Grieving: A Handbook for Those who Care'. St Louis, Mo: MMB Music Inc.

BROWN, G. W. and HARRIS, T. (1978). *Social Origins of Depression: A Study of Psychiatric Disorder in Women*. London: Tavistock

BROWNSTEIN, M. (1992). 'Contacting the Family after a Suicide'. *Canadian Journal of Psychiatry*, 37(3): 208–12

BUNCH, J. (1972). 'Recent Bereavement in Relation to Suicide'. *Journal of Psychosomatic Research*, 37(3): 208–12

BUNCH, J., BARRACLOUGH, B., NELSON, B., and SAINSBURY, P. (1971). 'Suicide Following the Death of Parents'. *Social Psychiatry*, 6: 193–9

BURGOINE, E. (1988). 'A Cross-cultural Comparison of Bereavement among Widows in New Providence, Bahamas and London, England'. Paper read at International Conference on Grief and Bereavement in Contemporary Society, London, July 12–15

CAIN, A. C. (1966). 'The Legacy of Suicide: Observations on the Pathogenic Impact of Suicide upon Marital Partners'. *Psychiatry*, 29: 26–8

CALABRESE, J. R., KLING, A. and GOLD, P. W. (1987). 'Alterations in Immuno-competence during Stress, Bereavement and Depression: Focus on Neuro-endocrine Regulation'. *American Journal of Psychiatry*, 144: 1123–34

CAMERON, J. and PARKES, C. M. (1983). 'Terminal Care: Evaluation of Effects on Surviving Family of Care Before and After Bereavement'. *Postgraduate Medical Journal*, 59: 73–8

CANNON, W. B. (1929). *Bodily Changes in Pain, Hunger, Fear and Rage*. Second edition. London and New York: Appleton

CAPLAN, G. (1961). *An Approach to Community Mental Health*. London: Tavistock

—— (1964). *Principles of Preventive Psychiatry*. New York: Basic Books; London: Tavistock

CATLIN, G. (1993). 'The Role of Culture in Grief'. *Journal of Social Psychology*, 133: 173–89

CERNEY, M. S. (1985). 'Imagery and Grief Work'. In *Psychotherapy and the Grieving Patient* (ed. E. M. Stern). New York and London: Harrington Park

CHAMBERS, W. N. and REISER, M. J. (1953). 'Emotional Stress in the Precipitation of Congestive Cardiac Failure'. *Psychosomatic Medicine*, 15: 38–50

CLAYTON, P. J. (1980). 'Bereavement and Its Management'. In E. S. Paykel *et al.*, *Handbook of Affective Disorders*. Edinburgh: Churchill

CLAYTON, P., DESMARAIS, L., and WINOKUR, G. (1968). 'A Study of Normal Bereavement'. *American Journal of Psychiatry*, 125: 168

CLAYTON, P. J., HALIKAS, J. A., and MAURICE, W. L. (1972). 'The Depression of Widowhood'. *British Journal of Psychiatry*, 120: 71–8

CLAYTON, P. J., HERJANIC, M., MURPHY, G. E., and WOODRUFF, R. A. (1974). 'Mourning and Depression: Their Similarities and Differences'. *Canadian Psychiatric Association Journal*, 79: 309–12

CLEGG, F. (1988). 'Grief and Loss in Elderly People in a Psychiatric Setting'. Ch. in *Grief and Mourning in Contemporary Society*, vol 1, *Psychodynamics* (ed. E. Chigier). London and Tel Aviv: Freund

CLEIREN, M. P. H. D. (1992). *Bereavement and Adaptation: A Comparative Study of the Aftermath of Death*. Washington, Philadelphia and London: Hemisphere

COCHRANE, A. L. (1936). 'A Little Widow is a Dangerous Thing'. *International Journal of Psycho-Analysis*, 17: 494

COOLEY, C. H. (1909). *Social Organization*. New York: Scribner

COOPER, C. L. and FARRAGHER, E.B. (1993). 'Psychosocial Stress and Breast Cancer: The Inter-relationship between Stress Events, Coping Strategies and Personality'. *Psychological Medicine*, 23(3): 653–62

COTTINGTON, E. M., MATTHEW, K. A., TALBOTT, E., and KULLER, L. H. (1980). 'Environmental Events Preceding Sudden Death in Women'. *Psychosomatic Medicine*, 42: 567–74

DALGARD, O., BJORK, S., and TAMBS, K. (1994). 'Social Supports, Negative Life Events and Mental Health'. *British Journal of Psychiatry*, 166: 29

DARWIN, C. (1872). *The Expression of the Emotions in Man and Animals*. London: Murray

DEMBO, T., LADIEU-LEVITON, G., and WRIGHT, B. A. (1952). 'Acceptance of Loss – Amputation'. In J. F. Garret (ed.), *Psychological Aspects of Physical Disabilities*. Washington DC: US Government Printing Office

DILLENBERGER, K. (1992) *Violent Bereavement: Widows in Northern Ireland*. Aldershot, Brookfield, Hong Kong, Singapore and Sidney: Avebury

DOKA, K. (ed.) (1989). *Disenfranchised Grief*. Lexington, Mass.: Lexington Books

DUKE, D. M. (1980). 'A Study of the Effects of Bereavement in a Sample of Those Bereaved in the Area Covered by Horton Parish, South Shields'. Thesis submitted for M.Phil. Degree (CNAA). *Unpublished*

DURAN, A., TURNER, C. W. and LUND, D. A. (1989). 'Social Support, Perceived Stress and Depression following the Death of a Spouse in Later Life'. In D. A. Lund (ed.), *Older Bereaved Spouses: Research with Practical Applications*, 69–78. New York: Hemisphere

ENGEL, G. (1971). 'Sudden and Rapid Death During Psychological Stress'. *Annals of Internal Medicine*, 74: 771–82

ERIKSON, E. H. (1950). *Childhood and Society.* New York: Norton; London: Imago, 1951; revised edition, New York: Norton, 1963

FAGIN, L. and LITTLE, M. (1984). *The Forsaken Families.* Harmondsworth: Penguin Books

FASCHINGBAUER, T. R. (1981). *Texas Revised Inventory of Grief Manual.* Houston, Texas: Honeycomb

FASCHINGBAUER, T. R., DE VAUL, R. A. and ZISOOK, S. (1977) 'Development of the Texas Inventory of Grief'. *American Journal of Psychiatry* 134: 696–8

FASCHINGBAUER, T. R., ZISOOK, S. and DEVAUL, R. D. (1987). 'The Texas Revised Inventory of Grief'. In S. Zisook (ed.), *Biopsychosocial Aspects of Bereavement* 111–25. Washington, DC

FENICHEL, O. (1948). *Psychoanalytic Theory of the Neuroses.* New York: Norton

FISHER, S. H. (1960). 'Psychiatric Considerations of Hand Disability'. *Archives of Physical Medicine and Rehabilitation*, 41: 62

FRANKEL, S. and SMITH, D. (1982). 'Conjugal Bereavement Among the Huli People of Papua, New Guinea'. *British Journal of Psychiatry*, 141: 302–5

FREUD, S. (1894). 'The Neuro-Psychoses of Defence'. *Standard Edition*, vol. 3

—— (1917). 'Mourning and Melancholia'. *Standard Edition*, vol. 14

—— (1923). 'The Ego and the Id'. *Standard Edition*, vol. 19

—— (1933). 'New Introductory Lectures on Psycho-analysis'. *Standard Edition*, vol. 22

FRIED, M. (1962). 'Grieving for a Lost Home'. In L. J. Duhl (ed.), *The Environment of the Metropolis.* New York: Basic Books

FROST, N. R. and CLAYTON, P. J. (1977). 'Bereavement and Psychiatric Hospitalization'. *Archives of General Psychiatry*, 34: 1172–5

FULTON, R. and GOTTESMAN, D. J. (1980). 'Anticipatory Grief: A Psychosocial Concept Reconsidered'. *British Journal of Psychiatry*, 137: 45–54

GASS, K. A. (1989). 'Appraisal, Coping and Resources: Markers Associated with the Health of Aged Widows and Widowers'. In D. A.

Lund (ed.), *Older Bereaved Spouses: Research with Practical Applications*. London and New York: Hemisphere

GAUTHIER, J. (1979). 'Graduated Self-Exposure in the Management of Grief'. *Behavioural Analysis and Modification*, 3: 202–8

GAUTHIER, J. and MARSHALL, W. L. (1977). 'Grief: A Cognitive-Behavioural Analysis'. *Cognitive Therapy and Research*, 1: 39–44

GERBER, I., RUSALEM, R., and HANNON, N. (1975). 'Anticipatory Grief and Aged Widows and Widowers'. *Journal of Gerontology*, 30: 225–9

GIOVINCO, G. and MONAHAN, J. (1994). 'Logotherapy and Bereavement: A Comparison of the Grief Response of Survivors of Individuals who Died of AIDS and Individuals who Died of Other Causes'. Paper read at 4th International Conference on Grief and Bereavement in Contemporary Society, Stockholm. Abstract from Swedish Association for Mental Health

GLICK, I., PARKES, C. M. and WEISS, R. S. (1974). *The First Year of Bereavement*. New York: London, Sidney and Toronto: Wiley Interscience

GOLAN, N. (1975). 'Wife to Widow to Woman'. *Social Work*, 20: 369–74

GOODALL, J. VAN L. (1971). *In the Shadow of Man*. New York: Houghton-Mifflin

GORER, G. (1965). *Death, Grief and Mourning in Contemporary Britain*. London: Cresset

GRINBERG, L. (1964). 'Two Kinds of Guilt: Their Relationship with Normal/Pathological Aspects of Mourning'. *International Journal of Psycho-Analysis*, 45: 366

HADFIELD, J. H. (1954). *Dreams and Nightmares*. Harmondsworth: Penguin Books

HAMLIN, M. and HAMMERSLEY, D. (1988). 'Benzodiazepines following bereavement'. Paper read to the International Conference on Grief and Bereavement in Contemporary Society, London, July 12–15, and reported in Jacobs (1993)

HAMNER, M. B. (1994). 'Endogenous Opioid Peptides in Grief and Traumatic Stress: Review and Hypothesis'. Paper read at 4th International Conference on Grief and Bereavement in Contemporary Society, Stockholm. Abstract from Swedish Association for Mental Health

HARARI, E. (1981). 'Pathological Grief in Doctors' Wives'. *British Medical Journal*, 3 January, 282: 33–4

HARLOW, S. D., GOLDBERG, E. L., and COMSTOCK, G. W. (1991). 'A Longitudinal Study of Risk Factors for Depressive Symptomatology in Elderly Widowed and Married Women'. *American Journal of Epidemiology*, 134(3): 526–38

HE, M. (1991). 'A Prospective Controlled Study of Psychosomatic and Immunologic Change in Recently Bereaved People'. *Chung-Hua-Shen-Ching-Ching-Shen-Ko-Tsa-Chih*, 24(2): 90–3

HEINICKE, C. and WESTHEIMER, I. (1966). *Brief Separations*. New York: International Universities Press; London: Longmans

HELSING, K. J., COMSTOCK, G. W., and SZKLO, M. (1982). 'Causes of Death in a Widowed Population'. *American Journal of Epidemiology*, 116: 524–32

HELSING, K. J., SZKLO, M., and COMSTOCK, G. W. (1981). 'Factors Associated with Mortality after Bereavement'. *American Journal of Public Health*, 71: 802–9

HINTON, J. (1967). *Dying*. Harmondsworth: Penguin Books

HOBSON, C. J. (1964). 'Widows of Blackton'. *New Society*, 24 September, 13

HOPMEYER, E. and WERK, A. (1994). 'A Comparative Study of Bereavement Groups'. *Death Studies*, 18, 243–56

HOROWITZ, M. J. (1976). *Stress Response Symptoms*. New York: Jason Aronson

HOROWITZ, M. J., BONNANO, G. K., and HOLEN, A. (1993). 'Pathological Grief: Diagnosis and Explanation'. *Psychosomatic Medicine*, 55: 260–73

HOROWITZ, M. J., WILNER, N., and ALVAREZ, W. (1979). 'Impact of Event Scale: a Measure of Subjective Stress'. *Psychosomatic Medicine*, 41, 209–18

HOROWITZ, M. J., WILNER, N., MARMAR, C., and KRUPNICK, J. (1980). 'Pathological Grief and the Activation of Latent Self Images'. *American Journal of Psychiatry*, 137: 1157–62

HOUGHTON, P. and HOUGHTON, D. (1977). *Unfocused Grief: Responses to Childlessness*. Birmingham: The Birmingham Settlement

IDE, B. A., TOBIAS, C., KAY, M. and GUERNSEY-DE-ZAPIEN, J. (1992). 'Pre-Bereavement Factors Related to Adjustment among Older Anglo- and Mexican–American Widows. Special Issue; Hispanic Age and Mental Health'. *Clinical Gerontologist*, 11(3): 75–91

ILLICH, I. (1977). *Medical Nemesis*. Harmondsworth: Penguin Books

IRWIN, M. R. and WEINER, H. (1987). 'Depressive Symptoms and Immune Function during Bereavement'. In Zisook (ed.), *Biopsychosocial Aspects of Bereavement*. Washington DC: American Psychiatric Press

JACOBS, S. (1993). *Pathologic Grief: Maladaptation to loss*. Washington DC and London: American Psychiatric Press

JACOBS, S. C., HANSEN, F. F., BERKMAN, L. *et al.* (1989). 'Depressions of Bereavement'. *Comprehensive Psychiatry*, 30: 218–24

JACOBSEN, G. and RYDER, R. (1969). 'Parental Loss and Some Characteristics of the Early Marriage Relationship'. *American Journal of Orthopsychiatry*, 39: 779–87

JAMES, W. (1892). *Psychology*. New York: Holt

JANIS, I. L. (1958). *Psychological Stress: Psychoanalytic and Behavioural Studies of Surgical Patients*. London: Chapman & Hall

JONES, D. R. (1979). 'The Grief Therapy Project: The Effects of Group Therapy with Bereaved Surviving Spouses on Successful Coping with Grief'. Ph.D. Thesis, University of Southern California. *Unpublished*

JONES, D. R. and GOLDBLATT, P. O. (1987). 'Cause of Death in Widow(ers) and Spouses'. *Journal of Biosocial Science*, 19: 107–21

JONES, E. (1953). *Sigmund Freud: Life and Work*, vol. 1; vol. 2 (1955). London: Hogarth; New York: Basic Books

KALISH, R. A. and REYNOLDS, D. K. (1973). 'Phenomenological Reality and Post-Death Contact'. *Journal for the Scientific Study of Religion*, 12: 209–21

KAMINER, H. and LAVIE, P. (1991). 'Dream Repression in Adjusted Holocaust Survivors'. *Journal of Nervous and Mental Disease*, 179: 664–9

KAPRIO, J., KOSHKENVUO, M., and RITA, M. (1987). 'Mortality after Bereavement: A Prospective Study of 95,647 Widowed Persons'. *American Journal of Public Health*, 77: 283–7

KAY, D. W., ROTH, M., and HOPKINS, B. (1955). 'Aetiological Factors in the Causation of Affective Disorders in Old Age'. *Journal of Mental Science*, 101: 302

KEDDIE, K. M. G. (1977). 'Pathological Mourning After the Death of a Domestic Pet'. *British Journal of Psychiatry*, 131: 21–5

KEMMENY, M. E., WEINER, H., TAYLOR, S. E., SCHNEIDER, S. *et al.* (1994). 'Repeated Bereavement, Depressed Mood and Immune Parameters in HIV Positive Seropositive and Seronegative Gay Men'. *Health Psychology*, 13(1): 14–24

KESSLER, H. H. (1951). 'Psychological Preparation of Amputee'. *Industrial Medicines*, 20: 107

KITSON, G. C. (1982). 'Attachment to the Spouse in Divorce: A Scale and its Application'. *Journal of Marriage and the Family*, May, 379–93

KLEIN, M. (1940). 'Mourning and its Relationship to Manic-depressive States'. *International Journal of Psycho-analysis*, 21: 125

KLERMAN, G. L. and IZEN, J. (1977). 'The Effects of Bereavement and Grief on Physical Health and General Well-being'. *Advances in Psychosomatic Medicine*, 9: 63–104

KOWALSKI, K. (1991). 'No Happy Ending: Pregnancy Loss and Bereavement'. *Clinical Issues in Perinatal Women's Health Nursing*, 2(3): 368–80

KREITMAN, N. (1964). 'The Patient's Spouse'. *British Journal of Psychiatry*, 110: 159

—— (1968). 'Married Couples Admitted to Mental Hospitals'. *British Journal of Psychiatry*, 114: 699

KRUPP, G. R. (1963). 'Notes on Identification as a Defence against Anxiety in Coping with Loss'. *International Journal of Psycho-Analysis*, 46: 303

KUHN, R. (1958). 'The Attempted Murder of a Prostitute'. In Rollo May (ed.), *Existence*. New York: Basic Books

KVAL, V. A. (1951). 'Psychiatric Observations under Severe Chronic Stress'. *American Journal of Psychiatry*, 108: 185

LEVY, L. H. (1992). 'Anticipatory Grief: It's Measurement and Proposed Reconceptualization'. *The Hospice Journal*, 7(4): 1–28

LEVY, L. H., MARTINOWKSI, K. S. and DERBY, J. S. (1994) 'Differences in Patterns of Adaptation in Conjugal Bereavement: Their Sources, and Potential Significance'. *Omega*, 29: 71–87

LEWIS, C. S. (1961). *A Grief Observed*. London: Faber (first published as by N. W. Clerk)

LIEBERMAN, M. A. and YALLOM, I. (1992) 'Brief Group Psychotherapy for the Spousally Bereaved: A Controlled Study'. *International Journal of Group Psychotherapy*, 42(1): 117–32

LIEBERMAN, S. (1978). 'Nineteen Cases of Morbid Grief'. *British Journal of Psychiatry*, 132: 159–63

LIFTON, R. J. (1961). *Thought Reform and the Psychology of Totalism: A Study of 'Brainwashing' in China*. New York: Norton

LINDEMANN, E. (1944). 'The Symptomatology and Management of Acute Grief'. *American Journal of Psychiatry*, 101: 141

—— (1945). 'Psychiatric Factors in the Treatment of Ulcerative Colitis'. *Archives of Neurology and Psychiatry*, 53: 322

—— (1960). 'Psychosocial Factors as Stress Agents'. In J. M. Tanner (ed.), *Stress and Psychiatric Disorders*. Oxford: Blackwell

LONGFORD, E. (1964). *Victoria R. I.* London: Weidenfeld and Nicolson

LOPATA, H. Z. (1979). *Women as Widows*. New York: Elsevier

LORENZ, K. (1937). 'Uber die Bildung des Instinktbegriffs'. *Naturwissenschaften*, 25

—— (1954). *Man Meets Dog*. London: Methuen

—— (1963). *On Aggression*. London: McEwan

LOVELL, D. M., HEMMINGS, G. and HILL, A. B. (1993) 'Bereavement Reactions of Female Scots and Swazis; a Preliminary Comparison'. *British Journal of Medical Psychology*, 66(3): 259–74

LOWELL, J. R. (1819–91). 'After the Burial'. In A. Whitaker (ed.), *All in the End is Harvest: An Anthology for Those Who Grieve* (1984). London: Darton, Longman and Todd

LUND, D. A., CASERTA, M. S., and DIMOND, M. F. (1989). 'Impact of Spousal Bereavement on the Subjective Well-being of Older Adults'. In D.. A. Lund (ed.), *Older Bereaved Spouses: Research with Practical Applications*. London and New York: Hemisphere

LUND, D. A., DIMOND, M. F., CASERTA, M. S., JOHNSON, M. S., POULTON, R. J., and CONNELLY, J. R. (1985). 'Identifying Elderly with Coping Difficulties after Two Years of Bereavement'. *Omega*, 16, 213–24

LUNDIN, T. (1984a). 'Morbidity Following Sudden and Unexpected Bereavement'. *British Journal of Psychiatry*, 144: 84–8

—— (1984b). 'Long-term Outcome of Bereavement'. *British Journal of Psychiatry*, 145: 424–8

LYNN, E. J. and RACY, J. (1969). 'The Resolution of Pathological Grief after Electro-convulsive Therapy'. *Journal of Nervous and Mental Disease*, 148: 165–9

MADDISON, D. C. (1968). 'The Relevance of Conjugal Bereavement for Preventive Psychiatry'. *British Journal of Medical Psychology*, 41: 223

MADDISON, D. C. and VIOLA, A. (1968). 'The Health of Widows in the Year following Bereavement'. *Journal of Psychosomatic Research*, 12: 297

MADDISON, D. C., VIOLA, A., and WALKER, W. (1969). 'Further Studies in Conjugal Bereavement'. *Australian and New Zealand Journal of Psychiatry*, 3: 63

MADDISON, D. C. and WALKER, W. L. (1967). 'Factors Affecting the Outcome of Conjugal Bereavement'. *British Journal of Psychiatry*, 113: 1057

MAIN, M. (1991) 'Metacognitive Knowledge, Metacognitive Monitoring, and Singular (Coherent) vs. Multiple (Incoherent) Model of Attachment: Findings and Directions for Future Research'. In C. M. Parkes, J. Stevenson-Hinde, and P. Marris (eds), *Attachment Across the Life Cycle*. London and New York: Routledge

MAKER, E. L. (1982). 'Anomic Aspects of Recovery from Cancer'. *Social Science and Medicine*, 16: 907

MANN, J. R. (1987). 'Psychosocial Aspects of Leukaemia and other Cancers during Childhood'. In N. K. Aaronson and J. Beckmann (eds), *The Quality of Life of Cancer Patients*, 135–9. New York: Ravens Press

MARRIS, P. (1958). *Widows and their Families*. London: Routledge and Kegan Paul

MAWSON, D., MARKS, I. M., RAMM, L., and STERN, L. S. (1981). 'Guided Mourning for Morbid Grief: A Controlled Study'. *British Journal of Psychiatry*, 138: 185–93

MCCRAE, R. R. and COSTA, P. T. JR (1993). 'Psychological Resilience among Widowed Men and Women: A 10-year Follow-up of a National Sample'. Chapter 13 in M. Stroebe, W. Stroebe, and R. O. Hansson (eds), *Handbook of Bereavement*. Cambridge: Cambridge University Press.

MCMAHON, B. and PUGH, T. F. (1965). 'Suicide in the Widowed'. *American Journal of Epidemiology*, 81: 23–31

MELLSTROM, D., NILSSON, A., ODEN, A., RUNDGREN, A., and SVANBORG, A. (1982). 'Mortality among the Widowed in Sweden'. *Scandinavian Journal of Social Medicine*, 10: 33–41

MEYER-HOLZAPFEL, M. (1940). 'Triebbedingte Ruhezustände als Ziel von Appetenzhandlungen'. *Naturwissenschaften*, 28: 273

MILLER, D. F. (1961). *Program for Widows*. Liguarian Pamphlets. Redemptarist Fathers, Liguari, Missouri

MITFORD, J. (1963). *The American Way of Death*. London: Hutchinson

MOSS, M. S. and MOSS, S. Z. (1995). 'Death and Bereavement'. Chapter 20 in R. Blieszner and V. H. Bedford (eds), *Handbook of Aging and the Family*. Westport, Conn. and London: Greenwood

MUNOZ, L. (1980). 'Exile as Bereavement. Socio-psychological Manifestations of Chilean Exiles in Britain'. *British Journal of Medical Psychology*, 53: 227–32

MURPHY, G. (1958). *Human Potentialities*. New York: Basic Books

NEIDIG, J. R. and DALGAS, P. P. (1991). 'Parental Grieving and Perceptions Regarding Health Care Professionals' Interventions'. *Issues of Comprehensive Pediatric Nursing*, 14(3): 179–91

NUSS, W. S. and ZUBENKO, G. S. (1992). 'Correlates of Persistent Depressive Symptoms in Widows'. *American Journal of Psychiatry*, 149(3): 346–51

OSTERWEIS, M., SOLOMON, F., and GREEN, M. (eds) (1984). *Bereavement: Reactions, Consequences and Care*. Washington DC: National Academy Press

PARKES, C. M. (1964a). 'Recent Bereavement as a Cause of Mental Illness'. *British Journal of Psychiatry*, 110: 198

—— (1964b). 'The Effects of Bereavement on Physical and Mental Health: a Study of the Case Records of Widows'. *British Medical Journal*, (2): 274

—— (1965). 'Bereavement and Mental Illness': part I, 'A Clinical Study of the Grief of Bereaved Psychiatric Patients'; part 2, 'A Classification of Bereavement Reactions'. *British Journal of Medical Psychology*, 38: 1

—— (1970). 'The First Year of Bereavement: A Longitudinal Study of the Reaction of London Widows to the Death of their Husbands'. *Psychiatry*, 33: 444

—— (1972a). 'Accuracy of Predictions of Survival in Later Stages of Cancer'. *British Medical Journal*, 1 April, 29–31

—— (1972b). 'Components of the Reaction to Loss of a Limb, Spouse or Home'. *Journal of Psychosomatic Research*, 16: 343–9

—— (1973). 'Factors Determining the Persistence of Phantom Pain in the Amputee'. *Journal of Psychosomatic Research*, 16: 343–9

—— (1976). 'The Psychological Reaction to Loss of a Limb: The First Year after Amputation'. Ch. 24 in *Modern Perspectives in the Psychiatric Aspects of Surgery* (ed. J. G. Howells). New York: Brunner Mazel

—— (1981). 'Evaluation of a Bereavement Service'. *Journal of Preventive Psychiatry*, vol. 1, 179–88

—— (1991a). 'Attachment, Bonding and Psychiatric Problems after Bereavement in Adult Life'. Chapter 14 in C. M. Parkes, J. Stevenson-Hinde, and P. Marris (eds), *Attachment Across the Life Cycle*. London and New York: Routledge

—— (1991b). 'Planning for the Aftermath'. *Journal of Royal Society of Medicine*, 84, 22–5

—— (1993a). 'Psychiatric Problems following Bereavement by Murder or Manslaughter'. *British Journal of Psychiatry*, 162, 49–54

—— (1993b). 'Bereavement as a Psycho-social Transition: Processes of Adaptation to Change'. Chapter 6 in M. S. Stroebe, W. Stroebe, and R. O. Hansson (eds) *Handbook of Bereavement*. Cambridge, New York and Victoria: Cambridge University Press

—— (1995a) 'Attachment and Bereavement'. Second John Bowlby Memorial Lecture. In T. Lundin (ed.), *Grief and Bereavement: Proceedings from the Fourth International Conference on Grief and Bereavement in Contemporary Society, Stockholm, 1994*. Stockholm: Swedish National Association for Mental Health

—— (1995b). 'Psychiatric Problems following the Death of a Parent in Adult Life'. *Bereavement Care* 14(3): 26–8

—— (1996a). 'Psychiatric Problems following the Death of a Child'. *Bereavement Care*, 14(3): 26–8

—— (ed.) (1996b). *Loss in Medicine: Helping Patients and their Families to Cope with Loss*. Awaiting publication as a series and book by the *British Medical Journal*.

PARKES, C. M. and BROWN, R. (1972). 'Health After Bereavement: A Controlled Study of Young Boston Widows and Widowers'. *Psychosomatic Medicine*, 34

PARKES, C. M. and WEISS, R. S. (1983). *Recovery from Bereavement*. New York: Basic Books

PARKES, C. M., BENJAMIN, B., and FITZGERALD, R. G. (1969). 'Broken Heart: A Statistical Study of Increased Mortality Among Widowers'. *British Medical Journal*, March, 740–3

PARKES, C. M., LAUNGANI, P., and YOUNG, W. (1996). *Cross-cultural Aspects of Death and Bereavement*. London: Routledge

PASTERNAK, R. E., REYNOLDS, C. F., HOUCK, P. R., and SCHLERNIZAUER, M. (1994a). 'Sleep in Bereavement-related Depression during and after Pharmacotherapy with Nortriptyline'. *Journal of Geriatric Psychiatry and Neurology*, 7(2): 69–73

PASTERNAK, R. E., REYNOLDS, C. F., MILLER, M. D., FRANK, E. *et al.* (1994b). 'The Symptom Profile and Two-year Course of Subsyndromal Depression in Spousally Bereaved Elders'. *American Journal of Geriatric Psychiatry*, 2(3): 210–19

PENNEBAKER, J., KIECOLT-GLASER, J. K., and GLASER, R. (1988) 'Disclosure of Traumas and Immune Function: Health Implications for Psychotherapy'. *Journal of Consulting and Clinical Psychology*, 56, 239–45

PEPPERS, L. G. and KNAPP, R. J. (1980). *Motherhood and Mourning*. New York: Praeger

PERKINS, W. H. and HARRIS, L. B. (1990). 'Familial Bereavement and Health in Adult Life Course Perspective'. *Journal of Marriage and the Family*, 52, 233–41

PETTINGALE, K. W., HUSSEIN, M. and TEE, D. E. H. (1994). 'Changes in Immune Status Following Bereavement'. *Stress Medicine*, 10(3): 145–50

PONZETTI, J. J. and JOHNSON, M. A. (1991). 'The Forgotten Grievers: Grandparents' Reactions to the Death of Grandchildren'. *Death Studies*, 15(2): 157–67

PRICE, J. (1967). 'The Dominance Hierarchy and the Evolution of Mental Illness'. *Lancet*, (2): 243

PRUDO, R., BROWN, G. W., HARRIS, T., and DOWLAND, J. (1981). 'Psychiatric Disorder in a Rural and Urban Population: Sensitivity to Loss'. *Psychological Medicine*, 11: 601–16

PYNOOS, R. S., NADER, K., FREDERICK, C., GONDA, L., and STUBER, M. (1987a). 'Grief Reactions in School-age Children following a Sniper attack at School'. *Israel Journal of Psychiatry and Related Sciences*, 24, 53–63

PYNOOS, R. S., FREDERICK, C., NADER, K., ARROYO, W *et al.* (1987b). 'Life Threat and Post-Traumatic Reactions in School-Age Children'. *Archives of General Psychiatry*, 44, 1057–63

RAMSEY, R. W. (1979). 'Bereavement: A Behavioral Treatment for Pathological Grief'. In P. O. Sioden, S. Bates, and W. S. Dorkens III (eds), *Trends in Behavior Therapy*. New York: Academic Press

RANSFORD, H. E. and SMITH, M. L. (1991). 'Grief Resolution in Hospice and Hospital Wards'. *Social Science and Medicine*, 32(3): 295–304

RAPHAEL, B. (1977). 'Preventive Intervention with the Recently Bereaved'. *Archives of General Psychiatry*, 34: 1450–4

—— (1984). *The Anatomy of Bereavement: A Handbook for the Caring Professions*. London: Hutchinson

—— (1986). *When Disaster Strikes*. New York: Basic Books

REES, W. D. (1971). 'The Hallucinations of Widowhood'. *British Medical Journal*, 2 October, 4: 37–41

REES, W. D. and LUTKINS, S. G. (1967). 'Mortality of Bereavement'. *British Medical Journal*, (4): 13

RELF, M. (1994). 'The Effectiveness of Volunteer Bereavement Support: Reflections from the Sobell House Bereavement Study'. Paper read at the 4th International Conference on Grief and Bereavement in Contemporary Society, Stockholm, June 12. Abstracts from Swedish National Association for Mental Health

RICHARDS, J. G. and MCCALLUM, J. (1979). 'Bereavement in the Elderly'. *New Zealand Medical Journal*, 89: 210–14

ROBERTSON, J. (1953). 'Some Responses of Young Children to Loss of Maternal Care'. *Nursing Times*, 49: 382

ROBERTSON, J. and BOWLBY, J. (1952). 'Responses of Young Children to Separation from their Mothers'. *Courier of the International Children's Centre*, Paris, II: 131–40

ROCHLIN, G. (1965). *Griefs and Discontents: The Forces of Change*. Boston: Little, Brown

ROGERS, C. R. (1961). *On Becoming a Person*. Boston: Houghton Mifflin

ROSENBLATT, P. C., WALSH, R. P., and JACKSON, D. A. (1976). *Grief and Mourning in Cross-cultural Perspective*. New York: HRAF Press

ROSENBLATT, P. C., SPOENTGEN, P., KARIS, T. A., DAHL, C., KAISER, T., and ELDE, C. (1991). 'Difficulties in Supporting the Bereaved'. *Omega*, 23(2): 119–28

ROSENBLOOM, C. A. (1993). 'The Effects of Bereavement on Eating Behaviors and Nutrient Intake in Elderly Widowed Persons'. *Journal of Gerontology*, 48(4): 223–9

ROSKIN, M. (1984). 'A Look at Bereaved Parents'. *Bereavement Care*, 3: 26–8

RUBIN, S. S. (1992). 'Adult Child Loss and the Two-track Model of Bereavement'. *Omega*, 24, 183–202

RUSH, B. (1835). *Medical Inquiries and Observations upon the Diseases of the Mind*. Philadelphia: Grigg and Elliott

RYNEARSON, E. K. (1978). 'Humans and Pets and Attachment'. *British Journal of Psychiatry*, 133: 550–5

SABLE, P. (1991). 'Attachment, Loss of Spouse and Grief in Elderly Adults'. *Omega*, 23: 129–42

SANDERS, C. M., MAUGER, P. A., and STRONG, P. A. (1991). *A Manual for the Grief Experience Inventory*. Palo Alto, Calif.: Consulting Psychologists Press

SANDLER, I. N., WEST, S. G., BACA, L., PILLOW, D. R., GERSTEN, J. C., ROGOSCH, F. *et al.* (1992). 'Linking Empirically Based Theory and Evaluation: The Family Bereavement Programme'. *American Journal of Community Psychology*, 20(4): 491–521

SANUA, V. D. (1974). 'Psychological Effects of the Yom Kippur War'. *New York State Psychologist*, August

SAVAGE, G. (1993). 'The Use of Hypnosis in the Treatment of Complicated Bereavement'. *Contemporary Hypnosis*, 10(2): 99–104

SCHLEIFER, S. J., KELLER, S. E., KAMERINO, M., THORNTON, J. C., and STEIN, M. (1983). 'Suppression of Lymphocyte Stimulation Following Bereavement'. *Lancet*, 1: 834–6

SCHLEIFER, S. J., KELLER, S. E., MEYERSON, A. T., RASKIN, M. D., DAVIS, K. L. and STEIN, M. (1984). 'Lymphocyte Function in Major Depressive Disorder'. *General Psychiatry*, 42: 129–33

SCHMALE, A. H. J. and IKER, H. P. (1966). 'The Affect of Hopelessness and the Development of Cancer: I, Identification of Uterine Cervical Cancer in Women with Atypical Cytology'. *Psychosomatic Medicine*, 28: 714

SCHNEIDER, S. G., TAYLOR, S. E., KEMMENY, M. E. and HAMMEN, C. (1991). 'AIDS-Related Factors Predictive of Suicidal Ideation of Low and High Intent among Gay and Bisexual Men'. *Suicide and Life-Threatening Behaviour*, 21: 313–28

SCHUT, H., DE KEIJSER, J., and VAN DEN BOUT, J. (1991). 'A Controlled Efficacy Study into Short-term Individual Counselling: Client Variables'. Paper read at the Third International Conference on Grief and Bereavement in Contemporary Society, Sydney, Australia, June 30 – July 4

SCHUT, H. A. W., DE KEIJSER, J., and VAN DEN BOUT, J. (1994). 'Short-term Inpatient Therapy in Groups'. Paper read at the Fourth International Conference on Grief and Bereavement in Contemporary Society, Stockholm, Sweden, June 12. Abstracts from Swedish National Association for Mental Health

SEGAL, N. L. and BOUCHARD, T. J. (1993) Grief Intensity following the Loss of a Twin and Other Relatives: Test of Genetic Kinship Hypothesis. *Human Biology*, 65(1): 87–105

SELIGMAN, M. E. P. (1975). *Helplessness*. San Francisco, Calif: Freeman

SELYE, H. and HORAVA, A. (1950 *et seq.*). *Annual Reports on Stress*. Montreal: Acta, Inc

SHANFIELD, S. B. (1979). 'Social and Emotional Determinants of the Death Process'. *Arizona Medicine*, 36: 602–3

SHANFIELD, S. B. and SWAIN, B. J. (1984a). 'Death of Adult Children in Traffic Accidents'. *Journal of Nervous Mental Disease*, 172(9): 533–8

SHANFIELD, S. B., BENJAMIN, G. A. H., and SWAIN, B. J. (1984b). 'Parents' Reactions to the Death of an Adult Child from Cancer'. *American Journal of Psychiatry*, 141(9): 1092–4

SHANFIELD, S. B., SWAIN, B. J., and BENJAMIN, G. A. H. (1985). 'Parents' Responses to the Death of Adult Children from Accidents and Cancer: A Comparison'. *Draft*

SHAPIRO, F. (1989). 'Eye Movement Desensitization; a New Treatment for Post-Traumatic Stress Disorder'. *Journal of Behaviour Therapy and Experimental Psychiatry*, 20: 211–17

SIEGAL, R. L. and HOEFER, D. D. (1981). 'Bereavement Counselling for Gay Individuals'. *American Journal of Psychotherapy*, 35: 4

SILVERMAN, E., RANGE, L., and OVERHOLSER, J. (1994). 'Bereavement from Suicide as Compared to other forms of Bereavement'. *Omega*, 30(1): 41–52

SILVERMAN, P. (1967). 'Services for the Widowed: First Steps in a Programme of Preventive Intervention'. *Community Mental Health Journals*, 3: 37

SIMON, R. (1982) 'Bereavement Art'. *American Journal of Art Therapy*, 20, 135–43

SMITH, E. W. L. (1985). 'A Gestalt Therapist's Perspective on Grief'. In

Psychotherapy and the Grieving Patient (ed. E. M. Stern). New York and London: Harrington Park

SMITH, K. R. (1990). *Risk of Mortality following Widowhood: Sex Differences between Sudden and Expected Bereavement*. Paper presented at the 1990 annual meeting of the Society for Epidemiological Research, Birmingham, Al

SMITH, P. C., RANGE, L. M., and ULMER, A. (1992). 'Belief in an After Life as a Buffer in Suicide and other Bereavements'. *Omega*, 24(3): 217

SOLOMON, R. M. (1994). 'Eye Movement Desensitisation and Reprocessing and the Treatment of Grief'. Paper read at 4th International Conference on Grief and Bereavement in Contemporary Society, Stockholm. Abstract from Swedish Association for Mental Health

SPRATT, M. L. and DENNET, D. R. (1991) 'Immune Variables, Depression, and Plasma Cortisol over Time in Suddenly Bereaved Patients'. *Journal of Neuropsychiatry and Clinical Neuroscience*, 3: 299–306

STEIN, Z. and SUSSER, M. W. (1969). 'Widowhood and Mental Illness'. *British Journal of Preventive and Social Medicine*, 23: 106

STENGEL, E. (1939). 'Studies on the Psychopathology of Compulsive Wandering'. *British Journal of Medical Psychology*, 18: 250

—— (1943). 'Further Studies on Pathological Wandering'. *Journal of Mental Science*, 89: 224

STERN, K., WILLIAMS, G. M., and PRADOS, M. (1951). 'Grief Reactions in Later Life'. *American Journal of Psychiatry*, 108: 289

STROEBE, M. S., SCHUT, H., and VAN DEN BOUT, J. (1994). 'The Dual Process Model of Bereavement'. Paper read at the Fourth International Conference on Grief and Bereavement in Contemporary Society, Stockholm, 12–16 June

STROEBE, M. S., STROEBE, W., and HANSSON, R. O. (eds) (1993). *Handbook of Bereavement*. Cambridge, New York and Victoria: Cambridge University Press

STROEBE, W. and STROEBE, M. S. (1987). *Bereavement and Health: The Psychological and Physical Consequences of Partner Loss*. Cambridge, New York and Sydney: Cambridge University Press

STROEBE, W., STROEBE, M., and DOMITTNER, G. (1988). 'Individual and Situational Differences in Recovery from Bereavement: A Risk Group Identified'. *Journal of Social Issues*, 44, 143–58

STRUHSAKER, T. T. (1967). 'Auditory Communication among Vervet Monkeys'. In S. A. Altmann (ed.), *Social Communication among Primates*. Chicago: University of Chicago Press

SWIGAR, M. E., BOWERS, M. B., and FLECK, S. (1976). 'Grieving and Unplanned Pregnancy'. *Psychiatry*, 39: 72–9

THEUT, S. K., JORDAN, L., ROSS, L. A., and DEUTSCH, S. I. (1991).

'Caregiver's Anticipatory Grief in Dementia'. *International Journal of Ageing and Human Development*, 33(2): 113–18

THOMAS, V. and STRIEGEL, P. (1995). 'Stress and Grief of a Perinatal Loss: Integrating Qualitative and Quantitative Methods'. *Omega*, 30(4): 299–311

TINBERGEN, N. (1951). *The Study of Instinct*. London: Oxford University Press

TUDIVER, F., HILDITCH, J., and PERMAUL, J. A. (1991). 'A Comparison of Psychosocial Characteristics of New Widowers and Married Men'. *Family Medicine*, 23(7): 501–5

TUDIVER, F., HILDITCH, J., PERMAUL, J. A. and MCKENDREE, D. J. (1992). 'Does Mutual Help Facilitate Newly Bereaved Widowers? Report of a Randomized Control Trial'. *Evaluation and the Health Professions*, 15(2): 147–62

TYHURST, J. S. (1957). 'The Role of Transition States – Including Disasters – in Mental Illness'. Symposium on Preventive and Social Psychiatry, Walter Reid Army Institute of Res., Washington DC

VACHON, M. L. S., SHELDON, A. R., LANCEE, W. J., LYALL, W. A. L., ROGERS, J., and FREEMAN, S. J. J. (1980). 'A Controlled Study of Self-help Intervention for Widows'. *American Journal of Psychiatry*, 137: 1380–4

—— (1982). 'Correlates of Enduring Distress Patterns Following Bereavement: Social Network, Life Situation, and Personality'. *Psychological Medicine*, 12: 783–8

VAN DEN BOUT, J. (1994). 'Cognitive Therapy and Rational-Emotive Therapy of Grief-related Problems'. Paper read at 4th International Conference on Grief and Bereavement in Contemporary Society, Stockholm. Abstract from Swedish Association for Mental Health

VAN DER HART, O. (ed.) (1988). *Coping with Loss: The Therapeutic Value of Leave-taking Rituals*. New York: Irvington

VAN ROOIJEN, L. (1978). 'Widows' Bereavement: Stress and Depression After One-and-a-half Years'. Paper read at Advanced Study Institute on Environmental Stress, Cambridge. *Unpublished*

VEBER, L. L. DE (1977). 'Families, Children and Death: Lessons we have Learned'. *University of Western Ontario Journal*, December

VOLLMAN, R. R., GANZERT, A., RICHER, L., and WILLIAMS, W. V. (1971). 'The Reactions of Family Systems to Sudden and Unexpected Death'. *Omega*, 2, 101–6

WALLER, W. (1951). The Family: A Dynamic Interpretation. New York: Dryden

WAUGH, E. (1948). *The Loved One: An American Tragedy*. London: Chapman and Hall; New York: Grosset (1949)

WEINBERG, N. (1994). 'Self-blame, other Blame and Desire for Revenge: Factors in Recovery from Bereavement'. *Death Studies*, 18(6): 583–93

WEISMAN, A. D. (1972). *On Dying and Denying: A Psychiatric Study of Terminality.* New York: Behavioral Publications

WESTERMEYER, J. (1973). 'Grenade Amok in Laos: A Psychological Perspective'. *International Journal of Social Psychiatry,* 19(3): 251

WIENER, A., GERBER, I., BATTIN, D., and ARKIN, A. M. (1975). 'The Process and Phenomenology of Bereavement'. In B. Schoenberg, I. Berger, A. Wiener, A. H. Kutscher, D. Peretz, and A. C. Carr, *Bereavement: Its Psychosocial Aspects.* New York: Columbia University Press

WITTKOWER, E. (1947). 'Rehabilitation of the Limbless: Joint Surgical and Psychological Study'. *Occupational Medicine,* 3: 20

WORTMAN, C. B. and SILVER, R. C. (1989). 'The Myths of Coping with Loss'. *Journal of Consulting and Clinical Psychology,* 57(3): 349–57

WRETMARK, G. (1959). 'A Study in Grief Reaction'. *Acta Psychiatrica et Neurologica Scandinavica Supplement,* 136: 292

YAMAMOTO, T., OKONOGI, K., IWASAKI, T., and YOSHIMURA, S. (1969). 'Mourning in Japan'. *American Journal of Psychiatry,* 125: 74

YERKES, R. M. (1943). *Chimpanzees: A Laboratory Colony.* New Haven, Conn.: Yale University Press; London: Oxford University Press

YOUNG, M., BENJAMIN, B., and WALLIS, C. (1963). 'Mortality of Widowers'. *Lancet,* (2): 454

ZISOOK, S. (ed.) (1987). *Biopsychosocial Aspects of Bereavement.* Washington, DC: American Psychiatric Press

ZISOOK, S., DE VAUL R. A., and CLICK, M. A. (1982). 'Measuring Symptoms of Grief and Bereavement'. *American Journal of Psychiatry,* 139, 1590–3

INDEX

READ MORE IN PENGUIN

In every corner of the world, on every subject under the sun, Penguin represents quality and variety – the very best in publishing today.

For complete information about books available from Penguin – including Puffins, Penguin Classics and Arkana – and how to order them, write to us at the appropriate address below. Please note that for copyright reasons the selection of books varies from country to country.

In the United Kingdom: Please write to *Dept. EP, Penguin Books Ltd, Bath Road, Harmondsworth, West Drayton, Middlesex UB7 ODA*

In the United States: Please write to *Consumer Sales, Penguin Putnam Inc., P.O. Box 12289 Dept. B, Newark, New Jersey 07101-5289*. VISA and MasterCard holders call 1-800-788-6262 to order Penguin titles

In Canada: Please write to *Penguin Books Canada Ltd, 10 Alcorn Avenue, Suite 300, Toronto, Ontario M4V 3B2*

In Australia: Please write to *Penguin Books Australia Ltd, P.O. Box 257, Ringwood, Victoria 3134*

In New Zealand: Please write to *Penguin Books (NZ) Ltd, Private Bag 102902, North Shore Mail Centre, Auckland 10*

In India: Please write to *Penguin Books India Pvt Ltd, 11 Community Centre, Panchsheel Park, New Delhi 110017*

In the Netherlands: Please write to *Penguin Books Netherlands bv, Postbus 3507, NL-1001 AH Amsterdam*

In Germany: Please write to *Penguin Books Deutschland GmbH, Metzlerstrasse 26, 60594 Frankfurt am Main*

In Spain: Please write to *Penguin Books S. A., Bravo Murillo 19, 1° B, 28015 Madrid*

In Italy: Please write to *Penguin Italia s.r.l., Via Benedetto Croce 2, 20094 Corsico, Milano*

In France: Please write to *Penguin France, Le Carré Wilson, 62 rue Benjamin Baillaud, 31500 Toulouse*

In Japan: Please write to *Penguin Books Japan Ltd, Kaneko Building, 2-3-25 Koraku, Bunkyo-Ku, Tokyo 112*

In South Africa: Please write to *Penguin Books South Africa (Pty) Ltd, Private Bag X14, Parkview, 2122 Johannesburg*

READ MORE IN PENGUIN

PSYCHOLOGY

How the Mind Works Steven Pinker

This brilliant and controversial book explains what the mind is, how it evolved, and how it allows us to see, think, feel, interact, enjoy the arts and ponder the mysteries of life. 'To have read [the book] is to have consulted a first draft of the structural plan of the human psyche ... a glittering *tour de force*' *Spectator*

The Uses of Enchantment Bruno Bettelheim

'Bruno Bettelheim's tour of fairy stories, with all their psychoanalytic connotations brought out into the open, is a feast of understanding' *New Statesman & Society*. 'Everything that Bettelheim writes about children, particularly about children's involvement in fiction, seems profound and illuminating' *Sunday Times*

Evolution in Mind Henry Plotkin
An Introduction to Evolutionary Psychology

Evolutionary theory holds a vital key to understanding ourselves. In proposing a more revolutionary approach to psychology, Professor Plotkin vividly demonstrates how an evolutionary perspective brings us closer to understanding what it is to be human.

The Man Who Loved a Polar Bear Robert U. Akeret

'Six fascinating case histories related with wit and humanity by the veteran psychotherapist Robert Akeret ... a remarkable tour to the wilder shores of the human mind' *Daily Mail*

Private Myths: Dreams and Dreaming Anthony Stevens

'Its case for dreaming as something more universally significant than a tour across our personal playgrounds of guilt and misery is eloquently persuasive ... [a] hugely absorbing study – its surface criss-crossed with innumerable avenues into science, anthropology and religion' *Spectator*